Zone Offenses
for Women's Basketball

Zone Offenses for Women's Basketball

William E. Warren

Allyn and Bacon, Inc.
Boston • London • Sydney • Toronto

Copyright © 1980 by Allyn and Bacon, Inc., 470 Atlantic Avenue, Boston, Massachusetts 02210. All rights reserved. No part of the material protected by this copyright notice may be reproduced or utilized in any form or by any means, electronic or mechanical, including photocopying, recording, or by any information storage and retrieval system, without written permission from the copyright owner.

Library of Congress Cataloging in Publication Data

Warren, William E.   1941-
  Zone offenses for women's basketball.

  Bibliography: p.
  Includes index.
  1. Basketball for women — Offense.
2. Basketball for women — Coaching.   I. Title.
GV889.W345   796.32'38   79-23194
ISBN 0-205-06800-6

Managing Editor: Paul Solaqua
Series Editor: Hiram Howard
Production Editor: Paula Carroll
Preparation Buyer: Patricia Hart
Manufacturing Buyer: Linda Jackson

Printed in the United States of America

for
Clara, Faye, and BooBoo
and a host of other young women who taught me
that winning is a state of mind,
not points on a scoreboard

Contents

Preface   ix

Acknowledgments   xi

Diagram of Courts Positions   xiii

Explanation of Diagrams   xv

1 THE THEORY AND PRACTICE OF ZONE DEFENSE   1

Reasons for Using Zone Defense   Attacking the Weaknesses of a Zone Defense   Guidelines for Constructing Zone Offense   Variations on a Theme: The Versatility of Zone Defenses   Basic Zone Defensive Coverage   The Even-Front Zone Defenses   The Odd-Front Zone Defenses   Laning Defense   Matchup Zone Defense   Trapping Zone Defenses   Combination Defenses   Conclusion

2 TEAM STRATEGY IN ZONE OFFENSE   41

Nine Principles of Zone Offensive Strategy   Where the Zone Weaknesses Occur   Provide an Inside Scoring Threat   Rotate Players Around the Outside of the Zone   Overload One or More Zones   Set Screens   Stress Automatics and Freelancing   Urge Players to Drive Whenever Possible   Be Patient   Consider Offensive Rebounding and Defensive Balance   Conclusion

3 OVERLOAD OFFENSES   51

Overload Positions and Strategy   Basic Overload Movements   Other Approaches To Overload   Maintaining the Overload   Rotation Patterns (Once the Overload Has Been Established)   A Revolving Rotation Overload Offense   Four-Player Overloads   Variations of the Basic Overload Technique   Conclusion

4 SPLITTING PATTERNS   89

Basic Splitting Patterns   Splitting the Even-Front Zone Defenses   Splitting Patterns Against Odd-Front Zone Defenses: The 1–1–3 Zone Defense   Splitting Patterns Against Odd-Front Zone Defenses: The 1–2–2 Zone Defense   Splitting Patterns Against Odd-Front Zone Defenses: The 3–2 Zone Defense   Conclusion

5 SPECIAL ZONE OFFENSES AND TECHNIQUES   117

A 2–3 Baseline Screening Offense   The "V" Offense   A High-Low Screening Offense   Weak Side Screening Offense   Keying in a Zone Offense   Attacking Matchup Zone Defenses   Attacking the Trapping Zone Defenses   Offenses Against Combination Zone Defenses   Control Offenses: Slowdowns, Stalls, and Freezes   Conclusion

6 BEATING THE ZONE PRESSES   157

Considerations in Combatting Zone Presses   Advice for Ballhandlers Against Zone Presses   The Inbounds Pass   Trapping Techniques   Combination Presses   Passing to Beat the Presses   Fast Breaking   Combatting the Half-Court Zone Presses

7 ZONE OFFENSIVE DRILLS   231

Glossary   251

Bibliography   259

Index   261

Preface

At first glance, the problems involved in organizing the material in a book on zone offenses do not appear to be significant. After all, the vast majority of zone offensive alignments and patterns fall into three general categories: *overload offenses, cutter patterns,* and *splitting and spreading patterns.* (For present purposes, we also considered attacking the full- and half-court zone presses as within the scope of zone offenses as a whole.)

Unfortunately, the process is not quite so cut and dried as all that. For instance, many splitting and spreading patterns involve cutters moving through or around the defense and often result in overload formations as well. Additionally, the author found in organizing the material that, for one reason or another, many of the patterns simply defied categorization. Because these miscellaneous offenses offer new and/or varied techniques for attacking zone defenses, particularly specific zone defenses (e.g., attacking a 2–1–2 or 2–3 zone from a "V" offensive alignment), they were grouped loosely under the all-inclusive heading, "Special Offenses and Techniques" in Chapter 5. Therefore, we have included an extensive index at the end of the book as an aid for the reader in locating material in the book.

A final point concerns the photographs used in the book. In some cases technical considerations forced us to alter the players' actual court positions slightly. For example, the positions occupied by offensive wing and/or corner players are sometimes actually wider than that shown in the photographs. We trust that this disparity, however slight, will not impair the reader's perception of the effectiveness of the various zone offenses discussed.

Acknowledgments

"No man is an island," John Donne wrote, and his words are particularly relevant to the writing of a book. Seldom, if ever, does a writer compose his works independent of the efforts, encouragement, and assistance of other people.

So it is with this book. First, since no one person can claim to have all the answers concerning zone offenses, I wish to express my gratitude to the many coaches whose pioneering efforts in the formulation of basketball coaching theory provide the basis for the styles of zone offensive attack outlined in this book.

Three coaches in particular influenced my thinking in many respects: the late Joe Bell, who coached girls and boys basketball at Milner (Georgia) High School; Coach Bill Shaw, presently coaching at Walker High School in Atlanta, Georgia; and Coach Mac Morrison, coach at Jenkins County High School in Millen, Georgia.

The author also wishes to thank the lovely and talented young ladies of the 1978 Toombs Central Jackette basketball team who appear in the photos in this book: team captains Clara Harden, Faye Edgerton, Edie Bennett, and Brenda Clark, along with teammates Lisa Hart, Daisy Gaffney, Debbie Pittman, Rosenda Mann, Laverne Harden, Elaine McKenna, Sabrina Berry, and Twanda Mobley.

Three other outstanding young ladies, graduates of Toombs Central, could hardly be omitted from these acknowledgments. They are: Mary McCall, Elaine Chambers, and Charlie Mae Edgerton.

There are others whose assistance proved invaluable in the preparation of this book. Mrs. Grace James, Athletic Director and women's basketball coach at South Georgia (Jr.) College in Douglas, Georgia, graciously permitted us to use the school's gymnasium to photograph the action shots appearing in the book. This often necessitated rescheduling and relocating classes during the two days' photography sessions.

A perceptive and thoroughly professional individual, Hiram Howard, sports book editor of Allyn and Bacon's Longwood Division provided invaluable guidance.

Talbot Lovering, staff photographer for Allyn and Bacon, managed in the brief two days not only to take more than two hundred difficult action photos of excellent quality, but also to become a close friend.

And last to be thanked, but certainly first in every other respect, my wife Louise, whose long-suffering support, encouragement, and assistance included typing the entire manuscript three times as well as serving as a second mother to the many players I have coached.

DIAGRAM OF COURT POSITIONS

As will be explained in greater detail, the court positions in which offensive players set up, or to which they cut, are, in most cases, extremely flexible. The diagram below is intended to exemplify those positions, not define them.

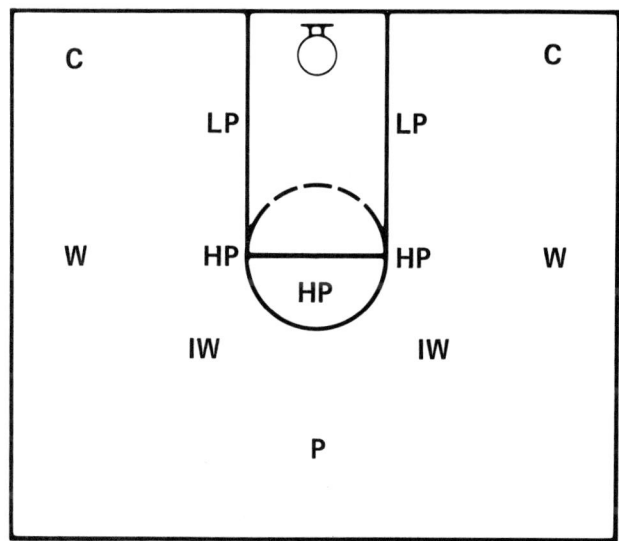

C = Corner   W = Wing
LP = Low Post   IW = Intermediate Wing
HP = High Post   P = Point

EXPLANATION OF DIAGRAMS

3   Offensive Player

③   Offensive Player with Ball

X₁   Defensive Player

◄‑ ‑ ‑ ‑②   Pass

├‑ ‑ ‑ ‑④   Fake Pass

◄‑ ‑ ‑③   Second Pass in a Series

◄∿∿∿②   Path of Dribbler

◄─── 5   Offensive Movement Without Ball

⌒ 4   Fake in One Direction, Cut in Another

├───①   Offensive Screen or Defensive Overguarding

◄─┼─ 3   Screen and Continued Movement

◄⌐ 2   Reverse Pivot

◄───   Sequential Movements

◄ OR ►   Alternative Movement*

(X)   One of Two or More Possible Defensive Positions

*Dotted lines indicate alternative passes.

Zone Offenses
for Women's Basketball

*He who, from zone to zone
Guides through the boundless sky thy certain flight,
   In the long way that I must tread alone
Will lead my steps aright.*
> William Cullen Bryant
> To a Waterfowl (1818), st. 8

1 The Theory and Practice of Zone Defense

We have met the enemy, and they are ours.
Oliver Hazard Perry

Although you wouldn't always know it from watching basketball games, ours is a rational, orderly universe governed by laws of cause and effect. When we see a team playing zone defense, we may assume that the coach has a reason for playing zone defense rather than player-to-player defense. Furthermore, without taxing too greatly our Holmesian powers of deductive reasoning, we can assert that teams using zone defense are faced with a defensive problem of some sort, or that they are trying to attack an offensive strength or weakness without surrendering defensive control. For example, teams with one or more players in the lineup who are inexperienced defensively will often be seen playing zone defense in order to reduce the likelihood and severity of mistakes made in player-to-player coverage; and teams with a single outstanding offensive performer will often play zone defense in order to protect that player from foul difficulty.

The best defense in basketball is, unquestionably, player-to-player defense. In its purest form, player-to-player defense issues a challenge to the offense: "We can beat you one-on-one. Wherever you go, we'll be there, too—before you, if possible—controlling your movements, giving you as little as possible, and making you work as hard as you can for everything you get." In player-to-player defense, it's *your* defensive strength against *my* offensive strength, one-on-one, which makes it doubly hard for me, since I have to protect the ball even as I'm attacking your defense.

In zone defense, however, you can be even more aggressive in your efforts to stop me, because even if I beat you one-on-one, I still have to face the rest of the defense. Zone defense involves players' defending *areas of the court* rather than specific offensive players, with defensive responsibilities delegated in terms of zones rather than players. At times a player may have no one at all to guard, while at other times she may be responsible for guarding two players simultaneously. Defensive players move around constantly within their zones, but they seldom leave their zones or guard players outside their zones for fear of giving up high-percentage shots (e.g., layups) within their own zones.

REASONS FOR USING ZONE DEFENSE

1. To Hide a Defensive Weakness. Player-to-player defense requires *five* capable defensive players, and if even one defender is fundamentally weak, the results can be catastrophic. Using a zone defense can at least partially hide one or more players' defensive shortcomings. However, it can never hide *all* of them.

If a team is inexperienced or fundamentally weak, zone defense can simplify the players' defensive movements and responsibilities and should serve to reduce the number of shots taken near the basket against them.

When players are in foul trouble, they sometimes go to extremes to avoid contact on defense. Zone coverage can keep a player in foul trouble in the game by reducing the likelihood of defensive confrontations in one-on-one situations.

Zone defense keeps players constantly in defensive rebounding position, an important consideration for teams with small or extremely slow players.

2. To Attack the Opponents' Offensive Weaknesses (or Strengths). Zone defenses are designed to keep the ball outside, and as a result there are more defensive players inside in zone coverage than in player-to-player defense. Zones tend to cut off passing lanes inside, even against teams that prefer to take the ball inside on offense.

Zone defense helps to provide coverage that ensures the defensive team of having more than one person between the ball and the basket at all times. Furthermore, transition from defense to offense is faster and more organized, since the defensive players are always in the same positions relative to the ball and the offensive players.

Finally, zone coverage helps to facilitate certain special defensive techniques such as trapping, switching, or sinking.

As mentioned earlier, every zone defense possesses weaknesses, although they are not always readily perceived. Players are guarding zones rather than players, and the defensive players' range of movement is therefore restricted largely to the areas of their zones. Offensive strategies such as overloading and sending cutters through the heart of the zones tend to confuse the defensive coverage and create matchups that favor the offense rather than the defense. Additionally, repeated outside rotation of the ball and players from one side of the court to the other tends to relax the defense into automatic movements and responses that further weaken their coverage, especially along the seams of the zone.

ATTACKING THE WEAKNESSES OF A ZONE DEFENSE

Having established that zone defenses have weaknesses, how does a team go about attacking, or taking advantage of, those weaknesses? First, by fast breaking to obtain high-percentage shots before the defense can become organized. Even two-on-two or three-on-three coverage is more difficult for the defense than five-on-five zone coverage.

Not all teams are capable of fast breaking, however. Other strategies against zone defenses include: spreading the offense to take advantage of the zone's tendency to sag inside; splitting the zone by setting offensive players along the outside seams and sending cutters into the zone to keep the defensive players inside; moving the ball quickly with short, crisp passes to find openings inside, or along the perimeters of the zone; and overloading zones with two or more players in order to confuse the defensive coverage or create one-on-one matchups favorable to the offense.

Overloading. The term *overloading* refers to the offensive strategy of setting or moving two or more players into a single zone, or setting or moving three or more players onto one side of the court to confuse defensive coverage. Figures 1-1, 1-2, and 1-3 illustrate the differences between balanced and overloaded offensive alignments. (Other balanced alignments include 1-3-1, 1-2-2, 2-1-2, and 2-3.)

In any overload situation, the number of offensive players is greater than the number of defensive players in certain areas of the court, and the offense's objective is to move the ball to players in these areas to gain higher percentage shots than would be possible elsewhere.

Ball or Player Rotation. As used within the context of this book, the term *rotation* refers to either the ball or players moving from one side of the court to the other. As the ball, and thus the zone defense, moves farther to one side of the court, the defensive player(s) left on the weak side, or side of the court away from the ball and the overload, tend to become more and more vulnerable to rapid rotation of the ball. For example, if low post in Figure 1-2 is double-teamed when the ball is at the wing, it is likely that only one defensive player will be left on weak side. Rotation involves passing from wing to point to weak side before the defense adjusts to the movement of the ball.

One aspect of zone coverage deserving further consideration con-

Figure 1-1 Balanced Offense, 1–3–1 Alignment.

Figure 1-2 Three-Player Overload Alignment.

cerns overloading and ball rotation: when the offensive team overloads one side of the court, either three or four defensive players may shift to the ball side of the court, depending upon whether the ball side low post receives single or double coverage. One defensive player assumes responsibility for the ball, one player is responsible for guarding the low post, and at least one player is responsible for weak side coverage, as shown in Figures 1–4, 1–5, and 1–6.

Although these defensive alignments will be analyzed in greater

The Theory and Practice of Zone Defense 5

Figure 1-3 Four-Player Overload Alignment.

Figure 1-4 Overload Offense with Single Coverage Inside (1–2–2).

detail later in this chapter, it should be mentioned that ball rotation is faster and more effective when the defense is in double coverage (Figure 1–6) than in single coverage (Figures 1–4 and 1–5). In the latter case, the weak side defensive player may move out to hinder the pass to the point guard that begins the rotation.

Ball and/or player rotation are integral parts of all continuity patterns, both zone and player-to-player.

Splitting Patterns. In splitting patterns, offensive players set up

Figure 1-5 Overload Offense with Single Coverage Inside (1–3–1).

Figure 1-6 Overload Offense with Double Coverage Inside.

along the outside seams of a zone and either cut into or across the zone, or set screens inside or along the perimeters of the zone. Splitting patterns are designed to freeze one or more defensive players and free certain offensive players for high-percentage shots. When cutters enter a zone, they force the defensive player or players in that zone to choose between guarding the cutter or guarding offensive players already in the zone. Figure 1–1 depicts a 1–3–1 offensive alignment used to split a 2–1–2 zone defensive alignment.

GUIDELINES FOR CONSTRUCTING A ZONE OFFENSE

1. Know Your Personnel. The simplicity inherent in this statement is deceptive; of course coaches know their personnel—or do they? How many times have you seen the opponents' tallest player and only inside scoring threat setting up in the corner to receive the ball? Or watched a team struggling to run a complicated pattern beyond their experience, skills, or capabilities?

"Fit the pattern to your personnel." "Diagrams don't win ballgames, players do." Every coach has heard these epigrams many times. But every coach who has ever been frustrated in her attempts to beat zone defenses also knows that necessity mothers some pretty strange inventions. For instance, for reasons that will be outlined later, I have always disliked even-front offenses and defenses. Yet recently after much brain-wracking and soul-searching I switched to a 2–3 zone offense against odd-front zone defenses because my players simply couldn't operate effectively from the 1–3–1 and 1–2–2 offensive alignments I'd been trying to use against 1–3–1 and 1–2–2 zone defenses.

2. Give Your Patterns a KISS. Charles G. ("Lefty") Dreisell, the superlative basketball coach of the University of Maryland's men's team, has a sign in his office that reads "K.I.S.S." That's "Keep It Simple, Stupid." One of the gravest mistakes a coach can make is using patterns that are beyond the capabilities of her players.

The revolving rotation overload offense is as diverse and sophisticated in its approach to attacking zone defenses as any, but only a team with experienced, knowledgeable players should attempt to run it. Some teams simply run patterns better than others, but it is in no way demeaning for a team to run simple patterns.

Sophisticated offenses look good on paper. They offer "evidence" of the coach's scholarly approach to the game, but they are of little help if the players involved are incapable of carrying them out properly. Complicated patterns may look impressive and attest to the coach's knowledge; but if they don't win games, they should be simplified or discarded. In the majority of cases a team is better off learning to "keep it simple," with a basic offensive pattern supplemented by increased attention to detail and execution and a few offensive automatics arising out of defensive adjustments.

If you don't believe me, ask Lefty.

3. Provision Must Be Made for Some Kind of Inside Offensive Thrust, Even When It Isn't Likely to Succeed. If no inside scoring threat exists, as in outside patterns without cutters, the defense will simply match up with the offense and move outside to harass the shooters along the perimeters of the zone. The defenders will not collapse inside unless the offensive team makes them do so by posting a player high or low, screening, sending cutters through the defense, or otherwise indicating willingness to work for inside shots.

4. Both the Coach and the Players Should Be Fully Aware of the Areas of Weakness Within the Zone Defense Being Used. Merely setting players in a 1–3–1 alignment against a 2–1–2 zone defense, for example, does not ensure that openings will appear, or remain, in the zone. Different teams cover their zones in different ways: one team may send its guards to cover wing passes, while another team sends a forward from an inside defensive position.

A perfect example of instructing players where to look for openings in a zone defense is shown in Figure 1–7. Point guard 1 has passed to 3 and cut to the weak side high post position. Player 2 is at weak side low post, and 3 has passed to 5 in the corner. Where should 5 look for openings in the zone?

First, since she is guarded and cannot shoot, she should look inside to 4 at low post. Next, she looks to 3, in case X_3 has dropped back to double-team 4. (Of course, these "looks" should be quick glances rather than stares.) Then, with the coverage shown in Figure 1–7, 5 should look to the weak side of the court, first to 1 and then to 2. Diagonal passes to the weak side are often effective in combatting zone defenses.

But how does 5 know to look to the weak side? She should be coached to look: (1) to the ball side low post, (2) to the ball side wing, (3) to the ball side high post. If they (as well as she) are all covered, one of the weak side players must be open. The defense does not have enough players to cover the corner, the wing, the low post, and the high post, all

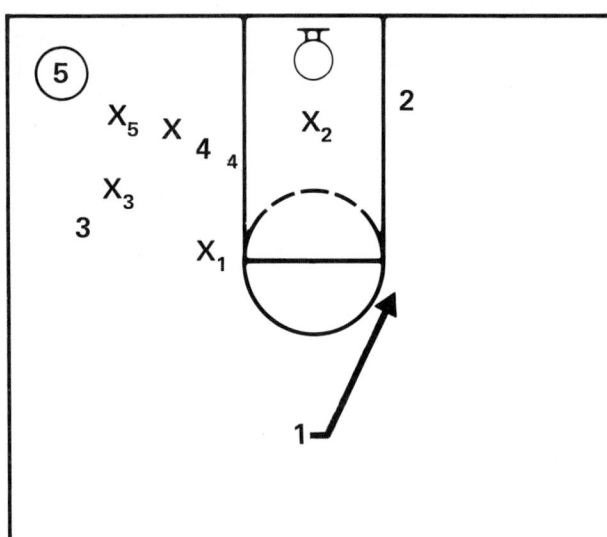

Figure 1-7 Looking For Openings in the Zone Defense, Ball in Corner.

on the ball side of the court, and still have two players left to cover the weak side wing and point, or the weak side low post and high post. X_1 may drop back into the lane to defense the long cross-court diagonal pass, but her movement opens the ball side high post area for 2 to cut into. And the defensive coach who would have X_2 follow 2 all the way across the lane will have a hard time teaching her players the difference between zone and player-to-player defense.

There are five basic outside offensive positions: the point, or top of the circle; the wings on either side of the court; and the corners, with the two intermediate wing positions between the point and wings in even-front offenses. Players should be shown repeatedly how different zone defenses adjust to the ball at each of the five (or seven) positions, so there will be no question as to the defensive coverage after each pass.

5. Players Should Be Coached to Break the Pattern Whenever Scoring Opportunities Arise. At first glance, it seems obvious that players will try to score whenever they are presented with opportunities, but if you believe that, you haven't coached junior high players before. Young or inexperienced players who are incapable of concentrating on more than one thing at a time sometimes fail to capitalize on scoring opportunities in their haste to run the pattern properly, and thereby pass up countless opportunities to drive, shoot layups, or open jump shots, etc. It is not uncommon for junior high players even to forget to turn and face the basket before shooting.

6. Offensive Rebounding and Defensive Balance Should Be Taken into Account in Constructing a Zone Offense. In addition to keeping at least one person in position to rebound offensively, at least one other player should remain outside as a potential deterrent to the opponents' fast break.

Zone offenses, especially overloads, offer unique advantages concerning offensive rebounding. In Figures 1–4 and 1–5, for example, it should be noted that, when the wing or corner players have the ball, *there are no defensive players in rebounding position on the weak side of the court!* If 2 moves to weak side low post and concentrates on blocking defensive players away from the weak side when shots are taken, a surprisingly large number of rebounds can be taken from overshots. When players shoot too hard, or overshoot, their teammates can often rebound effectively on offense if they block out away from the ball rather than merely going to the boards to rebound.

VARIATIONS ON A THEME: THE VERSATILITY OF ZONE DEFENSES

There are numerous zone defenses—the 2–1–2, 2–3, 2–2–1, 1–2–2, 1–3–1—and combination zones such as the box-and-one, diamond-and-one and triangle-and-two, which combine zone and player-to-player coverage within a single defense. Additionally, a team may use its zone in any of several different ways:

1. As a basic defense, covering the ballhandler, the ball side low post[1], the weak side low post, and any two of several other ball side or weak side positions (or the point).

2. As a matchup defense, with player-to-player coverage of all five offensive players within the context of zone defense.

3. As a trapping defense, double-teaming the ballhandler outside and cutting off the passing lanes in order to force bad passes, steal the ball, or otherwise pressure the offense into ball-handling mistakes and turnovers.

Generally, the difference between the various zone defensive alignments is found in their approach to initial ball movement. Odd-front alignments (e.g., 1–3–1) tend to force the ball wide of the point and give up the corner shot, a relatively low percentage shot in most cases. The greatest advantages to be found in using odd-front zones are that: (1) the areas involved in splitting the zone do not yield as high percentage outside shots as those afforded by even-front zone defenses, and (2) having an odd number of guards outside lessens the effectiveness of the offensive point guard's penetrating dribble to freeze the defense and free a wing for an open shot.[2] In other words, if the defense sets only one guard at the top of the circle, the offense cannot penetrate toward the basket as easily. And if the dribbler penetrates diagonally between the point guard and a defensive wing, the pass to the weak side wing can be stolen more easily, since it must be either a long bounce pass or a lob pass.

Trapping within the odd-front zone defenses occurs most often in the four corners of the half-court. Coach Joe B. Hall's University of Kentucky Wildcats have had great success in recent years with their 1–3–1 half-court trapping zone defense.

On the other hand, even-front alignments (e.g., 2–3, 2–2–1, or 2–1–2) influence the ball toward the middle of the court or the wings, with trapping occurring most naturally at the top of the circle. Even-front zone defenses are strong inside, with the 2–3 zone particularly effective against teams with great inside offensive strength and relatively weak outside shooting efficiency.

Before analyzing the strengths and weaknesses of the various zone defenses, one point should be restressed, that *once the ball is definitely established on one side of the court, all basic zone defensive coverages are alike in principle, regardless of the zone alignment being used.* The

---

[1] Double-teaming the ball side low post is a form of basic zone defense.

[2] See Figures 1–12, 1–13, and 1–14 and accompanying text.

players covering the zones may differ, as may the areas in which the defensive team intends to deny the offense access to the ball, but the zones to be covered remain the same. Changes in the basic defensive pattern of coverage generally tend to reflect defensive strategy rather than differences in the various zone defenses.

BASIC ZONE DEFENSIVE COVERAGE

It's a sad, but true, fact of life for the defense that *all* basic zone defenses give up something in the process of assuming defensive coverage. Basic zone defense is passive rather than aggressive, negative rather than positive in its underlying philosophy. Teams use basic zone defense to hide weaknesses or to yield as little as possible to the offense while protecting against a greater menace elsewhere.

In situations where a team is too weak fundamentally to use player-to-player defense, or the offensive team is simply too strong to be held in check by aggressive player-to-player or zone coverage, basic zone defense is clearly indicated. If the opponents are going to get their shots regardless of whether or not the defense applies attacking principles, the defenders may elect to play passively, denying the ball inside and giving up certain shots in order to keep from giving up higher percentage shots in other areas of the court. At the same time they maintain defensive rebounding positions to deny the opponents second and third opportunities to score via offensive rebounding.

What exactly is basic zone defense? It is zone coverage in which defensive pressure is applied to the ball and to the low post position on the ball side of the court, with other areas receiving less aggressive coverage, except when the offense attempts to force the ball into high-percentage scoring areas. These "other areas" of reduced coverage may be the *corner* (if the opponents are relatively ineffectual shooting from there); the *high post* (if the offense uses only one player inside); the *point* (if they have no effective long-range shooters from the top of the circle); or the *weak side* (if the opponents tend to keep the ball on one side of the court).

Using basic zone defensive coverage, a team may elect to surrender part of the court to the opponents in the hope that they cannot take full advantage of it. For example, consider a situation in which you are preparing to face an opponent whose leading player scored 38 points against your team last time you played them, mainly on lob passes inside and offensive rebounding. One type of strategy to use is to send your players outside to apply defensive pressure to the opponents' ballhandlers, keeping the ball outside and forcing bad passes and turnovers. Unfortunately, you tried that last time you played them.

A second school of thought is evidenced in the old adage, "One player can't beat you!" Sadly, however, one player *can* beat you, by fouling out your best defensive players in the process of demoralizing your team with another 38 points and/or an equal number of rebounds.

Besides, that "one player" has four teammates who might decide that tonight is the night they are going to play defense, holding your high-scoring team to 36 points until you're 18 points down with thirteen seconds left to play. Match up with them? Forget it. You might as well match up with the Red Chinese Army!

This leads us to basic zone defensive coverage: you decide to double-team the tall inside player, fronting her on the ball side and alerting the weak side defender to double-team her on lob passes inside. If the inside player moves to the corner, single-guard her except when she tries to drive. Give her the outside shot—you probably won't stop it anyway—but block her away from the boards after her shot.

As for the rest of the team, give them whatever shot you think they can't make, apply defensive pressure in other areas to keep the ball away, and hope for the best. If their outside shooters are having a hot night, they'll beat you—but if they are superior to you inside *and* outside, you probably wouldn't beat them even with your entire squad on the court!

Basic zone defense is safe, conservative, percentage basketball—if any kind of defense can be called *safe!* Its proponents adhere to the dictum that, "If you're going to beat us, you're going to have to do it with your outside shooting." You don't take chances in basic defense, you try to keep the offensive players away from whatever it is that they do best, and at the same time you try to surrender as little as possible in terms of offensive control and unmolested shots from high-percentage scoring areas. Basic zone defense is far from foolproof; in fact, in its way it is as hazardous as matching up or trapping. But in certain situations, and for teams that have trouble matching up or trapping, it can be the *only* effective defensive strategy.

Using basic zone defense doesn't necessarily *win* games, but neither does it lose them.

Types of Basic Zone Defensive Coverage. As mentioned earlier, the distinguishing characteristics of basic zone defensive coverage are (1) stress upon stopping the inside game, and (2) diminished coverage of certain outside areas once the ball is established on one side or the other of the court.

Two basic considerations guide a team in its use of basic zone defense:

1. Will the ball side low post position be single-guarded or double-teamed?
2. Will the weak side be covered by one or two players?

When the defensive team single-guards the low post position, the players may guard the ball side corner and high post, or they may set a player in only one of those two positions in order to retain two players on the weak side of the court. The weaknesses of each method should be obvious: in the former case, rapid ball rotation to the weak side will yield a two-on-one offensive advantage, and in the latter case, the neglected corner or high post player will be open to receive passes.

However, both methods will be unlikely to yield as many unhindered outside shots as the double-teaming technique. Of course, a further method of double-teaming exists, that of dropping back the defensive point guard on the ball to form a diagonal even front that would facilitate coverage of passes to the wing, high post, or point guard. Regardless, the weak side defensive coverage is extremely weak when two defensive players are assigned to a single offensive player inside.

Time and extensive experimentation have changed our former attitudes about zone defenses. For instance, it was once accepted as fact that "A zone defense always retains its basic shape, regardless of the position of the ball." Aside from the fact that such advanced techniques as matching up and trapping obviously cannot conform to that concept of zone defense, most successful modern coaches use their basic zone defense to meet specific needs and attack specific strengths or weaknesses of their opponents, rather than blithely reasoning that "Since our 2–1–2 zone didn't work last night, we're gonna try a 1–3–1 zone tonight!"

But if all basic zone defensive coverage is alike in principle, why do some coaches swear by their 2–3 zones "that keep our players in rebounding position," while other coaches are at this very moment lauding the merits of the 3–2 zone as "the wave of the future" in basketball defense—despite the objections of still other coaches whose 1–3–1 or 1–2–2 zone defenses have brought it all together for *their* teams? The answer lies partly in the personal preferences and experiential levels of individual coaches, but it is also due in part to the absence of a vital phrase from the above statement: all basic zone defense is, or can be, alike in principle all right—*once the ball is established on one side of the court!* As long as the ball is in the middle of the court, however, defensive responsibilities may or may not be established.

The initial movement or pass by the offense that sets the ball clearly on one side of the court or the other can be dictated fairly well by the defense, and therein lies much of the value of different zone defensive alignments. (Other advantages of various zone alignments appear after a team reacts to the first pass or movement and prepares to counteract a *second* pass or movement—e.g., the pass from the wing to the corner or high post.)

Odd-Front vs. Even-Front Zone Defenses (Basic). Zone defenses are given names corresponding to the number of defensive players setting up at each level of the zone defensive alignment, beginning with those nearest to midcourt. Thus, a "2–3" zone defense has two players setting up outside and three players inside, while a "3–2" zone has three players outside and only two inside. A 1–3–1 zone has, obviously, three levels of zone coverage.

Moreover, zone patterns fall into two general categories, *odd-front* and *even-front*. Odd-front zones have either one or three players outside in their basic alignment, and even-front zones have two players outside. While odd-front zones tend to force the ball to the corners or to areas midway between the wings and the point (the intermediate wing positions), even-front zones tend to force the ball to the wings or corners. (Odd-front alignments do not *force* the ball to the middle—i.e., the top of the circle—since the ball arrives at the middle naturally in offensive splitting alignments. However, trapping movements by the two defensive guards will tend to force the ballhandler to pass the ball away, usually to the vicinity of the wings or corners when the defense denies the pass to high post.) The differences may appear inconsequential at first, but they can be considerable in terms of coverage and shooting effectiveness.

THE EVEN-FRONT ZONE DEFENSES

Basic 2-1-2 Zone Defense. The 2–1–2 zone defense was, until recently, the most widely used defense in basketball, although it is far from being the most effective in most cases. The basic movements and defensive adjustments with ball rotation are natural from 2–1–2 forma-

Figure 1-8 2-1-2 Zone Defensive Alignment.

tion—everybody moves toward the ball side of the court—and, therefore, they are easily learned even by inexperienced or unskilled players. The high post position receives ample coverage, especially when the ball is at the point, and an inside rebounding triangle of three defensive players is almost always present. Fast breaking is easily accomplished from a 2–1–2 alignment, and defensive balance is always in evidence.

On the other hand, the 2–1–2 zone defense is extremely weak at the wing positions, except when the outside defensive triangle shifts to 1–2–2 coverage. It is also vulnerable at the corners of the free-throw lane, since X_3 cannot possibly cover both high post positions.

Generally, the outside guards are responsible for stopping the dribbler's penetration and covering passes to the wing. However, when the offensive wings slide toward the baseline to make coverage by the outside guards more difficult, the forwards will usually come out to challenge the pass receiver. In such cases, the corner is left untended at least momentarily.

Basic 2-3 Zone Defense. Although apparently identical with the 2–1–2 zone defense, especially when the offense sets a player at high post, the 2–3 zone defense is far more versatile in terms of the types of coverage available. For example, the outside guards can come out to challenge the ball or trap the dribbler, or they can stay back as shown in Figure 1–9, helping to cover the high post position when the ball is at the point. (Of course, a good point shooter would destroy such tactics, but in that case the defense would find another means of protecting the high post.)

With three players deep rather than two, the 2–3 zone defense can

Figure 1-9 2–3 Zone Defensive Alignment.

be stronger than the 2–1–2 alignment in covering the corners, because the defenders' zones of responsibility are smaller. Or with the three inside defensive players moving 3–5 feet farther out from the basket, increased coverage of the medium- to high-post areas can be effected without drastically altering the basic coverage.

As a rule, teams using 2–3 zone defense have only two small guards, with three taller players performing the "3" inside coverage. However, there is another usage of the 2–3 zone defense other than as a basic, matching, or trapping defense: when the offensive team has not one, but *two* tall players who set up at the low post positions or move around inside, the defense may elect to operate from a 2–3 zone alignment, with the ball side low post being single-guarded. As shown in Figure 1–11, only two defenders remain outside to guard the point and wings, but a team uses such drastic measures only when other, safer measures have proven insufficient or have been discarded as ineffective.

Against such tactics, the offense may simply split the defense as shown in Figure 1–11, or they may send 1 to the corner to further widen the zone responsibilities of the outside defenders. If the inside defenders move out to cover the wings, the ball side low post will be single-guarded, and if the defense had wanted to single-guard either offensive low post position or player, they would have used matchup coverage in the first place rather than double-teaming.

Basic 2-2-1 Zone Defense. The 2–2–1 zone defense is a 2–1–2 zone with the "1-2" positions reversed inside. It is seldom seen on any level of

Figure 1-10 2–2–1 Zone Defensive Alignment.

play, which could be a good reason for using it. The 2–2–1 zone defense is best suited for teams with one tall player—especially one who is slow, immobile, or defensively inexperienced—and four small, quick defenders. It can also be used as a trapping defense, particularly at the high post or wing positions. As can be readily seen in Figure 1–10, the 2–2–1 zone defense is weak along the baseline, and setting a player at high post can sometimes confuse the defensive coverage.

THE ODD-FRONT ZONE DEFENSES

Basic 1-2-2 Zone Defense. The 1–2–2, or "Jug" defense, was popularized by the legendary Clair Bee of New York University. In its basic form, with one player outside guarding the ball and four players inside in rebounding position, the 1–2–2 alignment presents formidable obstacles for the offense: the high post position is apparently open (see Figure 1–12), but if the outside guard applies defensive pressure to the ballhandler, she will have to throw a lob pass to the high post player, and the wings can trap her when she catches the pass. Thus, the 1–2–2's most obvious weakness can also be its greatest strength.

Among the greatest advantages of odd-front defensive alignments is that they tend to force the ball to one side of the court or the other, and thus provide the defense with early adjustments to ball and player movements. It has already been established that basic coverage within practically every zone defense is the same once the ball is definitely

Figure 1-11 Double-Teaming Inside from a 2–3 Zone Defense.

established on one side of the court, and odd-front zone defenses force the ball to one side and farther out from the basket earlier than even-front zone defenses.

Basic 1-3-1 Zone Defense. Probably the most versatile of all zone defenses, the 1-3-1 zone defense is ideal as an aggressive defense in its

Figure 1-12 Basic 1-2-2 Zone Defense.

Figure 1-13 Basic 1-3-1 Zone Defense.

Figure 1-14 Basic 3-2 Zone Defense.

matchup or trapping form. It is possibly at its weakest in its basic form—but hardly anybody uses the 1-3-1 that way, anyway.

The 1-3-1 alignment is weakest in the corners, and supposedly in the outside positions diagonally between the defensive point guard and the wings. However, matching up or trapping can actually take advantage of the offensive splitting alignment to attack the offense. The basic 1-3-1 zone defense covers the point, high post and wing positions extremely well, although corner coverage is adequate at best.

Basic 3-2 Zone Defense. The 3-2 zone defense is, or can be, deceptive in its coverage. Its basic shape, with three players outside and two inside, can be transformed with facility into a 2-3, 2-1-2, or 1-2-2 zone defense, either by dropping back the player in the middle of the "3" to create a 2-1-2 or 2-3 zone defense, or moving her forward to form a 1-2-2 alignment.

Generally, however, coaches neglect such intricacies, preferring to play the 3-2 zone as a kind of 1-2-2 zone with the point guard sinking back toward the high post. As a result, offenses that attack the 1-2-2 zone defense usually can be used with equal facility against 3-2 zone defenses.

Thus, we can see that all basic zone defensive coverages have the same general objectives, namely, guarding: (1) the ball, (2) the low post position, (3) the weak side of the court, (4) the corner, and (5) the high post. The primary exception to this type of coverage occurs when the defense double-teams the low post position. Figures 1-15, 1-16, and 1-17 show how inside double-teaming varies in two types of zone coverage.

Figure 1-15 Inside Double-Teaming, Ball at Wing.

Figure 1-16 Inside Double-Teaming, Ball in Corner, X_3 Dropping Low.

Figure 1-17 Inside Double-Teaming, Ball in Corner, X_1 Sliding Low.

The Theory and Practice of Zone Defense 21

Figures 1-18, 1-19 Basic 1-3-1 Zone Defensive Alignment.

"LANING" DEFENSE

Whereas in basic defense the players tend to stay inside or near the lane except when covering the ball, some teams are of sufficient strength to broaden their outside coverage without weakening their inside coverage. On the college level, where outside shooting proficiency is the rule rather than the exception, concentrating on inside coverage within a given zone defense may prove impossible.

The first and most obvious alternative to basic defense is called *laning* and consists of setting one or more outside defenders in the passing lanes between offensive players.

The key to success of the 1–3–1 laning shown in Figure 1–20 lies in X_4's coverage of the high post position: if the ballhandler is able to pass to high post, the wing defenders will likely have to drop back to cover the corners, since the inside defender will be unable to reach either of them in time. When the high post defender is able to contain the inside game, however, the advantage swings to the defensive team, since the outside defenders are located in the passing lanes. The pass will have to be a lob pass, and the very act of lobbing will permit the defenders to cover the pass receiver—or, more importantly, to trap her.

Figure 1-20 Laning 1–3–1 Zone Defensive Alignment.

Generally, high school teams are less likely to use laning techniques when deploying zone defenses than are college teams, since a basic reason for using zone defense in high school is to keep as many defensive players as possible inside, or near the basket. It is not at all uncommon to find high school teams playing a 1–2–2 zone defense, with the point guard fronting high post rather than going out on the ballhandler when the ball is at the top of the circle. In other cases, the wings may elect to play a "tight" zone defense (Figure 1–21) when the point guard moves outside to cover the ballhandler at the point, in order to double-team high post if the ballhandler passes to her.

Both of these coverages are seen with far greater frequency than laning techniques at the junior high and high school levels. At the college level, defensive teams may use laning to force the outside shooters farther away from the basket than is necessary at the high school level; and laning in high school and junior high school basketball will often result in undesirable matchups inside favoring the offensive team—for example, at high post if the defensive wings are spread (Figure 1–20). Thus, while laning will initially tend to force the offensive players further away from the basket than more basic, conservative coverage, it also spreads the defensive coverage as well and tends to increase the likelihood of inside confrontations.

Screening techniques[3] are unlikely to work against laning zone defense. The defensive splits are simply too wide. Laning alignments

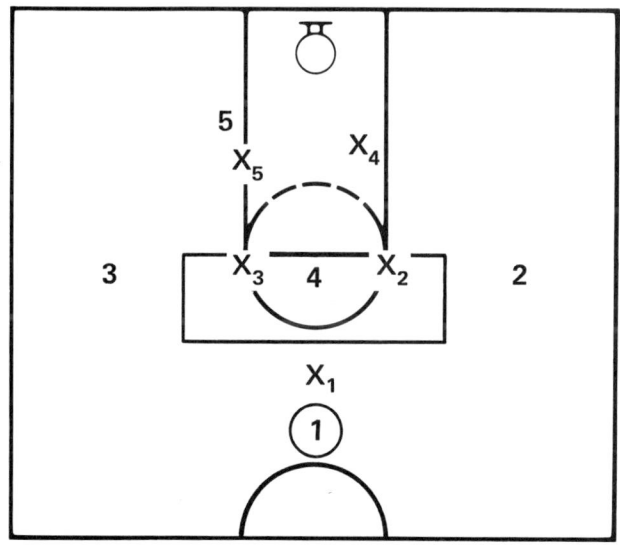

Figure 1-21 Setting Up a High Post Double Team Defense from Basic 1–2–2 Zone Defense.

---

[3] See Figures 4–22 through 4–30, 4–36, 4–37, 5–1, 5–2, 5–4, 5–13, and 5–14 and accompanying text.

generally are used for the purpose of trapping or matching up, and should be attacked as such. Preferred techniques for dealing with laning include: (1) working the ball inside for desirable one-on-one matchups; (2) penetrating into the seams of the defense and passing off; (3) sending outside cutters into, or through, the lane; (4) overloading; (5) using weak side cutter patterns and rapid ball rotation to take advantage of the broad areas of coverage required by the laning; and (6) generally approaching the laning strategy as if it were a trapping or matching zone defense.

MATCHUP ZONE DEFENSE

Against teams with no better-than-average offensive players, or teams who do not rely on multiple cutting patterns toward and away from the ball, the toughest defense to crack in basketball is a matchup zone.

Teams can match up defensively from any zone alignment; however, it is generally agreed that the 1–3–1 zone defense facilitates the act of matching up to a greater extent than any other zone defense. And, since all matchup zones operate from the same principles, we shall use the 1–3–1 zone to exemplify the objectives and methods of matchup defenses.

Since the offensive team usually "splits" the defense by setting players in the gaps between defenders in the zone—for example, setting up 2–1–2 against a 1–3–1 defense—the team using matchup zone coverage will shift its defensive alignment to create one-on-one matchups—in this case, shifting into a 2–1–2 alignment to combat the opponents' 2–1–2 offensive alignment. (See Figures 1–22 and 1–23.)

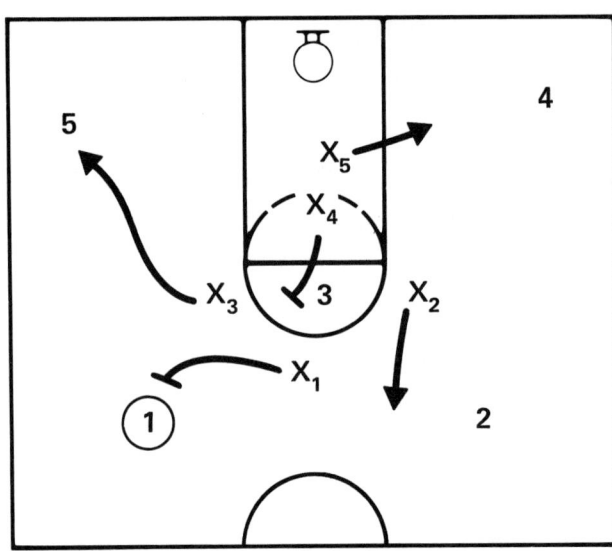

Figure 1-22 Matching Up from 1–3–1 Zone Defense.

Figure 1-23 Matching Up from 1-3-1 Zone Defense, Alternate Method.

Thus, a 1-3-1 zone defense suddenly becomes a 2-1-2 zone, or 1-2-2, or whatever offensive alignment the offense sets up in, and the resulting confusion can be disastrous to the offensive team.

There are two types, or directions, for the rotation to matchup to take: either point guard X_1 covers the ball (Figure 1-22), in which case X_3 drops back and everyone else except X_4 rotates in a clockwise direction to cover the 2-1-2 offensive alignment; or the ball side wing moves up to cover the ball (Figure 1-23), the point guard slides across to cover the other guard, and the inside defenders rotate in a counterclockwise direction to cover the corners. In both cases, X_4 covers the high post.

While any team from the most inexperienced to one of championship calibre may use basic zone defense, matchup defense is likely to be used only by experienced teams, since the basic objective in using a matchup zone is to force one-on-one confrontations within the context of zone defense. Teams that use matchup zone defense should not be taken too lightly, since they have announced their style of play by their choice of defenses.

Matching up from a zone defense may be the most devastating approach to defensive basketball ever devised: it permits player-to-player coverage within the greater context of the team's zone defense, and if the

26 Zone Offenses for Women's Basketball

Figures 1-24, 1-25 1-3-1 Zone Defense After Matching Up.

Figure 1-26 Matching Up Against 1-2-2 Offensive Alignment.

offensive player manages to achieve partial success against her defender, she still has to contend with the rest of the zone.

TRAPPING ZONE DEFENSES

Like matchup zone defenses, trapping presents unique problems for the offense beyond those found in basic zone defense. The first salient point to be made concerning trapping as a zone defensive strategy is that it differs in both execution and intent from double-teaming. Whereas double-teaming is used to keep the ball away from a certain player, trapping is an aggressive action designed to force bad passes or turnovers that will yield an easy layup for the defense.

As is the case with matchup zones, trapping can be effected from practically any zone defense, although the areas in which the traps occur vary with the type of zone defense being used. Trapping usually occurs along the very seams of the zone that the offense is splitting. For example, when a team sets up in a 1-3-1 zone defense, the opponents invariably set up 2-1-2 to split the defense. A team that traps on defense wants the opponents to set up in a splitting alignment, because the traps work better

Figure 1-27 Trapping Areas Within the 1–3–1 Zone Defense.

that way. With the possible exceptions of some of the forms of player-to-player defense, trapping zone defense is the most aggressive type of defense in basketball—and it is without a doubt the riskiest defense in the game, since the offense has a four-on-three advantage every time the trap fails to work!

Quickness, anticipation, and experience are prerequisites for successful trapping. Without at least two of these three attributes, a team is unlikely to resort to a trapping defense. A team will not use trapping defense unless the chances of successfully trapping the ballhandler outweigh the considerable risks involved. An exception to this occurs when the team is trailing at the end of a game and needs to regain possession of the ball.

Thus, trapping teams are likely to be very aggressive in going after the ball and in forcing errant or lob passes that can be picked off by teammates.

2-1-2, 2-3, and 2-2-1 Zone Trapping. A team does not set up in a "trapping" zone defense; rather, it sets up in a given zone defensive alignment (e.g., 2–3 or 2–1–2) and attempts to create situations conducive to trapping from that alignment.

The Theory and Practice of Zone Defense 29

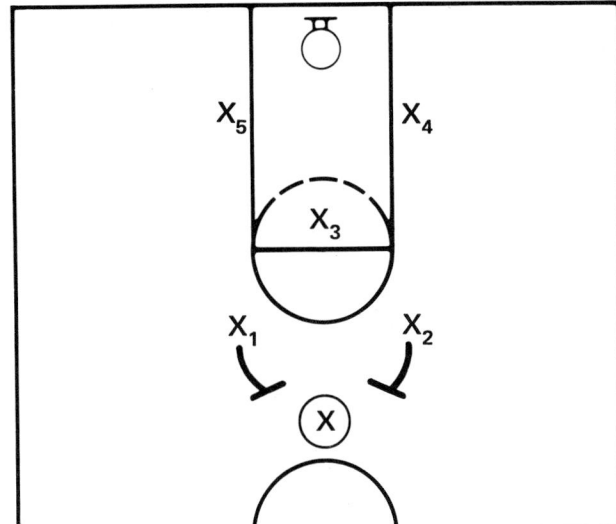

Figure 1-28 Point Trapping Area in 2-3 Or 2-1-2 Zone Defense.

Figure 1-29 Baseline Trapping Areas in 2-2-1 Zone Defense.

The areas of the court in which the traps are sprung depend upon the alignment used. In 2-1-2 and 2-3 zone defense, the traps occur most naturally at the top of the circle. The 2-2-1 zone defense is conducive to corner or baseline trapping.

The only really effective area for trapping from the 2-1-2 or 2-3 alignments is at the top of the circle, and even then the trap must take full

Figure 1-30 Intermediate Wing Position Trapping in 1–2–2 Zone Defense.

Figure 1-31 2–1–2 Trapping at the Point.

advantage of the element of surprise to deter the ballhandler from dumping the ball off to a teammate at a wing position.

Point trapping generally occurs when the dribbling point guard is turned by one defensive guard into the other outside (trapping) guard, as shown in Figure 1–31.

One can readily see the problems entailed in 2–1–2 or 2–3 point trapping from Figure 1–31: if the defensive forwards move outside to cut off the passing lanes; they risk surrendering inside passes for easy layups; and if they stay back, the wings serve as safety valves for outlet passes to avoid the trap.

However, most point trapping is done with the intention of stealing the ball, so the inside defenders will in all probability stay back anyway, since no harm is done if the ballhandler is able to elude the trap and pass to a teammate at the wing.

The defensive movements will differ with the alignment used in setting up the corner trap, but the areas in which trapping occurs will remain constant, as do the passing lanes.

1-3-1 Zone Trapping. In the system that follows, trapping occurs in one corner and at one wing; that is, assuming the ballhandler to be outside facing the basket from a 2–1–2 offensive alignment, the defensive team will trap the pass receiver at the intermediate wing every time she receives a pass, and the corner whenever the ballhandler passes to her. (The defense may elect to trap in any number of ways, of course, but the point is that the defenders will not trap every pass receiver every time she catches a pass.) Some teams trap only when the ballhandler is on the right side of the court passing to the other outside guard. At other times they match up with the offense.

In order to give the trapping defenders time to spring their trap, the point defensive guard positions herself between the opponents' outside guards, and thus forces the ballhandler to make a lob pass over her. The ballhandler has three other options available: she can pass to the ball side corner, work for her own shot, or attempt the dangerous diagonal cross-court pass to the weak side corner.

If the ballhandler passes to the ball side corner, the inside defender will move out to cover her, and the rest of the defenders will match up. If, however, the ballhandler elects to lob the ball over the point guard, the trapping movement will begin: the point and wing defenders trap the pass receiver, the weak side wing slides out slightly to steal any return pass, the high post defender moves around to cut off the pass to high post, and the inside defender moves toward the ball side corner to cut off that passing lane.

The corner player on the weak side will slide toward the basket in the clear, but if the trap is sprung quickly and aggressively, the ballhandler will likely be unable to see her, since four players will serve

Figure 1-32 Springing the Outside Trap in 1-3-1 Zone Defense.

to effectively block her vision, with the trapping guards forcing her to protect the ball rather than attacking the defense. The ballhandler will look to the ball side corner but will find that player covered. She looks to the high post. (She cannot see the weak side low post.) Unfortunately, that passing lane has been shut off as well. Finally, knowing that the referee is counting the seconds before calling a held ball, the ballhandler turns and passes blindly back across the zone to the other guard, who was in the clear the last time she looked.

Unfortunately, however, the weak side wing defender has moved into position to steal the pass and breaks downcourt for the easy layup.

That's the way it works. Weak side low post was open throughout, but the ballhandler has been coached not to throw passes to teammates she cannot see, especially cross-court, on the assumption that an offensive player will be there.

Some teams deploy corner trapping exclusively, for a very important reason: the passing areas and angles are more confined in the corners, as are the ballhandler's escape routes. Trapping often occurs in the right-hand corner, since the ballhandler will then have to dribble left-handed out of the trap. For purposes of the system being described, however, the trap will take place in the left corner of the court. (See Figure 1-33.)

Figure 1-33 Corner Trapping in 1–3–1 Zone Defense.

As the ball is passed to the corner, the inside and wing defenders move quickly to cover the receiver aggressively, waving their hands and forcing her to protect the ball. The point guard slides over to intercept the return pass, the weak side wing moves across the lane to the ball side low post position, and the high post defender covers that area. A player may be in the clear in the weak side corner, but she will be hidden behind three defenders in her line of sight. Even if she can spot that player in the confusion, the ballhandler will have to throw a high lob pass over the defenders and the basket as well, and the defense should have time to move back to cover the lob pass.

The weak side wing will be in the clear outside, too, but: (1) she is two passes away from the ball, (2) four players are positioned between the two of them, (3) the ballhandler is being pressured to do something, anything, with the ball before a held ball is called, and (4) even if she can get the ball outside, no damage is done to the defense. Lob passes outside seldom hurt a trapping defense.

It should be restated that the most successful corner trapping generally occurs in the offensive right corner rather than the left. Since the majority of players are right-handed, the ballhandler will almost always turn to her right to protect the ball from the trapping players, and

Figure 1-34 1-3-1 Corner Trapping, Right Side of the Court.

Figure 1-35 Corner Trapping, Alternate Coverage of Passing Lanes.

the act of turning will decrease the likelihood of her seeing the outside guard in the clear for the diagonal cross-court pass.

An alternate version of coverage of the passing lanes in trapping in either corner is for the high post defender to slide low to cover the low post on the ball side, with the weak side wing moving across the lane to cover the high post position. (See Figure 1-35.)

Thus, from the two examples given, an emerging pattern can be seen that applies to all trapping defenses: two players trap the ballhandler, while the three other players cut off the primary passing lanes in order to force bad passes, turnovers, or held balls. Someone is always in the clear when the defense traps one person, but finding that person when two players are grabbing for the ball and waving their arms wildly is not always as easy as it looks. Trapping is a gambling defensive technique, and teams who aren't aware of the risks involved seldom use it.

COMBINATION DEFENSES

Combination defenses are those in which principles of both zone and player-to-player defense are used within a single coverage; that is, while part of the team is in zone coverage, the rest of the defenders assume player-to-player coverage of certain offensive players.

The advantages of such defensive coverage are obvious: if a team has only one or two good ballhandlers or shooters, the defense may elect to assign one player to cover her player-to-player, and thus keep the ball away from her by overguarding and weakening the opponents' ballhandling or zone offensive rotation patterns. If the offensive team has an exceptional outside shooter, player-to-player coverage of her will deny her the ball while the rest of the team remains in zone defense. Additionally, many players are unused to playing without the ball and become frustrated when they are repeatedly denied access to the ball as teammates pass and cut outside freely without interference.

Teams seldom practice against combination defense, and therefore are often unused to the type of offensive game forced upon them by such coverage. Combination defenses are "gimmick" defenses used to combat specific offensive advantages. This does not mean that they should be taken lightly, but that, unless offensive players understand what is happening, they may find their patterns grinding to a standstill as the ball is forced repeatedly to weaker offensive players for longer and longer periods of time.

The major disadvantage of combination defense is that it is a special defense, and as such requires special attention. Occasionally, coaches might be able to get by with using a regular defense (e.g., a 2-1-2 zone), with certain players merely instructed to "guard so-and-so player-to-player" from that alignment, with the other players shifting in their zones accordingly. However, such coverage often presents more problems than it solves. (Note in Figure 1–36 the large openings at the corners of the free-throw lane if the defense plays its 2–1–2 zone normally when X_1 moves outside to cover 3 with the ball at the point.) The defense may elect to match up, of course, but they probably will prefer not to, or else they would have been in matchup coverage in the first place.

Too, combination defense sometimes forces the rest of the defensive team into player-to-player coverage, or into trapping situations which negate the initial advantages of the combination coverage. Before a coach decides to use combination defense, she should be fairly certain that the rest of the team isn't going to beat them.

Types of Combination Defenses. There are three basic styles of combination defense: (1) the box-and-one, (2) the diamond-and-one, and (3) the triangle-and-two. Of these three, the first two consist of four-player zones with one player in player-to-player defense; and the last features two players in player-to-player coverage and the other three in triangle zone defense inside. Some coaches use the rule of thumb that, "If the player-to-player defense is on a guard, use a diamond-and-one zone defense; and if the player-to-player coverage is on a forward or center, use a box-and-one zone." In Figures 1–37, 1–38, and 1–39, a 1–3–1 offensive alignment is used to exemplify the differences between the three types of defensive coverage. (It should be noted, too, that any offensive players may be guarded player-to-player, and not just positions 2 or 3.)

One final aspect of combination defense merits further considera-

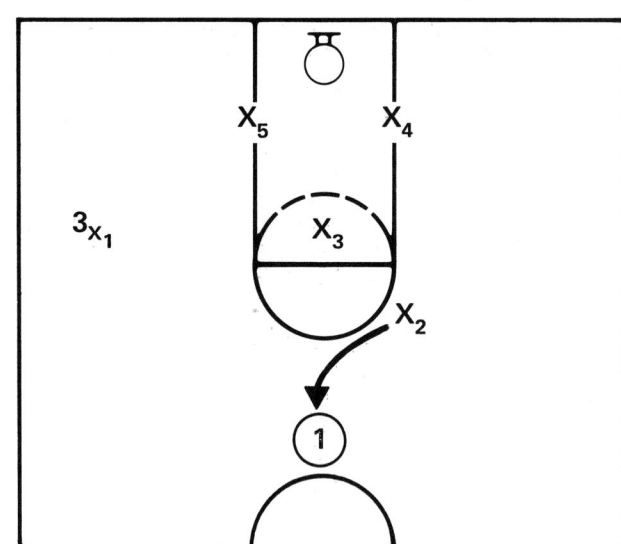

Figure 1-36 Combination Defense from Regular 2–1–2 Zone Coverage.

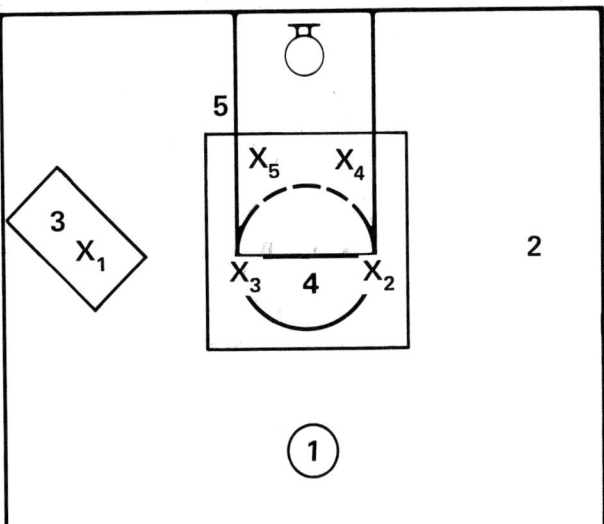

Figure 1-37 Box-and-One Combination Defense, 1–3–1 Offensive Alignment.

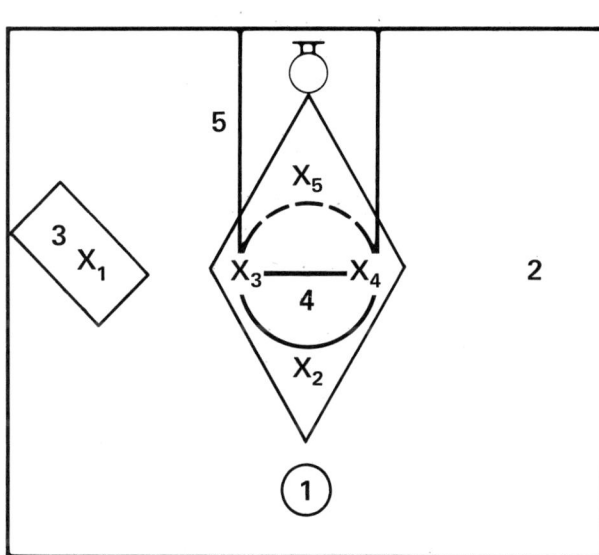

Figure 1-38 Diamond-and-One Combination Defense, 1–3–1 Offensive Alignment.

tion: practically without exception, the strategy will seldom be successful when an inside player or players receives the player-to-player coverage. In such cases, the offense will either attack the defense as a matchup zone, or force double-coverage by placing the "one" player being guarded player-to-player at low post where an inside defender is already playing zone defense.

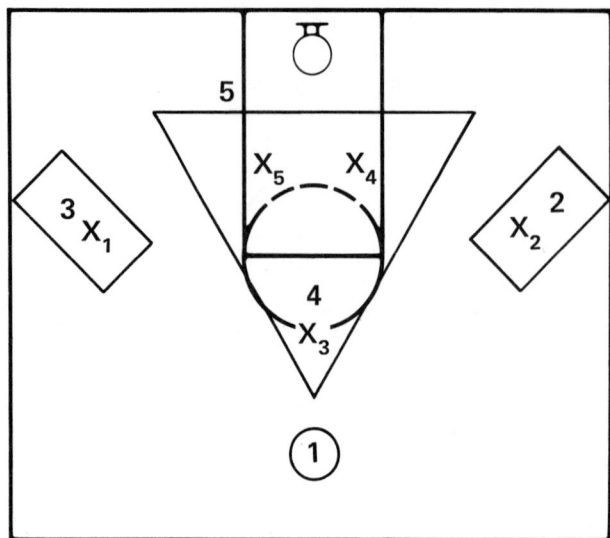

Figure 1-39 Triangle-and-Two Combination Defense, 1-3-1 Offensive Alignment.

CONCLUSION

Once upon a time when basketball was a simple, uncomplicated game in which Team A always beat Team B because Team B's material was better, it was thought sufficient to know that Team A ran a certain zone defense, or that wing shots were always available against even-front zones. Now, however, it is not enough to know that a team runs a 1-3-1 zone: the perceptive coach will also note which players cover passes to the corner (with an eye toward developing unhindered inside shots); whether the high, medium, and low post positions receive adequate defensive coverage in different ball positions; and whether the defense traps or matches up within their zone coverage.

If a team is unprepared to deal with trapping defenses or matchup zones, it is likely to have to settle for low-percentage shots dictated by the defense—or, indeed, to lose the ball to an organized, aggressive, well-disciplined team whose intentions are clearly evident to *them*.

The rest of this book is intended to deal with offensive alignments, patterns, and techniques designed to counteract the effectiveness of the various styles and techniques of zone defense. That no simple pattern will prove effective for any given team, or against all zone defenses, goes without saying. Still, the broad array of zone offensive patterns and techniques presented should be sufficient to provide the bewildered coach with a basic understanding of how zone defenses can and should be attacked. And zone defenses *must* be attacked!

Start with the basic assumption that *every zone defense and every team using zone defense has weaknesses, however slight, that can be at-*

tacked. Identify those weaknesses, and the battle is half won already. The final step is analyzing the strengths and weaknesses of your own team in terms of attacking the zone at its weakest (or strongest) points and organizing your zone offensive patterns in such a manner that you have something left in case your offensive thrust fails.

That is the basis for all zone offensive strategy.

2 Team Strategy in Zone Offense

O! My offense is rank; it smells to heaven;
It hath the primal eldest curse upon't...
                                William Shakespeare
                                Hamlet, III, iii, 36

As was explained in Chapter 1, zone defenses generally fall into two separate and easily discernible categories: basic, passive, wait-until-they-make-a-mistake zoning[1] in which the defense sets up inside (and stays inside) for rebounding purposes and to cut off inside passing lanes; and aggressive zone coverage that applies defensive pressure on the ball and primary receivers inside and outside.

Basketball coaches, too, fall into distinct categories concerning their reaction to zone defenses. The first type of coach uses the same offense against all zone defenses, making as few modifications as possible in the basic pattern, under the premise that simplicity, repetition, and proper execution are the hallmarks of successful offense. To see the effectiveness of this philosophy in action, one needs to look no farther than pro football's legendary Vince Lombardi and his famous "Lombardi Sweep" end-around play.

The second type of coach continually changes or adjusts her team's zone offensive patterns to adapt to the type of zone coverage the opponents are using. Since few coaches make wholesale changes in their offense from game to game merely for the sake of change, it becomes apparent that radical changes may result from the coach's dissatisfaction with either the patterns themselves or the team's inability to run them correctly (which amounts to practically the same thing). A pattern may appear to be foolproof on paper, but if a team cannot translate the movements into points on the scoreboard, it is as useless as screen doors on a

[1] Sometimes referred to as "containing" zone defense.

submarine. Personnel deficiencies can render any offensive pattern harmless.

But who is right, the coach who never changes offensive patterns or the one who switches at the drop of a pass? Personnel considerations aside, probably both are partly correct. With three All-Staters in the lineup and a starting team that averages 6'2" tall, *any* pattern will probably work; and with a team of 5'3" players for whom three consecutive dribbles or passes without a turnover is cause for celebrating, one may as well flip a coin in selecting offensive patterns as to spend sleepless nights maneuvering O's and X's on paper searching for the One True Zone Offense.

Is this not, then, an argument that defeats the purpose of this book? Not at all. Rather than serving as a panacea for a team's zone offensive ills, this book is intended to offer ideas, suggestions, and analyses of as many problems as possible concerning zone offense.

In fact, the previous arguments reinforce the need for such a book to clear away the haze of misunderstanding surrounding the entire problem of zone offenses. We coaches keep hoping to unearth the Universal Zone Offense, one that can be used with equal facility and success against sinking, switching, trapping or matchup zones, regardless of the quality of available personnel. But deep in our hearts we know we'll never find it, because it doesn't exist except on teams whose players are extremely effective inside or outside. The final answers concerning zone offenses will not be unearthed like the Dead Sea Scrolls in the form of this volume or any other.

There is no secret formula or short cut to success concerning zone offenses. If there were, basketball minds greater than yours or mine would have found and cashed in on them by now, and none of us would have the problems we face daily in trying to find patterns our teams can run.

Where, then, do we stand? Are we, according to existentialist Jean-Paul Sartre, standing on the brink of a great void with nothingness before us and behind us to guide our actions? No, we have the collected wisdom of those who have expended millions of reams of paper manipulating the same O's and X's with which we've struggled; and even more important, we have our own resources, including the desire to increase our own understanding of zone defenses and offenses by reading, attending coaching clinics, talking with other coaches, scouting opponents to study the ways they use their zone defenses and search for weaknesses in their coverage, and improving the fundamental skills our players will need in executing various zone offensive movements.

NINE PRINCIPLES OF ZONE OFFENSIVE STRATEGY

1. Know Where the Zone Weaknesses Occur. Although the wisdom of this statement appears self-evident, many coaches note in their scouting reports that a team used a 2–1–2 zone defense, for example, but fail to note exactly *how* the team played their 2–1–2; that is, which players covered the passes to the wings, how they covered cutters through the zone, whether or not they matched up, the areas where trapping occurred, or how many players covered the weak side in overloads. Coverage and movements within the same zone defense vary from team to team, and coaches scouting future opponents would be well advised to note the nuances and idiosyncracies of coverage rather than merely noting that, "They stayed in a 2–1–2 zone throughout the game." Any zone defense can be used in several different ways to accomplish various defensive goals.

Every zone defense has weaknesses. The coach must be aware of what the opponents are trying to do before she can attack those weaknesses, but she must also understand the theory and practice of zone defense before adopting offensive patterns designed to combat specific zone defensive coverages.

Studying the various zone defensive alignments shown in Chapter 1 will reveal that, with the single exception of matchup zone defense, *every zone defense has openings, or holes, in the basic coverage.* These openings occur inside and outside, varying with the alignment, but they always occur, except as noted above.

Peripheral Openings. The openings for outside shooting vary from zone to zone and will be investigated at length in Chapter 4, "Splitting Patterns," but the point is that players should receive ample time practicing shooting from the outside openings—the corners, the wings, and intermediate wing positions.

When game strategy is completed, a team should expect to have its best outside shooters setting up in, or cutting to, the outside openings.

Inside Openings. Since a basic objective of most zone defenses is to provide additional defensive strength near the basket, the inside openings are found in those areas between defensive players in which defensive responsibilities overlap. These inside openings, known as the seams of a zone, shift with the movement of the defensive players, and players should be taught where the seams are to be found in various zone alignments and ball positions. Sliding or cutting into or through the seams provides the basis for much of the inside game in zone offenses.

When offensive overloads are established, the defense will leave either one or two players to guard the weak side of the court. Any of several offensive maneuvers (e.g., sending cutters through the lane to the weak side) combined with rapid ball rotation can produce two-on-one offensive advantages or situations in which weak side matchups favor the offensive team.

Finally, every team using zone defense has players who are less effective defensively than others, and it is often possible to attack these players one-on-one within the zone offensive pattern. On the other hand, some coaches prefer to attack the opponents' *strength* by playing to the best defensive player in hopes of getting her into foul trouble. Cutter patterns or screening can foil the defense's desired matchups and create matchups favoring the offensive team.

2. Provide an Inside Scoring Threat. Offensive patterns without cutters or outside movement are sometimes effective in cases where the defenders are totally committed to passive defense, staying inside and giving up the outside shot completely, but such instances are few and far between. In most cases, the defense will provide at least a modicum of outside coverage, hoping to entice the offensive player into taking the outside shot, but from farther out than desired and with greater defensive pressure than was expected. If a team sets up offensively with five players outside and does not send cutters inside, the defense will gradually move outside to increase defensive pressure on the perimeter shooters.

The most elementary form of inside strategy is to place a player at high or low post and tell her to follow the movement of the ball from one side of the free-throw lane to the other. The countless other patterns of inside movement may be grouped under two general headings, *splitting the defense* and *outside cutter patterns*.

Splitting the Defense. In terms of a team's inside game, splitting the defense refers to setting players at both low post positions when the defense has only one player deep (e.g., 1–3–1 defense), or using a high post player when the defensive team has no one guarding the high post in its basic zone defensive alignment (e.g., 1–2–2 zone defense).

Outside Cutter Patterns. An outside cutter is any outside offensive player who cuts through the middle of a zone defense, whether from weak side to ball side or vice versa. The defenders must react to every outside movement and cut or risk the possibility of inside passes and layups or unhindered shots.

The outside cutter does not have to be an effective inside player to be a scoring threat. Regardless of a player's size or shooting ability, her inside movement forces the defense to guard her at least perfunctorily, whereas keeping her outside may ease the defense's inside coverage problems.

Perhaps the easiest way for any team to provide an inside scoring threat against zone defenses, however, is to fast break whenever possible. Fast breaking provides high-percentage shots, wears the opponents down physically, and takes advantage of any tendency on the part of the opponents' tall players to take their time getting back on defense.

Fast-breaking techniques and philosophy are described in greater detail in Chapter 6.

3. Rotate Players Around the Outside of the Zone. Along with sending cutters into or through the zone, outside players should rotate around toward the ball and fill the positions left by the cutters. The cutter's inside movement tends to draw her outside guard inside toward the basket, and outside rotation can sometimes yield a good shot from the area vacated by the cutter.

4. Overload One or More Zones. The term *overload* may refer to either having more players on one side of the court than the other (see Figures 3-2, 3-3, and 3-4), or to setting or cutting more than one offensive player in the area of the court covered by a single defender.

Overload alignments and patterns offer the offensive team several advantages over balanced alignments. First, the overload forces defensive players far out of their basic positions in addition to forcing them to cover more than one player in their area and generally tends to weaken coverage of the weak side of the court. Second, overloading tends to force one-on-one defensive coverage—which, although, it may or may not be to the offensive team's advantage, reduces the possibility of double-teaming or trapping. Third, rotation of the overload and the players involved can effectively combat matchup zone defense by altering both the defenders' intended matchups and the areas in which the matchups occur.

5. Set Screens. Coaches and players alike often forget that screening, or blocking defensive players away from the ball or cutters, can sometimes prove as effective against zone defenses as against player-to-player defense.

To be successful against zone defense, however, screening generally occurs along the perimeters of the zone (e.g., the baseline or the corners of the free-throw line) rather than directly in the heart of the defense. A sim-

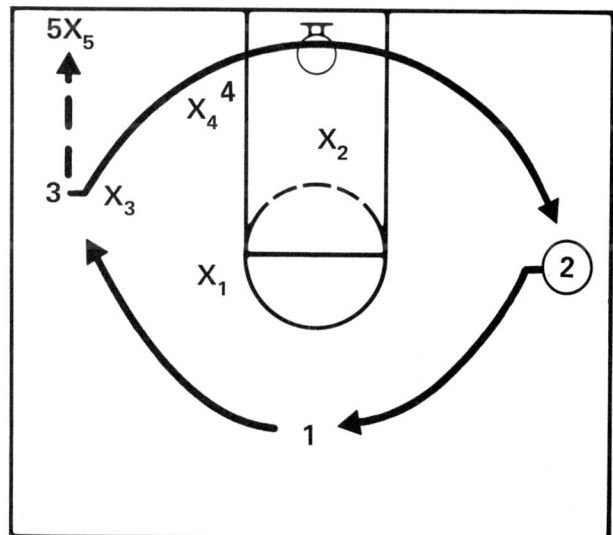

Figure 2-1 Outside Rotation Toward the Ball with Cutter in Overload Offense.

ple inside screen is far more likely to work against player-to-player coverage than against zone defense.

The difference between player-to-player and zone defensive coverage is that in player-to-player coverage the defense may or may not switch defensive assignments, depending upon the type of player-to-player coverage involved (i.e., pressure defense, switching, sinking, or trapping), while in zone coverage the defenders will switch automatically, *regardless of whether the screen is set.* In zone defense, the high–low post interchange itself is as likely to free the players involved to receive a pass as the act of screening inside.

This is not to say, however, that inside screening cannot work against zone defenses. In Chapter 4, numerous inside screening movements and cuts are shown, but inside screening is generally thought to be more difficult to accomplish than screening along the perimeters of the zone.

6. Stress Automatics and Freelancing. A common mistake found among many players and teams, especially on the junior high level, is slavish adherence to the basic movements of an offensive pattern, even when the defense overplays or exaggerates its coverage to stop the pattern. Players should be coached as thoroughly as possible in the automatics of a given pattern, including the options available and where they are likely to occur on the court.

We are not asserting that players should freelance as opposed to running patterns, but if a team fails to avail itself of freelancing movements when opportunities arise, the pattern is likely foreordained to failure. Personnel considerations aside, practically any zone offensive pattern can be defeated by overplaying—*but not without creating other opportunities for the offensive team to take advantage of.* It goes without saying that not every opportunity for freelancing will succeed even when players break the pattern to go one-on-one; however, without resorting to such tactics at least occasionally to keep the defense honest, the basic offensive pattern is unlikely to succeed.

7. Urge Players to Drive Whenever Possible. Although driving against zones is often risky and difficult, it does not follow that players should never drive against zone defenses, as some old-time coaches insisted. Driving the baseline, for example, can yield baskets when an inside defender's baseline coverage is extremely aggressive, and it can also provide an excellent means of getting defensive players in foul trouble or attacking players already in foul trouble. Additionally, it can set up the corner shooter for open shots when the defender drops back to stop the drive: if a defender respects the ballhandler's driving ability, she is likely to stay back and surrender the outside shot rather than risk the chance of fouling her on the drive.

Driving against zone defenses is most dangerous to the offensive team when the ballhandler sacrifices ball control for speed in getting around the defender and to the basket as quickly as possible. Ballhandling violations or charging fouls often result from a player's failure to slow down slightly once having gotten around the defender, forgetting that once she has passed the first line of defense, she still has to contend with the rest of the zone defense.

Penetrating the zone on the dribble is sometimes highly advantageous to a team. When used with discretion and an understanding of how the defenders are playing their zone defense, the penetrating dribble through two defenders into the heart of the zone can create more offensive possibilities than any other maneuver in zone offense. Often, a defensive team will spread its outside guards to increase coverage of the wings, especially when covering overload patterns; and an alert ballhandler can take advantage of the spread to penetrate as shown in Figure 2–2.

With the ball at the wing, X_1 has moved over to help cover the high post area, and the rotation pass to the point guard permits penetration between X_1 and X_2. If X_2 stays back, 1 will take the layup, and if X_2 moves up to cover the dribbler, 2 will be open for the pass and layup.

8. Be Patient. Two of the worst habits a team can get into are taking the first shot it gets against defenses and forcing bad shots when good shots do not appear immediately. First shots may or may not be the best shots available, but acquiring the habit of taking shots simply for the sake of shooting or because they're available is to be avoided at all costs.

All teams that use zone defenses normally have some kind of defen-

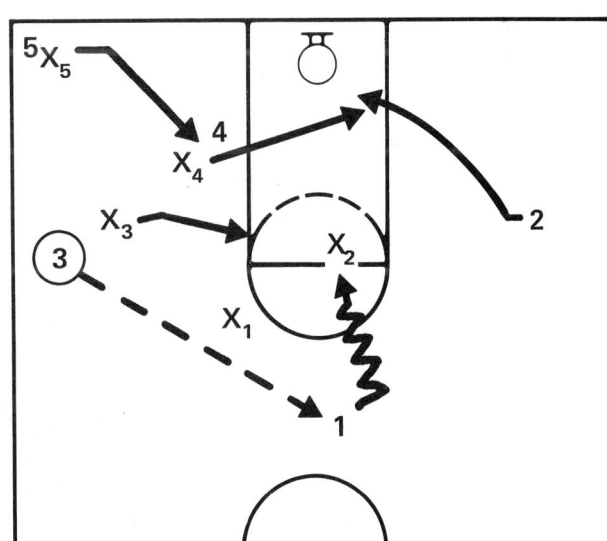

Figure 2-2 Point Guard Penetrating from Overload.

sive problem or weaknesses, or else they would be in player-to-player defense. Still, patience is often required to find the weaknesses in a particular zone coverage. A team need not pass up good shots in order to display its patience; however, the ability to wait for openings to occur within the zone coverage is a hallmark of all good basketball teams.

9. Consider Offensive Rebounding and Defensive Balance. Teams are often guilty of ignoring the possibilities of offensive rebounding against zone defenses. Figure 2–2 shows a situation that occurs frequently in zone offense, yet players seldom take advantage of the defensive coverage to rebound effectively in this situation.

When the shot is taken, the weak side low post player (3 in Figure 2–3) can greatly increase her chances of rebounding offensively by blocking the weak side defender (No. 10) away from the weak side of the court rather than going directly to the boards to rebound. Rebounding away from the ball is often overlooked, yet it can provide many points for alert players. Zone offensive patterns should take into account opportunities for weak side rebounding, especially since the ball side rebounding is likely to be sporadic at best.

The term *defensive balance* refers to the offensive team's keeping at

Figure 2-3 Blocking Inside Defenders Away from Rebounds in Zone Offense.

Team Strategy in Zone Offense   49

Figure 2-4 Defensive Balance in a Zone Offense.

least one player outside to stop the opponents' fast break when the ball changes hands. If, for example, the ballhandler passes to the wing and cuts to the corner to create an overload as shown in Figure 2–4, another offensive player will, in all likelihood, move to the area of the top of the circle for defensive balance. Otherwise, the defensive guard (21) will have an unhindered fast break layup when the ball changes hands.

CONCLUSION

There are very few absolutes in basketball. Perhaps we might even be permitted to assert that the *only* absolutes in basketball are the referees' decisions and the final score. The rest of basketball is based on contingencies, on a universe of *ifs* and *buts* that, as someone said, "If *ifs* and *buts* were candy and nuts, every day would be Christmas." Defense wins ballgames—*but not always!* You can't win without the tall player—except that every year thousands of teams do just that! The only thing you can count on is that winning is going to be even tougher than you thought it would be.

Every coach needs to develop a personal basketball philosophy, and the zone offenses she intends to use should reflect that philosophy. In order to communicate her expectations to her players, a coach must understand the limitations of both her players and the offensive patterns she hopes to teach them. If hers is a racehorse, run-and-gun style, she must develop racehorses capable of playing the high-speed transition game. If she is an exponent of careful, deliberate play, she must be aware of the offensive styles of play that most nearly achieve that goal. If she advocates freelancing or one-on-one situations, she must be able to find ways to structure one-on-one situations that lessen or eliminate the possibility of defensive double-teaming (e.g., clearout patterns).

There is an ancient maxim that "familiarity breeds contempt," but familiarity in terms of *awareness* also breeds success against zone defenses.

Chapters 3 and 4 deal with the two basic styles of zone offensive play, *overload offenses* and *splitting patterns*. Chapter 5 covers special situations and patterns with which a coach may have to contend.

3 Overload Offenses

Against the side she would defend...
Jonathan Swift
The Furniture of a Woman's Mind

Overloading is one of two basic systems for attacking zone defenses. Its defining characteristics include: (1) ball side low post and wing players; (2) a player setting up in, or cutting to, the corner and/or high post positions; and (3) one or two weak side players, depending upon whether or not the offense uses both the ball side corner and high post positions.

An offense is said to be overloaded when three or more players set up on, or cut to, one side of the court at one time, or when two or more players are in the zone of responsibility of a single defensive player.

The primary objective of such alignments is, of course, to create uncertainty concerning defensive coverage and to force the defensive players far outside from their basic positions in shifting with ball and player movement. Rapid ball rotation to the weak side of the court further spreads the defense, and sending cutters through the lane alters the defensive matchups.

Overloading with three players provides an excellent means for combatting defensive trapping or double-teaming inside, since the spread formation stretches the defensive coverage to its limits when only two players are left to defend the ball side corner and high post, the point, and the entire weak side of the court. (The players in Figure 3–1 indicate areas of the court that the defense may attempt to cover— and *could* cover, if they were permitted to use seven players on the court at the same time!)

Before analyzing the merits, virtues, and strengths of overload offenses, however, perhaps we should discuss reasons why a team might *not* want to create or use overload situations:

Figure 3-1 Overloading to Spread Defensive Coverage When the Low Post Is Double-Teamed.

1. Although practically all teams use overload offenses at least occasionally against zone defenses, a surprisingly large number of teams misuse the offense, failing to grasp the finer implications of its use. For example, some teams overload one side of the court in order to achieve the open corner shot, then compound their error by abandoning the offense whenever the defense matches up. In isolated cases, a team's best shooter may excel from the corner and prefer that area to shooting from the wing or point positions; however, it is generally true that the corner shot is one of the lowest percentage shots in basketball. Depth perception is difficult without the visual cues provided by the backboard, and shooters sometimes lose sight of the rim in the mottled background of the crowd. Too, while errant shots from the wing or point sometimes bounce in off the backboard, the corner shooter is seldom so lucky.

2. Overload offenses with four offensive players on the strong side of the court reduce the area available for one-on-one confrontations and increase the likelihood of double-teaming or trapping by the defense. Even when the defense does not double-team, however, they can match up rather easily, and a team with poor ballhandlers may find the ball confined to one side of the court.

3. Teams with no legitimate inside scoring threats will have difficulty combatting matchup zones by overloading, since the defense will be able to cover the outside positions more easily than when the offense is using some kind of splitting pattern.

4. Finally, overload offenses are relatively slow in rotating the ball from one side of the court to the other, especially in junior high and girls' basketball where the players simply cannot make the long, crisp chest or

overhead passes necessary to move the ball around the perimeter of the zone to the opposite wing or corner before the defense has time to adjust. In fact, in many cases the players are unable to make the long diagonal cross-court passes necessary to defeat the zone coverage.

Strengths of Overload Offenses. Overloads practically guarantee one-on-one coverage, and when such matchups are to the advantage of the offensive team, especially inside matchups, overloading can be the answer to a team's prayers.

Overloads force the defensive team out of its basic positioning, and whenever defensive players are moving they are more likely than when stationary to make mistakes in judgment and coverage.

Overload offenses, especially three-player alignments, tend to spread the defense while retaining inside positions close enough to the basket to facilitate offensive rebounding while making outside shooting feasible.

When a team has good ballhandlers capable of moving the ball quickly, overloads can create two-on-one offensive advantages away from the ball.

Overloads may be used against all types of zone defenses, even trapping or matchup zones, with minimal changes.

The rhythmic movements of cross-court rotation tend to lull the defense into automatic movements, which an alert offensive team can take advantage of.

The movements of most overload rotation patterns are simple and are easily learned by beginning players as well as by veterans.

OVERLOAD POSITIONS AND STRATEGY

While splitting patterns put offensive players into the gaps between the defensive players and attempt to *freeze* the defense into immobility, overload offenses rely upon defensive movement to either: (1) force matchups unfavorable to the defense, or (2) move the defense out of position to adequately protect the weak side of the court.

Although it is technically true that *any* offensive pattern is an overload pattern when a majority of the offensive players are on one side of the court, in terms of practical usage and the goals outlined above, an offense is an overload offense only when the overload is on the ball side of the court and possesses a wing, a corner, and at least one post player. (See Figures 3–2, 3–3, and 3–4.)

Thus, the basic 1–3–1 offensive alignment is not really an overload, although the players can shift into an overload with facility.

At first glance the overload concept appears limited in potential, with only one three-player alignment and two four-player alignments.

54 Zone Offenses for Women's Basketball

Figure 3-2 Three-Player Overload.

Figure 3-3 Four-Player Overload, Box-and-One Alignment.

Overload Offenses 55

Figure 3-4 Four-Player Overload, Diamond-and-One Alignment.

Figure 3-5 False Overload (1–3–1 Alignment).

Figure 3-6 False Overload Shifting into Overload Alignment.

Figure 3-7 Basic Overload Positions.

However, its simplicity is the clue to its widespread misuse: Team A works for a corner shot, and Team B responds by matching up, with their superior inside defensive player shutting off the inside pass. Frustrated, Team A calls time out and switches to an outside splitting pattern. End of experimentation with overload offenses.

As we shall see, however, the overload principle is extremely versatile, even with teams of limited experience or ability. In fact, with young or inexperienced players the use of overloads is often more effective than splitting patterns.

Perhaps the most important aspect of teaching overload offensive patterns is stressing the players' setting up in, and cutting to, the proper positions. It is, therefore, vital for the coach to understand why, as well as where, the corner, wing, and high-low post positions are stressed.

The Low Post. The proper positioning at low post is just outside the free-throw lane, with the player's feet adjacent to the solid colored lane

Figure 3-8 Foot Positioning at Low Post.

divider. Players should be coached to look at their feet when learning to cut to the low post position, in order to avoid setting up too low (near the baseline), too high (near the free-throw line), or with one or both feet in the lane. If a player sets up too low, she will be out of position for a turnaround jump shot off the backboard; and if she sets up too high, she invites double-teaming by sinking guards or forwards.

Inside players should be taught to always face the ball and keep their hands up to receive passes. Incidentally, the term *facing the ball* refers to an offensive player's setting up with her entire body, including her feet, facing the ball. Many young players think that "facing the ball" means *looking* at it, whether their bodies are turned toward the ball or not. Thus, they are off-balance when they attempt to catch passes. Perhaps this is one reason for dropped passes.

In three-player overloads, the low post is usually the preferred shooter, with the corner or wing players shooting from the outside only when they cannot pass inside, or when the defense refuses to come out to challenge them. (It should be noted in passing that the low post player may not be the primary receiver in overloads, as in four-player overloads, serving instead as a decoy to free a teammate cutting to high post for a pass.) (See Figure 3–12.) In such cases, the low post may set up nearer the baseline than previously, not to receive the pass but to keep the high post from being double-teamed.

The Corners. The distance from the basket that an offensive player sets up in the corner varies with the defensive coverage, of course, but the average distance is usually 15–18 feet from the basket. What *is* important, however, although it is usually overlooked by both coaches and players, is the distance the inside player sets up *from the baseline.* Players often want to set up 6–9 feet from the baseline in order to achieve a slightly better shooting angle, but the recommended distance from the baseline is no more than 3 feet—or, put more simply, even with the edge of the backboard. This position reduces shooting efficiency to a certain extent, but more importantly, it facilitates the inside pass to the low post from the corner, as shown in Figure 3–10. (In order to avoid double-teaming or trapping, the corner player will merely back away from the nearest inside defender. If that defender continues outside, the inside pass to low post from the wing will be facilitated.)

When the wing passes to the corner, the inside defensive player (55) will always move straight to her, and if she is too far from the baseline, the quick bounce pass or chest pass inside will be eliminated. (See Figures 3–9 and 3–10.) The lob pass may still be made, but the idea is to pass inside quickly while the defense is still adjusting to the wing's pass to the corner. Players should not be permitted to move to the general vicinity of the corner in practice; rather, they should learn to move to the *exact spot* where the coach wants them to set up in the corner. Taped or chalked X's on the floor can help them to learn where they are supposed to go.

In overload offenses, the corner shooter must be able to make the unchallenged shot often enough to bring the defense out, or else they will stay back to defend the inside game and give away the low-percentage shots from the corner. The coach desiring to implement an effective overload offense will drill her players in shooting from the corners as well as from other areas of the court.

The Wings. The positioning of the wings is not so invariable as the low post or corner positions. The only real considerations are that they must be far enough from the corner to spread the defense and far enough from the low post (and high post in four-player overloads) to permit inside offensive players to maneuver. As a general rule of thumb, however, it is suggested that they set up somewhere outside along the invisible extensions of the free-throw line. (In splitting patterns, they may set up 6–8 feet closer to the baseline than in overloads, since *they* may be the primary shooters rather than the corner shooters or inside players.)

If the wing player sets up 15 feet out from the basket along the free-throw line extended, it may be argued she will be too far out to shoot high-

Overload Offenses 59

Figure 3-9 Results of Incorrect Corner Positioning.

Figure 3-10 Correct Corner Positioning

percentage shots. This is, unfortunately, true, but it stresses the importance of getting the ball inside to the high or low post player—the first consideration of all overload offenses.

The High Post. The position we are analyzing here is not that taken by a player setting up at high post (e.g., the middle of the free-throw line), but rather *the position at which the high post player expects to receive the ball,* which may be anywhere within 6 feet of the corner of the free-throw lane on the ball side of the court. That this position seems nebulous is due to the varieties of zone coverage of the pass from the point guard to the wing. In Figure 3–2, for example, when 25 passes to the wing, the defensive wing will guard the pass receiver, but either X_{21} or X_{23} will guard the high post on the ball side of the court, depending upon whether low post is single-guarded or double-teamed.

In the former case, with X_{21} responsible for the high post position when the overload is established, a tall offensive player cutting to the high post will have a decided advantage over a small defensive guard. In the latter case, with X_{21} double-teaming inside and X_{23} covering the high post, the area in which the player cutting to high post catches the ball will vary greatly. Thus, coaches tell their players to "cut to the opening" in the zone wherever it occurs.

The most widely used cutting patterns in passing to high post are: (1) the high post player at the center of the free-throw line sliding to the opening, as shown in Figure 3–11, or (2) the weak side low post player's cutting across the lane to the opening, as shown in Figure 3–12.

High post players should be coached to turn to the middle of the court when they receive a pass from the wing. If they pivot to the outside of the court, they are almost certain to be double-teamed, or possibly even triple-teamed. Upon receiving the pass from the wing, their alternatives are to: (1) shoot from the high post position, (2) drive, or (3) pass to the weak side wing, who may or may not be cutting to the basket. Young players have a tendency to turn to their right after receiving a pass (if they turn at all), which is fine for the left side of the court, but on the right side of the court they are almost certain to confront fierce opposition.

The Point Guard. The primary responsibilities of the point guard are usually: (1) to protect against the opponents' fast break, (2) to rotate the ball to the weak side of the court, and (3) to penetrate or take the 12–15 foot shot whenever possible. (Notice that shooting is the third option, not the first.) From time to time the point guard may be able to get the ball inside to the high or low post, but such cases are comparatively rare in overload offenses—except when *the offensive players and the ball are rotating to the weak side of the court.* An alert point guard sometimes can pass back across the zone as it is shifting or find teammates cutting across the lane for easy inside shots.

Overload Offenses 61

Figure 3-11 High Post Sliding.

Figure 3-12 Cut to High Post.

Depending upon the offensive strategy, the point guard may slide toward or away from the ball, cut or screen away from the ball, or even cut through the lane to the ball side corner.

BASIC OVERLOAD MOVEMENTS

Four of the simplest methods of setting up a three-player overload are shown in Figures 3-13, 3-14, 3-15, and 3-16. The movements involved in each of the patterns are easily learned by players on any skills level, regardless of their experience. In Figure 3-13, 2 cuts behind 5 to the ball side corner after 1's pass to wing 3—or 3 cuts to the corner behind 4/5 at low post—whomever the coach wants at low post on ball side, as 1 passes to 2. Players cutting to the corner should be coached to go *behind* the defensive players inside, who may not be looking for cutters until it is too late to stop the pass.

In Figure 3-14, 4 slides in a semicircular route along high post to low post, looking for an inside pass from 3 as 5 cuts to the corner.

A third method of setting up the overload (Figure 3-15) is superior when the point guard is a poor passer. Instead of passing directly to the wing, she dribbles to the wing position as the wing player slides to the corner.

The most effective of the four methods of overloading in terms of confusing the defensive assignments is that shown in Figure 3-16. Player 1 passes to 3, setting the defensive adjustments. Then player 1 moves to an outside position approximately along the side of the free-throw line ex-

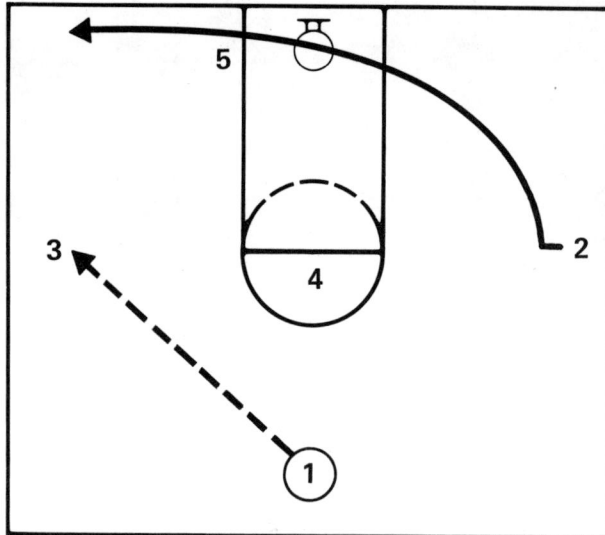

Figures 3-13, 3-14, 3-15, 3-16
Basic Overload Movements.

Overload Offenses 63

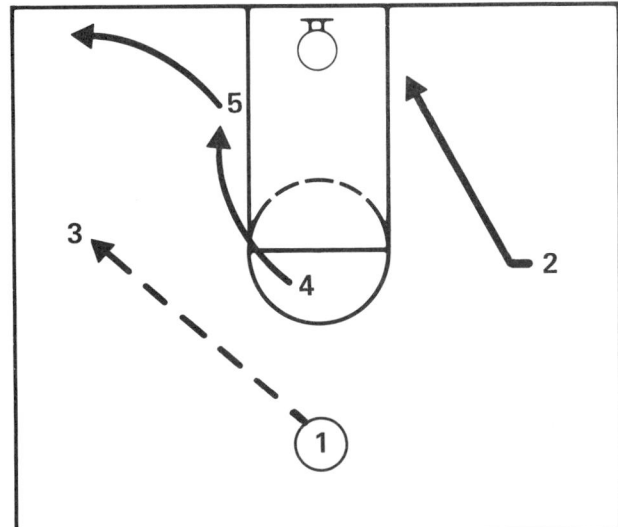

Figure 3-14.

Figure 3-15.

64 Zone Offenses for Women's Basketball

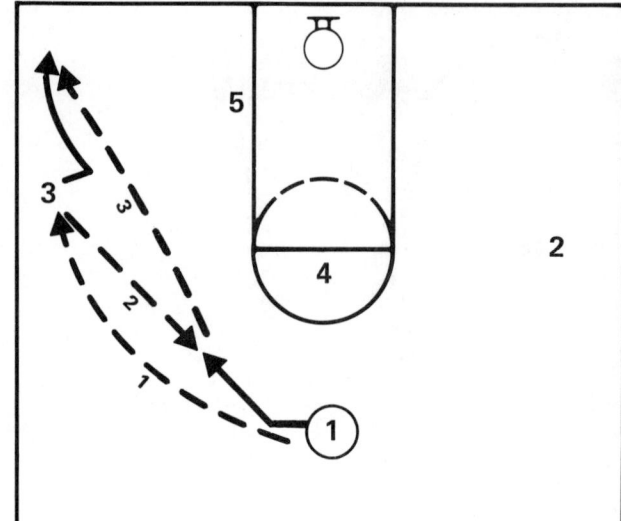

Figure 3-16.

tended, and 3 passes back to 1. In almost every case, the defensive guard or forward shifting to guard 3 after the first pass will continue to guard her until it becomes apparent that an inside defensive player will have to cover the corner. Similarly, when the inside defender comes out, she will usually be off-balance and out of position to stop the outside shot or inside pass.

OTHER APPROACHES TO OVERLOAD

The following diagrams are largely self-explanatory, with the exception that in Figure 3–17, the coach may prefer that her team set up in a four-player overload by sending 2 through to the corner, with 4 cutting across to high post instead of cutting behind the zone to the corner. The only problem associated with using 2 as the cutter to the corner is that the offense tends to bog down while waiting for 2 to reach the corner.

Both 1-4 and 1-2-2 configurations are superior in terms of setting up overloads because their court balance forces the defense into the maximum range of defensive adjustments to the cutters. (In an unbalanced alignment, the defense would already have adjusted to the offense before the first pass was made.)

A variation of the movements shown in Figure 3–19 is for 4 to cut across to low post as 5 moves to the corner, with high post 3 cutting to low post away from the ball. Such movements tend to confuse defensive coverage of inside players.

Before leaving the discussion of setting up overloads from various of-

Overload Offenses 65

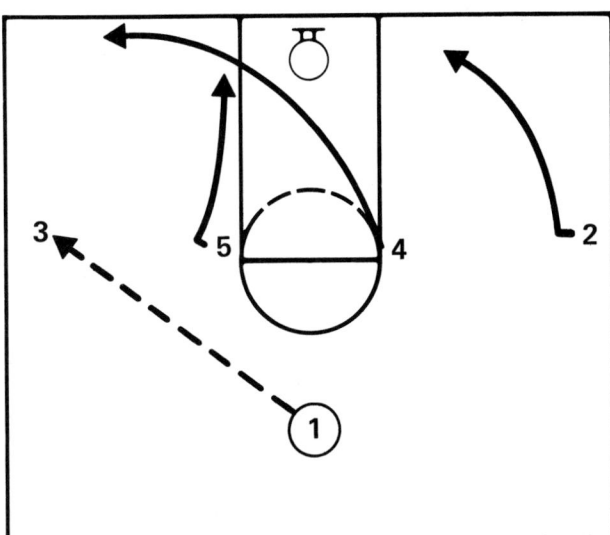

Figure 3-17 1-4 to Overload.

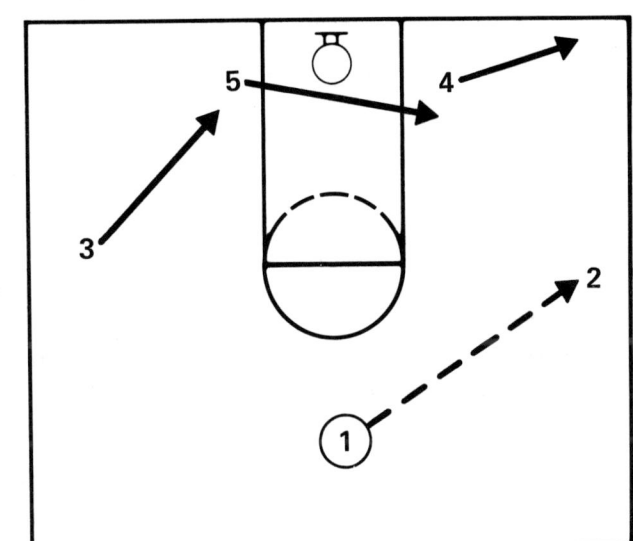

Figure 3-18 1-2-2 to Overload.

fensive alignments, it should be noted that any of the movements shown in Figures 3-13, 3-14, 3-15, and 3-16 can be made from 1-4, 1-2-2, 2-1-2, or other basic alignments.

A variation of the three-player overload sometimes used is the "cornerless" double post offense. Although seen more often than one would expect, such offenses are basically weak for two reasons: first, they tend to keep the opponents' taller defensive players inside, and thus reduce the effectiveness of the low post position; and second, the absence of a corner

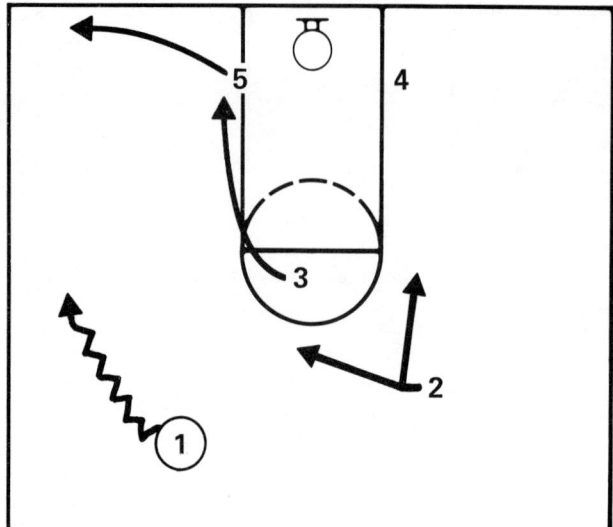

Figure 3-19 2-1-2 to Overload.

shooting threat facilitates defensive coverage of the wings.

On the other hand, the inside game afforded by the cornerless double post offense can be devastating as a rotation offense (see the section on multiple overload rotation system later in the chapter), especially when the inside players understand the automatics of zone offenses.

MAINTAINING THE OVERLOAD

For any of several reasons, a team may want to keep the ball (and the overload) on one side of the court rather than rotate to the other side. They may want to apply constant pressure offensively to a defensive player in foul trouble. Their outside ballhandling may be so weak as to limit their ability to rotate the ball quickly or with any degree of safety, or the defense may move outside to stop rotation passes to the point guard or weak side wing. Finally, the team may decide to use a passing game on one side of the court to delay, stall, or merely look for high-percentage shots for their best outside shooter.

Two methods exist for continuing movement without rotating the ball to the weak side once the overload has been established. If the defense's only tall player is at low post, the low post cutting to the corner, as shown in Figure 3–20, can create more favorable matchups inside, and at the same time draw the taller defensive player outside.

The third method of maintaining the overload is shown in Figure 3–21, an outside rotation pattern with a single cutter through the lane. Player 2 passes to the corner and cuts through the lane to the opposite wing (or to low post), anticipating a return pass from 4 as she cuts. Player

Overload Offenses   67

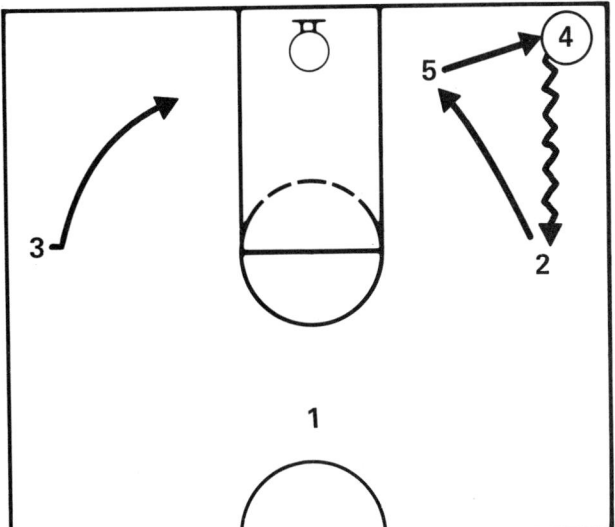

Figure 3-20 Maintaining the Overload by Dribbling Outside to the Wing.

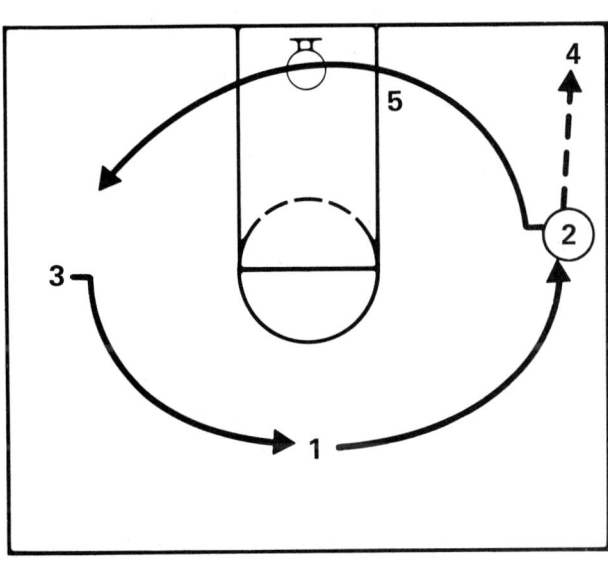

Figure 3-21 Outside Cutter through the Lane to Maintain Overload.

1 rotates around to 2's original wing position, and 3 moves to the point guard position. Outside rotation patterns are often used by teams with superior outside shooting and weak inside play.

ROTATION PATTERNS (ONCE THE OVERLOAD HAS BEEN ESTABLISHED)

Since the reason for using overload zone offenses is to move the defensive players out of their basic positions, and thus provide unhindered outside shooting or favorable inside matchups, the rotation patterns, or methods of moving the ball and offensive players from one side of the court to the other, are important to any overload offense. No overload offense will succeed regularly when the offensive team keeps the ball on only one side of the court. Ball rotation must be accomplished, despite any ballhandling shortcomings the offensive team may have; otherwise, the defense will require few or no adjustments after the pass from the point guard to the wing, or from the wing to the corner.

Therefore, the prerequisites for ball rotation include: (1) a good ballhandler, who must be responsible for moving the ball cross-court as offensive players shift; (2) the shift should be accomplished as economically as possible in terms of time required to make the rotation passes and cuts; (3) risky cross-court passes for the purpose of rotation (e.g., wing-to-wing passes) should be avoided at all costs; and (4) offensive players should be alert to inside passing situations at all times, including passing back against the zone as the defense shifts.

At higher levels of play the rotation may be rather involved, but with young or inexperienced players the simplest movements are usually best.

The most elementary form of overload rotation consists of the same person—player 5 in Figures 3-22 and 3-23—playing the corner on both sides of the court, with 4 playing low post on both sides. The weakness inherent in this strategy is the additional time necessary for 5 to go from one corner of the court to the other. For an inexperienced squad, or one with only one inside scoring threat, however, necessity might dictate such a rotation pattern.

Along with this rotation, an elementary form of outside rotation ex-

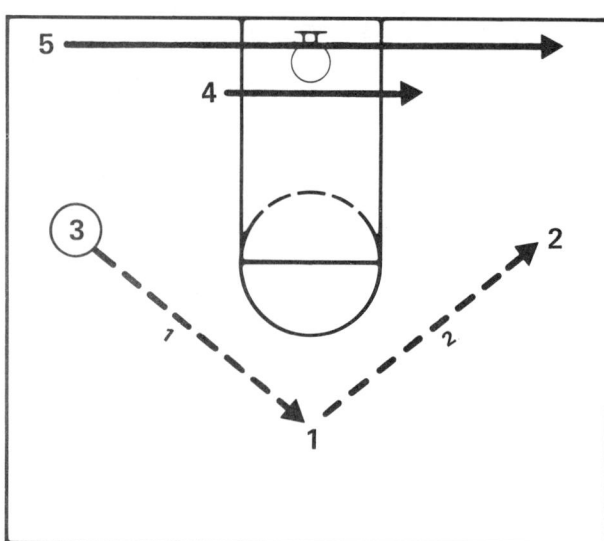

Figure 3-22 Elementary Inside Rotation.

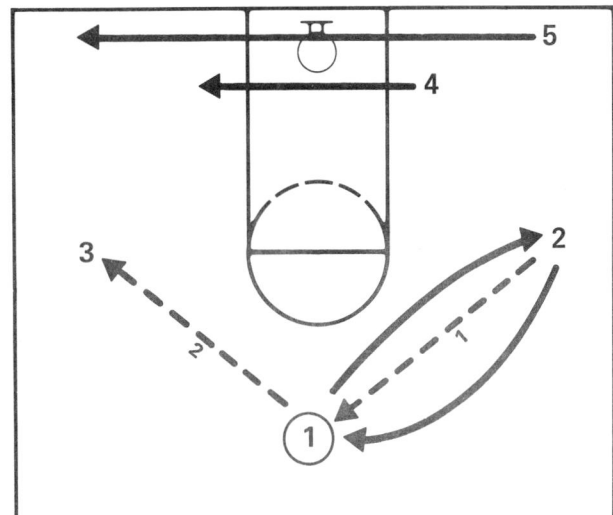

Figure 3-23 Elementary Outside Rotation.

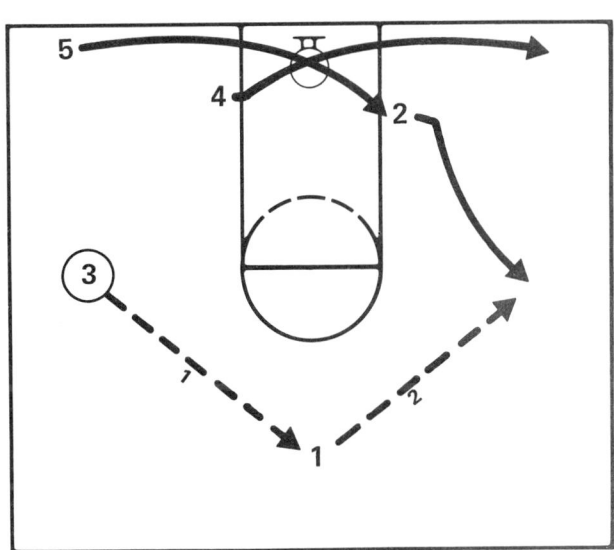

Figure 3-24 Criss-crossing Inside Rotation.

ists to add movement to the overload. After passing to one wing, the point guard cuts away from the ball toward the weak side wing, with that wing moving out to become the point guard. When the ball is rotated to the opposite side of the court, the point guard again cuts away from the ball to exchange with the weak side wing.

In addition to rotating the offense, players should be alert for opportunities to pass inside while rotation is in progress. One such opportunity occurs after the overload has been established and the ball has been passed back to the point.

Figure 3-25 Inside Movement and Pass in Overload Rotation.

While the wing player has the ball, the inside defender will usually front 4 inside at low post as shown in Figure 3-25. As 3 passes to 1 at the point, however, 4 will be clear momentarily for an inside pass as she begins her cut across the lane. If the weak side defender moves to cut off the inside pass to 4, 2 will be open on the weak side.

A REVOLVING ROTATION OVERLOAD OFFENSE

A more intricate system of "revolving rotation" can be extremely effective for combatting matchup zones, especially when the defense relies heavily upon the efforts of one defensive player inside, or when a team has a strong offensive inside game with two or three tall players.

Personnel Requirements. Player 3 may be either the weakest outside shooter or the poorest ballhandler. Her primary responsibility is to get the ball to the corner and cut through the lane, keeping her hands up and her eyes on the ball as she cuts, anticipating a return pass from the corner. A team whose wing players are roughly equal in outside shooting and ballhandling skill might use either 2 or 3 as the cutter, guided perhaps by the direction of 1's first pass.

The weak side wing (2 in Figure 3-26, although she moved inside with 1's pass to 3) should be prepared to play inside and in the corner as well, since 4/5's "revolving" movements in Figures 3-27 and 3-28 require that those positions be filled by someone other than 1 or 3.

Overload Offenses 71

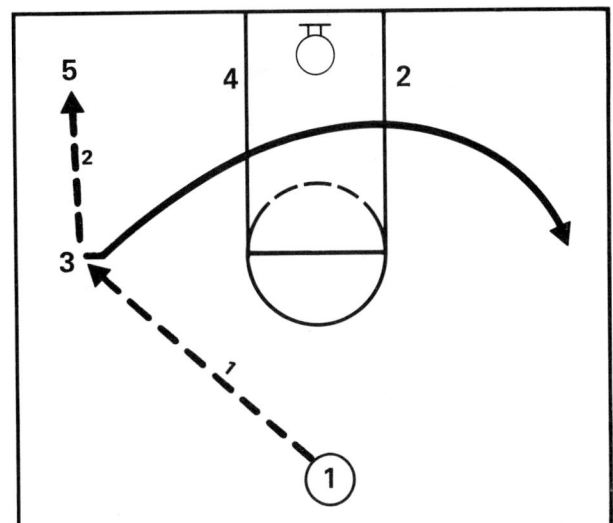

Figures 3-26, 3-27, 3-28, 3-29, 3-30 "Revolving Rotation" System.

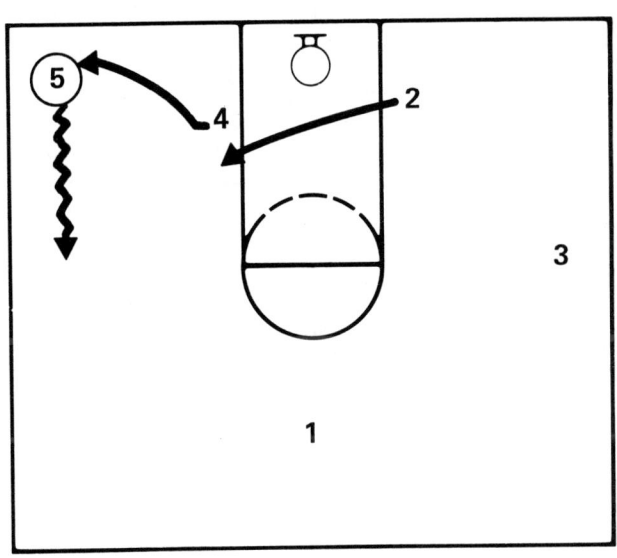

Figure 3-27.

Point guard 1's primary responsibility is rotating the ball from wing to wing. In order to take advantage of shooting opportunities afforded by the overload, 1 may move to an area near the corner of the free-throw lane away from the ball (see Figure 3–19). However, such movement increases the likelihood of the defense's intercepting the pass to the point guard.

Point guard 1 must be quick and maneuverable to break free when guarded closely, protecting the ball while dribbling when necessary, and

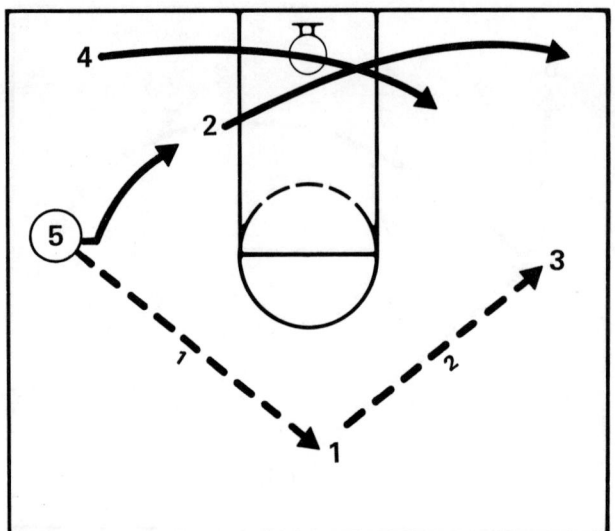

Figure 3-28.

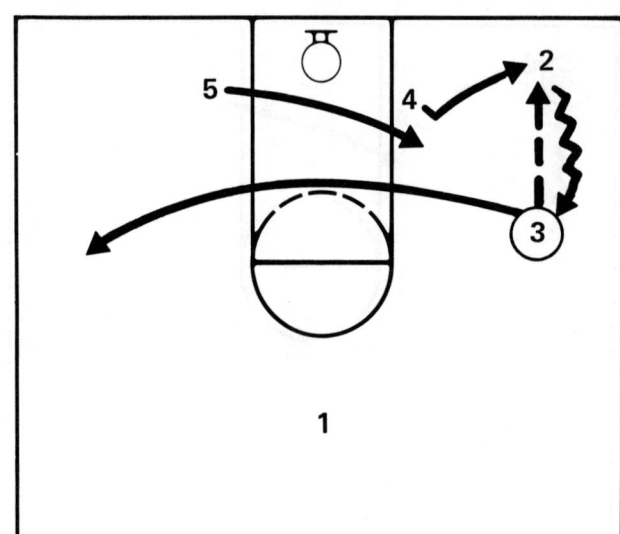

Figure 3-29.

capable of making quick, crisp passes without undue hesitation, since the defense will be shifting back to its original alignment with the pass from the wing to the point guard. Player 1 should be thoroughly familiar with the positions occupied by all of the players, both defensively and offensively, including those court positions to be filled by cutters in the offensive rotation. A thorough knowledge of court positions, together with the useful habit of glancing around while the ball is in the corner, will shorten the time necessary for the point guard to find the offensive cutters. If

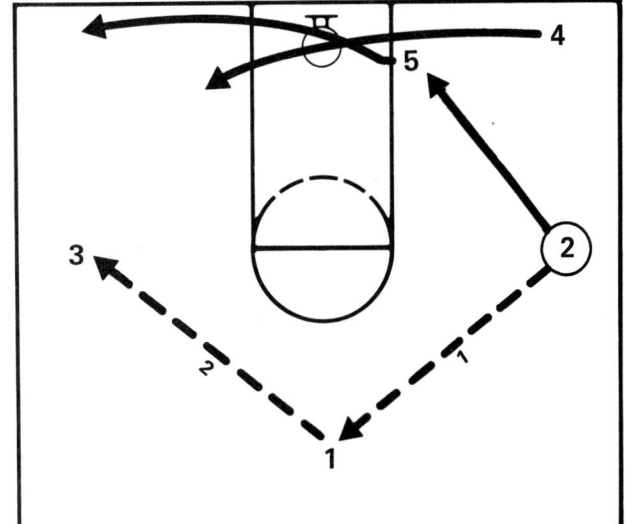

Figure 3-30.

possible, the point guard should be the team's best ballhandler.

Whenever possible, the inside offensive players should be effective corner shooters as well, since either the ball rotation or the players' revolving movements in Figures 3–27 or 3–28 may yield the open corner shot. Of course, it helps if they are also potent inside scoring threats, but even if they aren't especially aggressive inside, they must still occupy the inside positions as shown, since outside patterns by themselves are seldom effective. (If the offense relies solely upon outside patterns, the defense will simply match up and force the outside shots even farther out from the basket.)

FOUR-PLAYER OVERLOADS

There is a distinct tendency on the part of coaches to drastically over- or underestimate the effectiveness of four-player overload offenses. Enthusiastic supporters reason that, since four-player overloads are frequently encountered as double high-low post patterns, they must be twice as effective as overloads involving one inside player. Opponents argue that, because eight players are crowded into the same relatively small area of the court, the room available for one-on-one movements arising out of the overload is drastically limited. Furthermore, the ball (and the offensive players) takes longer to rotate to the other side of the court than in three-player overloads.

In truth, however, there are fallacies in *both* lines of reasoning. Four-player overloads require a minimum of two good inside players, depending upon the type of rotation used, and at least one of them must also be able to function effectively at high post in order to derive maximum benefit from the high-low post alignment. And, while it is generally true that the low post's effectiveness is curtailed to some extent by the presence of a high post player, the high post position affords offensive movements and penetration possibilities unknown to three-player overloads.

There are two basic types of four-player overload offenses: (1) the box-and-one overload and (2) the less-used diamond-and-one overload. The two may be run identically as continuity patterns. The two four-player alignments are shown in Figures 3–3 and 3–4.

The Box-and-One Overload. The variety of ways of setting up the box-and-one overload offense are limitless, as are the alignments from which the overload can be established. Figures 3–31 through 3–35 are representative of the various movements in setting up four-player overloads.

In Figure 3–31, weak side wing 2 cuts to the ball side corner simultaneous with 1's pass, and high post 4 slides to the opening in the zone. Point guard 1 may elect to cut opposite the ball, either to the corner of the free-throw line or to the weak side low post, or she may maintain position at the top of the circle in order to speed up ball rotation.

Figure 3–32 involves 1 dribbling to the wing position, 2 cutting through the lane to the ball side corner, 5 moving to high post, 4 cutting to ball side low post, and high post 3 cutting away from the ball to weak side low post. This pattern is less effective for several reasons: it has two offen-

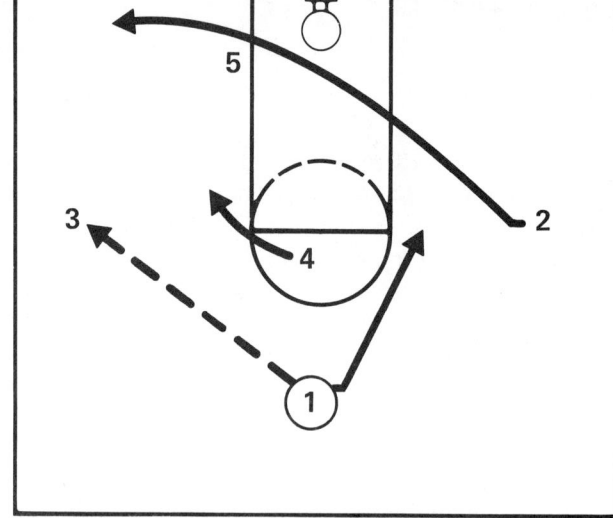

Figure 3-31 1–3–1 to Overload, Weak Side Wing Cut and High Post Slide.

Overload Offenses 75

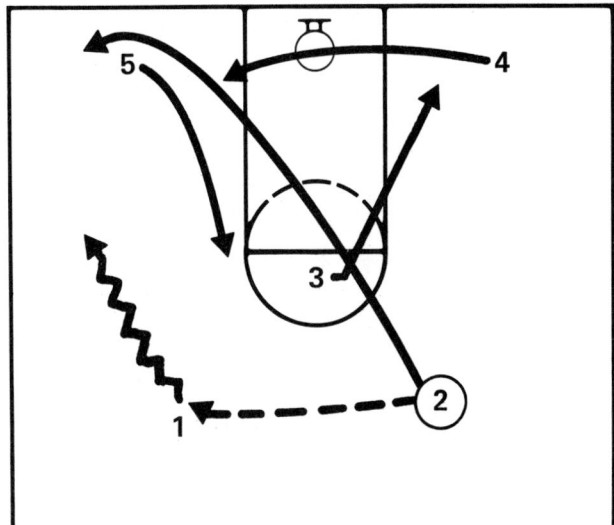

Figure 3-32 2-1-2 to Overload, Inside Rotation.

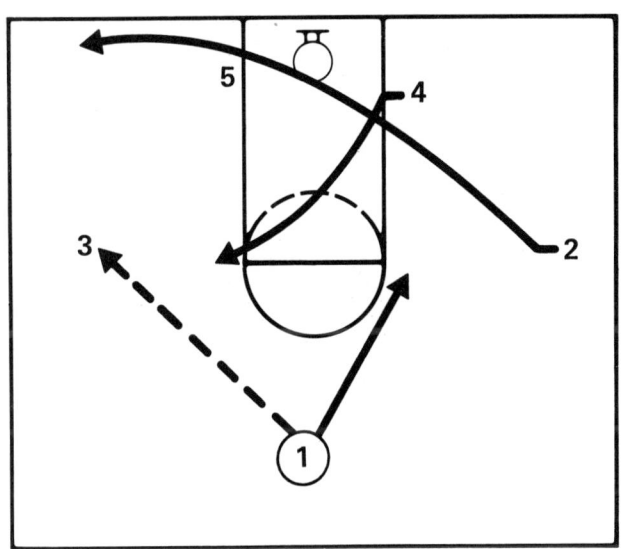

Figure 3-33 1-2-2 to Overload, Weak Side Wing and Low Post Cuts.

sive players cutting to the same general area; 5's move to high post is easily seen, and thus more easily defended than blind cuts such as 4's cut in Figure 3–33; 1's dribble to the wing position is slower than a pass would be, and therefore gives the defense ample opportunity to shift to optimal defensive positioning; and 3's cut away from the ball involves turning away from the ball, decreasing the likelihood of a surprise pass across the zone from the wing to weak side low post. However, the

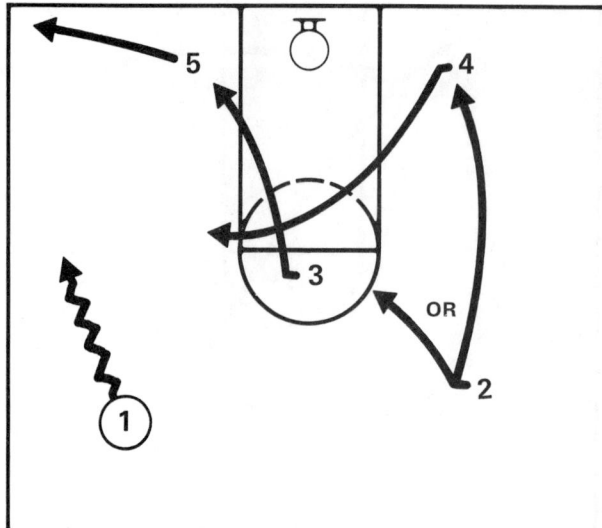

Figure 3-34 2-1-2 to Overload, High Post and Weak Side Low Post Cuts.

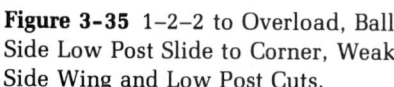

Figure 3-35 1-2-2 to Overload, Ball Side Low Post Slide to Corner, Weak Side Wing and Low Post Cuts.

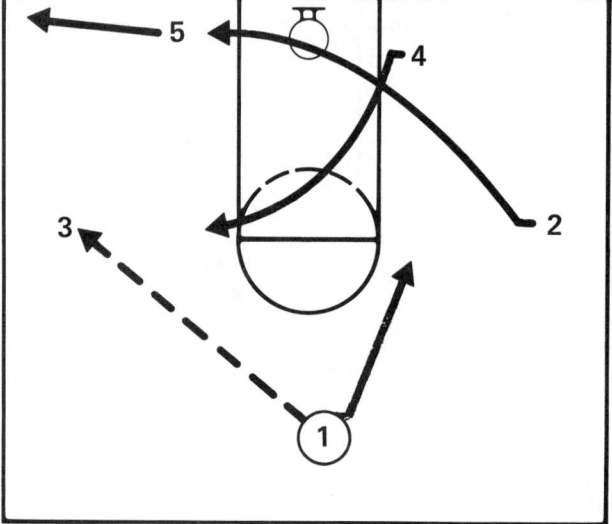

movements have been included to illustrate the range of options open to the offense.

The movements shown in Figure 3–33, on the other hand, are widely used and highly effective in setting up the four-player overload. While 2's cut is somewhat time consuming, the first option (4's cut through the lane to high post) will usually achieve either the corner shot or the pass inside to low post 5.

Player 4's cut in Figure 3-34 is identical to that shown in Figure 3-33, but 5 slides outside as 1 dribbles to the wing. Player 3 slides along the lane to low post. Player 2 may move inside or to the top of the circle, depending upon the defensive coverage and movement. Player 5's cut facilitates ball movement to the corner to a higher degree than that shown in the previous alignments. Thus, in cases where getting the ball to the corner is a primary offensive objective, a cut from ball side low post to the corner may be highly rewarding.

Finally, Figure 3-35 illustrates the same movements in different order and from a different alignment: simultaneous with 1's pass to wing 3, 5 cuts to the corner and 4 and 2 criss-cross to ball side high and low posts. Player 1's cut to the weak side corner of the free-throw line is optional.

Before discussing methods of rotating the four-player overload to the weak side of the court, 1's optional move to the weak side corner of the free-throw line should be mentioned. When the overload is established, the first offensive priority is to pass inside to the high post. When the high post player gets the ball, she should pivot toward the middle of the court rather than toward the baseline in order to avoid double-teaming, and because the defensive player guarding high post will almost surely overguard from the inside. (See Figure 3-36.)

When the high post pivots with the ball toward the center of the court and the point guard has moved to the opposite corner of the free-throw line, the two of them can force a two-on-one confrontation with the single defensive player away from the overload. (See Figure 3-36.)

Figure 3-36 Forcing Two-on-One from High Post in Four-Player Overload.

Rotating the Box-and-One Overload. Once the overload has been established, the inside rotation pattern is easily accomplished. Perhaps the simplest method is the criss-crossing "inside-outside" movement shown in Figure 3-37.

As 3 passes to 1, 2 and 4 criss-cross to the outside positions (corner and wing) on the other side of the court, and 5 and 3 criss-cross to the inside positions (high and low post) on the other side. Player 1 must wait for 4 to reach the wing before passing, of course, unless the rotation calls for

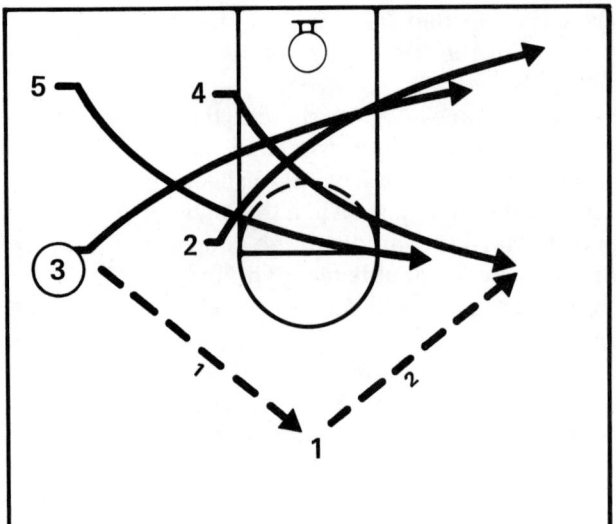

Figure 3-37 Inside-Outside Four-Player Rotation.

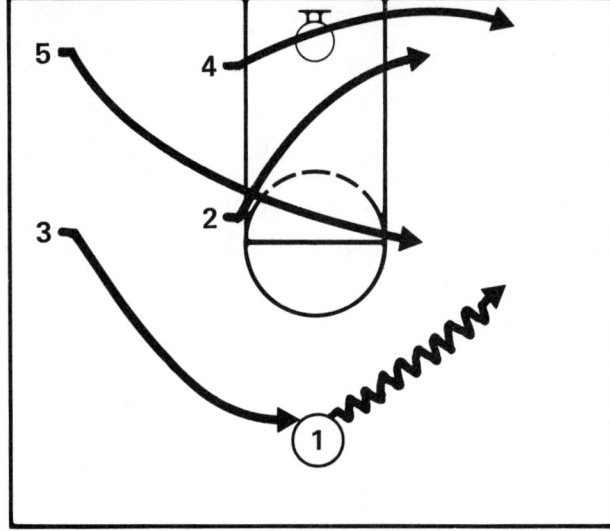

Figure 3-38 Variation of Inside-Outside Four-Player Rotation.

1 to dribble to the opposite wing, with 3 moving to the top of the circle. In this event, 4 moves to the corner, 2 slides through the lane to low post, and 5 cuts to high post. (See Figure 3–38.)

In either case, the rotation is slowed by the absence of a fifth player on the weak side of the court: not only must someone cut across to assume the wing position, but she must also turn around and face the ball before catching the pass. Thus, although circumstances, player skills, or coaching preferences might dictate that the same player cover both corners, or even cut to the weak side wing position from the ball side corner, it is generally preferable to have the nearest high or low post player cut or slide to the corner or wing, since she can reach the position more quickly.

VARIATIONS OF THE BASIC OVERLOAD TECHNIQUE

A Multiple Overload Rotation System. In describing the following system of setting up and rotating an overload, no attempt is made to describe it as better or worse in any respect than any of the previous alignments or systems. It is, in fact, composed of movements and options from the various rotation systems and is designed to take advantage of as many of the options as possible without surrendering speed of rotation.

The strengths of the overload formation shown in Figure 3–39 include: (1) the two inside players stay inside without rotating outside, (2) the outside players can concentrate on quick ball rotation and finding the outside openings rather than cutting to the corners and thus slowing down the rotation, and (3) the players' movements and positions are easily learned.

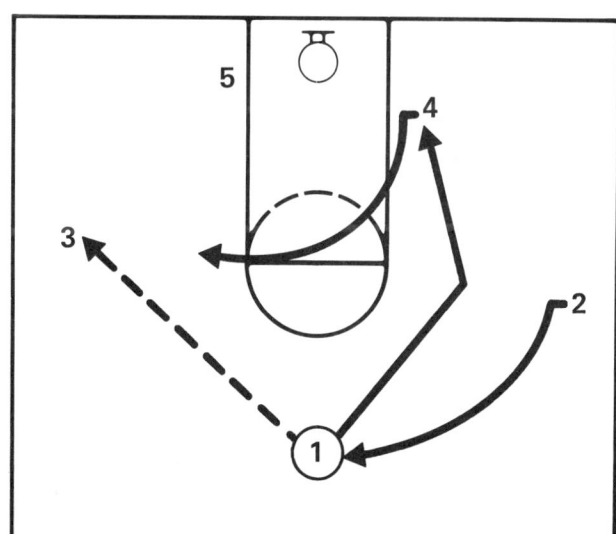

Figure 3-39 1–2–2 Multiple Overload Rotation System, Basic Movements.

80 Zone Offenses for Women's Basketball

Basic Alignments and Movements. The 1-2-2 alignment is extremely versatile in setting up the overload, since the overload can be established quickly with a pass to either wing.

If pressed for a preference as to the point guard's initial pass, we prefer the pass to 3, since 3's first option is to pass to 4 cutting across the lane, and 4's movement with the ball toward the middle will then be right-handed.

In order to provide greater movement for the defense to contend with, the point guard and weak side wing exchange positions. Player 1 may cut toward the basket, or 2 may slide toward the weak side low post for a return pass from 3.

The overload as established in Figure 3-39 has no corner player because the offensive emphasis is on ball movement and rotation rather than spreading. If the offensive team wishes to establish the regular three-player overload, 5 may cut to the corner and 4 will slide to low post.

When the ball is rotated back to the top of the circle and weak side wing, either of two methods of inside movement may serve to disconcert the defense. In the first method, shown in Figure 3-40, 5 cuts into the opening in or around the high post after 4 cuts across the lane to low post. When the ball rotates back to the left side, 5 will cut back to low post and 4 will then cut back to high post. (See Figure 3-41.) The outside rotation of point-to-weak side wing-to-point may or may not continue, depending upon offensive objectives and individual preferences.

The second method of rotating in the multiple overload rotation might be termed "Follow the Leader." After the first movements, shown in Figure 3-39, when 3 passes to 2, 4 slides across to ball side high post

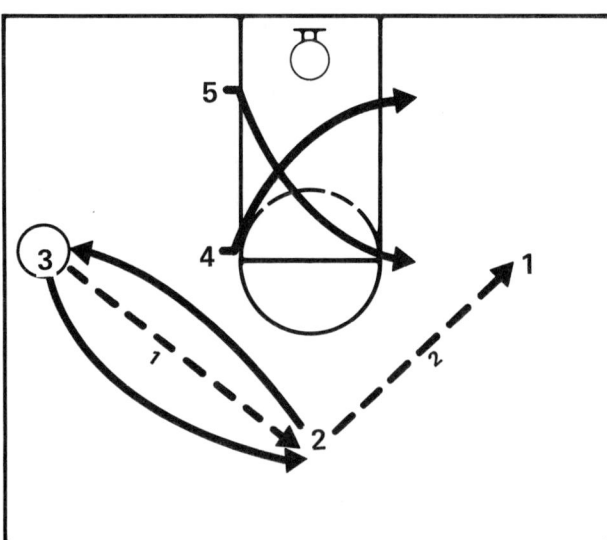

Figure 3-40 Multiple Overload Rotation, Criss-crossing Pattern.

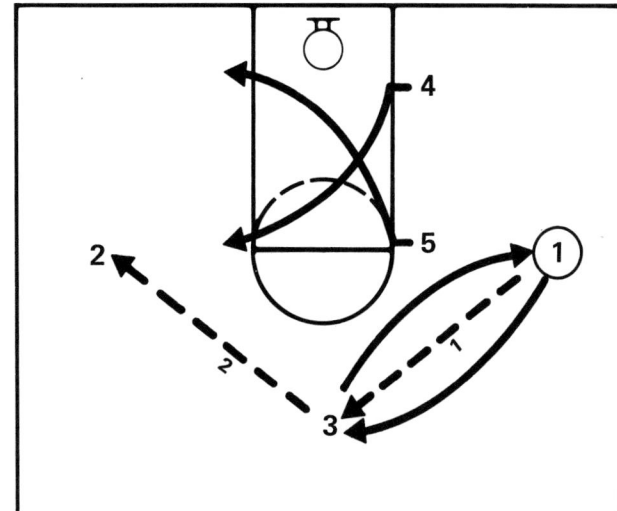

Figure 3-41 Multiple Overload Rotation, Criss-crossing Back to Original Overload.

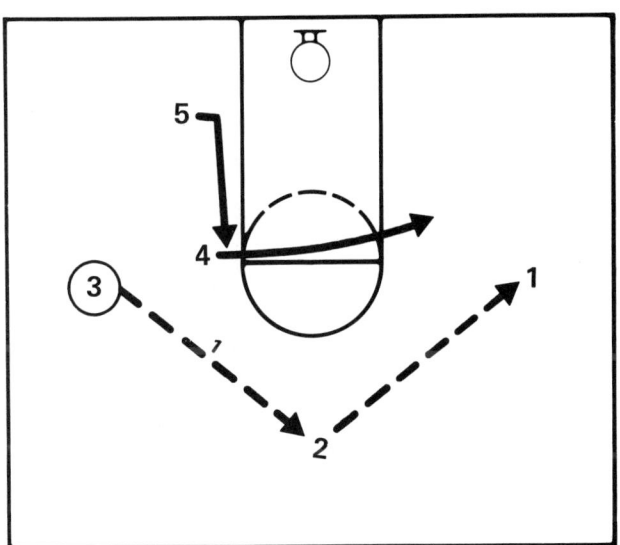

Figure 3-42 "Follow the Leader" Inside Rotation, 1-2-2 Overload Pattern.

and 5 moves up to the other high post position. (See Figure 3-42.) Then, when the ball continues to the opposite wing (Figure 3-43), 4 slides to low post and 5 cuts to high post. Player 4 may continue to the ball side corner, with 5 dropping to 4's vacated low post position.

Movements to the corner are the same as before. When one inside player cuts from low post to the corner, the high post player slides low. Otherwise, the inside players follow the movements of the ball.

The rotation may also be accomplished from a 1-4 alignment, as shown in Figure 3-44.

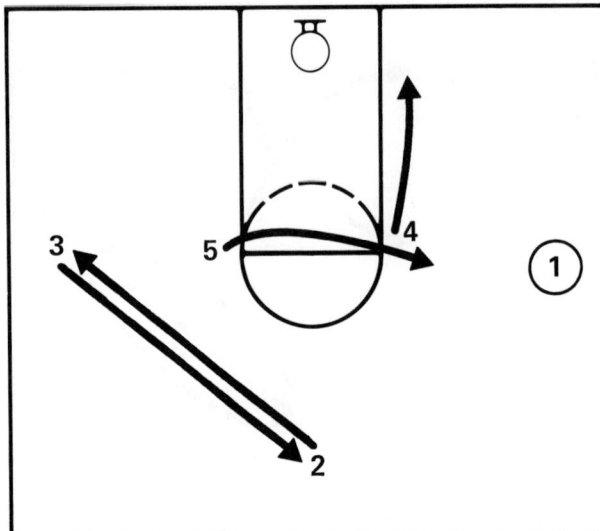

Figure 3-43 Continuing the "Follow the Leader" Movement, 1–2–2 Overload Pattern.

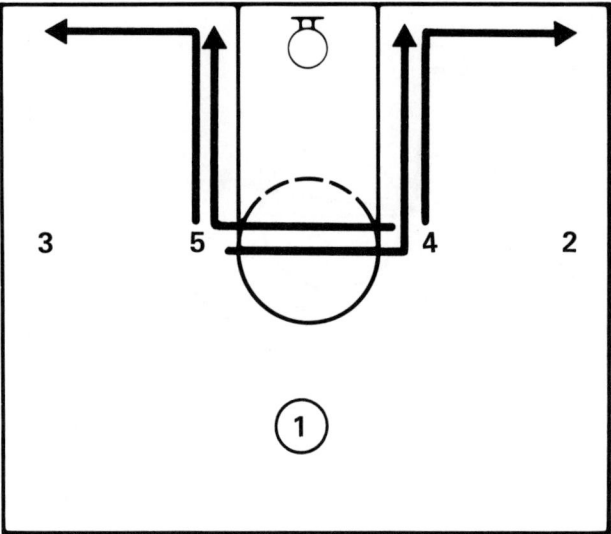

Figure 3-44 Rotation Pattern "Follow the Leader" from 1–4 Alignment. Say 1 passes to 2. Player 4 slides to low post and cuts to the corner. Player 5 cuts to high post, then slides to low post. Player 5 is, in essence, following 4. When the ball rotates to 3 on the other side, 5 moves around the lane following the ball, this time with 4 following her. (These movements are shown in part in Figures 3–42 and 3–43.)

Overload with Cutter Series. One type of overload movement not yet discussed is the pass-and-cut. In the following example, the point guard and wing pass and cut on either side of the court, with the inside double posts criss-crossing to the ball side of the court. The weakness of the pattern lies in the corner's (1 and 2) dribbling outside to the wing position to begin the rotation. The strength of the pattern is that the cuts and criss-crosses force the defense to constantly readjust its coverage, especially in defending against the inside movements.

Overload Offenses   83

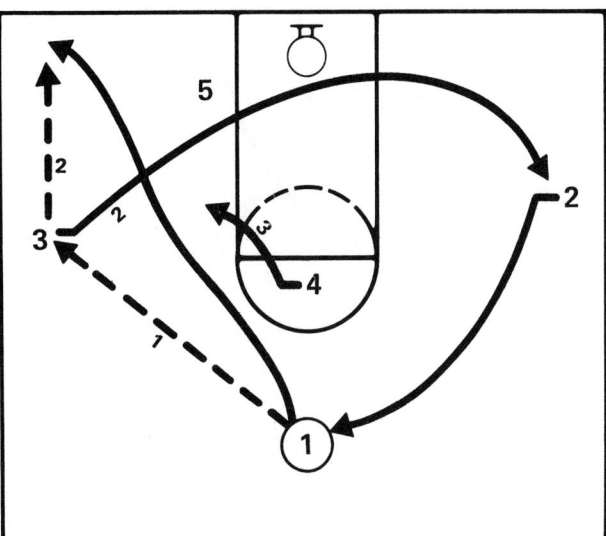

Figure 3-45 Establishing the Overload Cutter Pattern. Player 1 passes and cuts to the corner. Player 3 passes to the corner and cuts to weak side. Player 4 slides to the corner of the lane at high post, and 2 fills 1's position at the point.

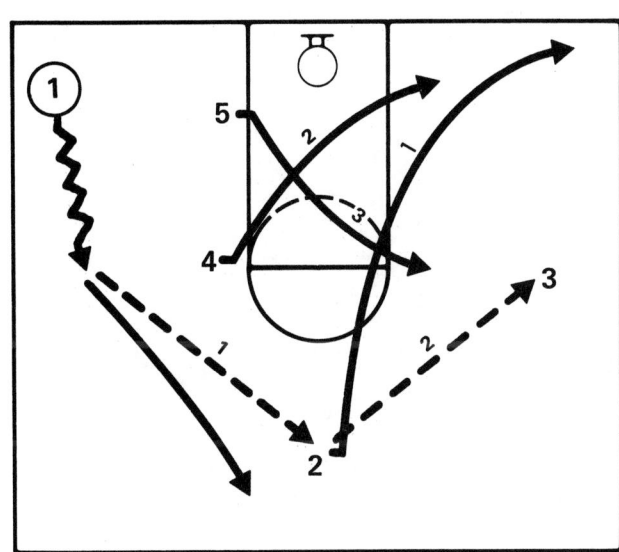

Figure 3-46 Rotating the Cutter Overload (continued from Figure 3-45). Player 1 dribbles out of the corner and passes to 2. Player 2 relays the ball to 3 and cuts to the corner. Player 4 cuts low, and 5 then cuts to high post. Player 4's cut is intended to draw the defense deep and open the lane or high post for 5's cut.)

Weak Side Cutter Series. One of the more important features of zone defenses is that, almost without exception, *every player in every zone defense shifts toward the ball or the ball side of the court*. Thus, sending cutters through the lane and away from the ball can speed up rotation and sometimes yield open shots for the offense.

The variety of ways to send cutters through or around the lane, toward or away from the ball, is as infinite as the number of positions players can occupy on a half-court. Many continuity patterns (e.g., the

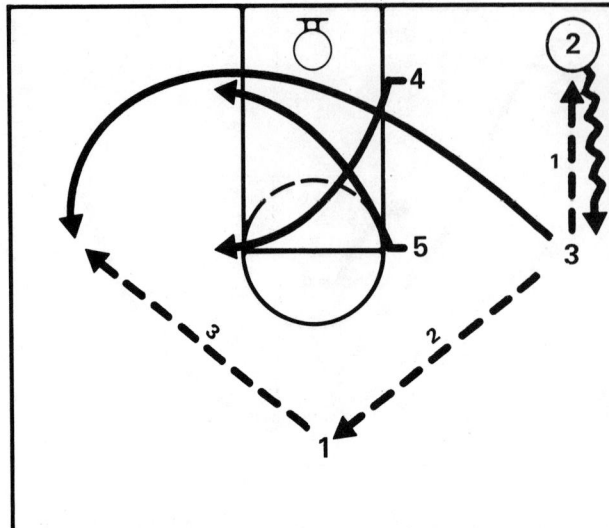

Figure 3-47 Re-establishing the Cutter Overload. Player 3 passes to 2 and cuts through the lane. Player 2 dribbles out to the wing and passes to 1, who relays the ball to 3 on weak side. Player 5 cuts to low post, and 4 then cuts to high post.

Figure 3-48 Point Guard Pass-and-Cut to Weak Side Corner. Player 1 passes and cuts through the lane to weak side corner. Player 4 slides low, and 5 cuts to high post. Player 2 moves outside, receives 3's pass and relays the ball to 1 in the corner.

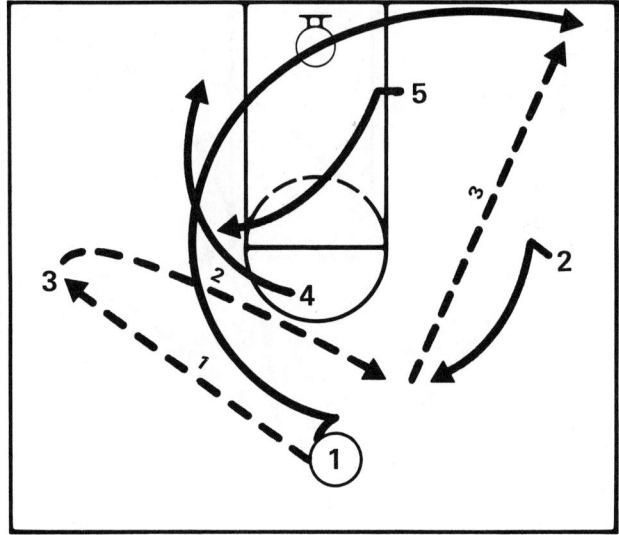

shuffle and wheel player-to-player offenses) feature cuts and screens away from the ball, the major difference being that zone offenses are not really designed to yield uncontested layups, regardless of the number of cuts and screens in the offense, whereas player-to-player patterns feature exactly those shots.

Generally, the optimal expectancy of zone offensive patterns is to achieve open 6–15 foot shots, or to create one-on-one matchups even closer to the basket. Sending cutters away from the ball can provide addi-

Overload Offenses   85

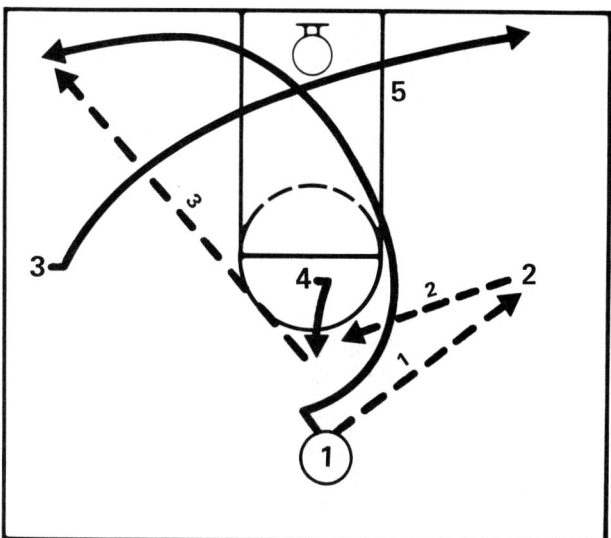

Figure 3-49 Pass-and-Cut to Weak Side, Alternate Rotation Method. Player 1 passes and cuts to weak side corner. Player 3 cuts to ball side corner. Player 4 steps out to receive 2's pass and relays the ball to 1 in the corner.

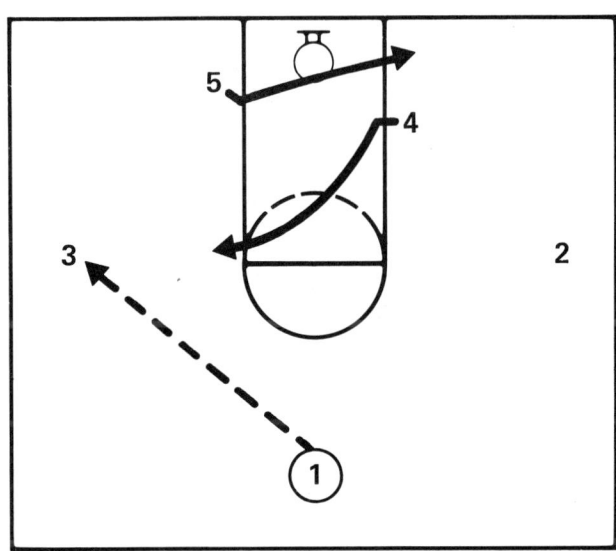

Figure 3-50 Setting Up the Inside Rotation Pattern.

tional scoring opportunities in both of the aforementioned categories.

Two of the more elementary cuts away from the ball are shown in Figures 3–48 and 3–49. (Cuts to the weak side may, of course, be made from any offensive alignment, and not just from those shown in the diagrams.)

It is important to note that the three-player overloads shown in Figures 3–50 and 3–51 change to four-player overloads with 3's dribble or 1's cut to the corner. Alternately, after 1 cuts to the corner and receives

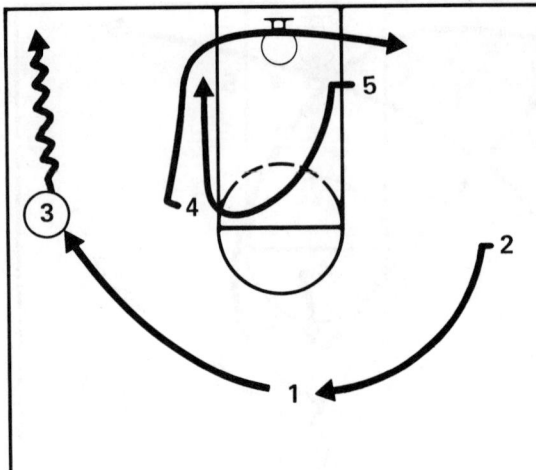

Figure 3-51 Filling the Corner Position, Inside Rotation Pattern.

Figure 3-52 Ball Rotation in Inside Rotation Pattern. Player 3 has the ball in the corner. She passes to 1 at the wing. Player 4 may cut to ball side high post now, or wait until 1 passes to 2. Player 5 cuts to weak side wing to receive 2's pass.

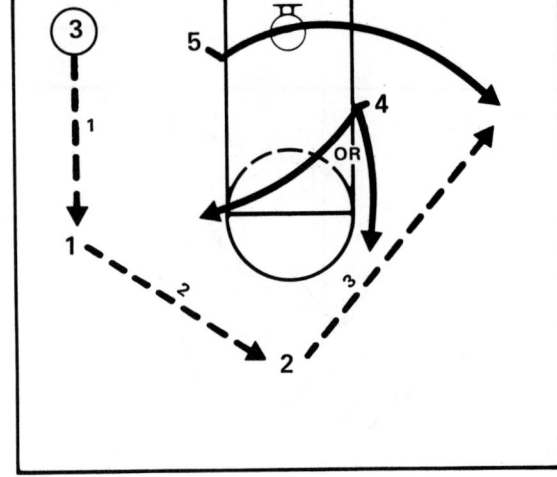

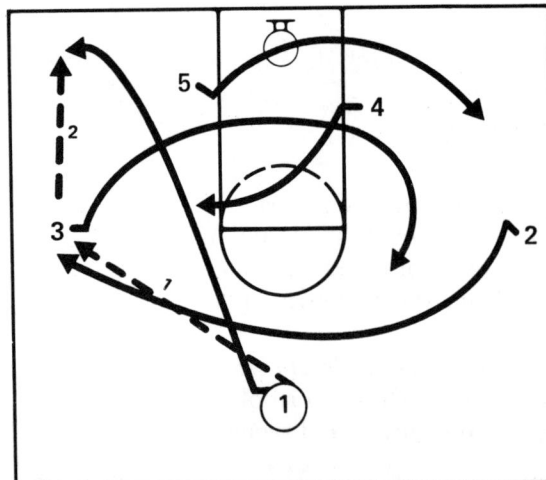

Figure 3-53 Player 3 Inside Cut with Inside Rotation Pattern. Player 1 passes and cuts to the corner. Player 3 passes to the corner and cuts through the lane. Player 2 moves across to ball side and 4 cuts to high post. Player 5 moves to weak side. Ball rotation is designed to free 5 for the weak side shot.

Overload Offenses 87

Figure 3-54 Inside Screen for 5 from Inside Rotation Pattern.

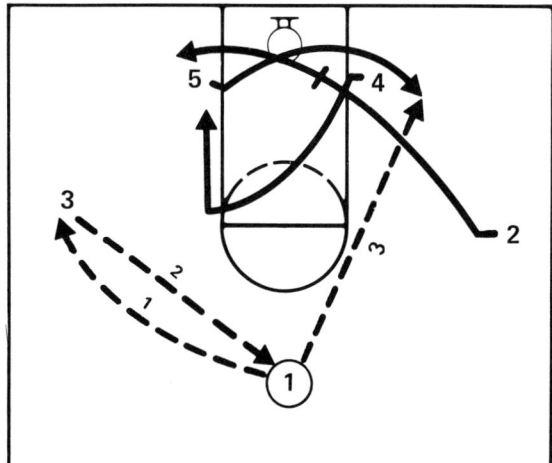

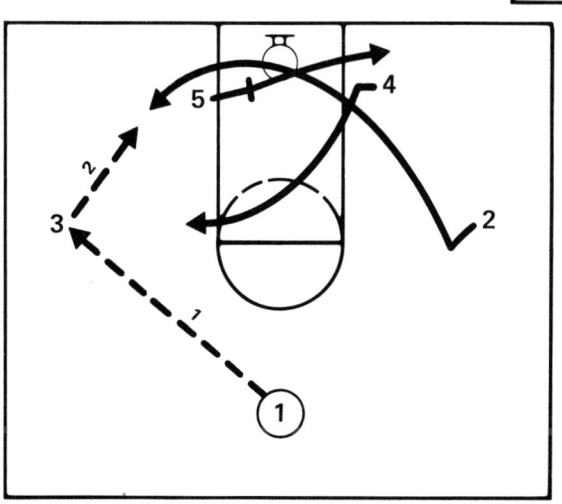

Figures 3-55, 3-56 Variations of Weak Side Screen from Inside Rotation Pattern.

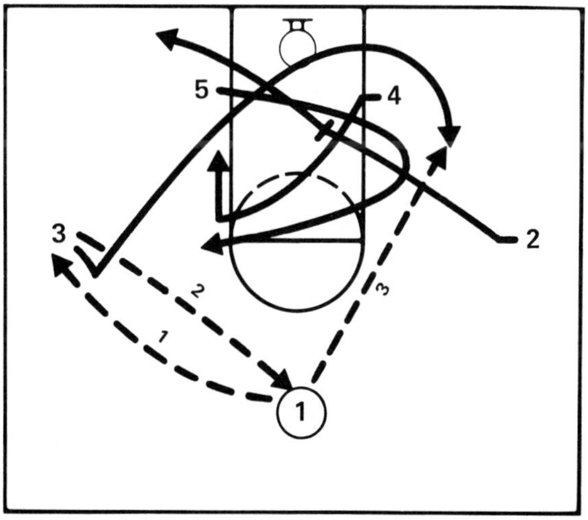

Figure 3-56.

3's pass, 3 may cut through the lane and back out to the point as 2 moves to the wing position.

Just as 4's cut to high post in Figure 3–50 can yield high-percentage shots on the ball side of the court, so 5's weak side cut can provide added dimensions to the offensive thrust. (In theory, at least, the cut to weak side low post will be open, but in practice the cut must be outside to a position 10–15 feet from the basket in order to complete the pass.)

A simple maneuver that can facilitate the rotation pass is shown in Figure 3–54.

As 1 passes to 3, 2 moves inside to screen for 5 cutting across the lane to the weak side. Player 3 passes quickly back to 1, and 1 passes to 5 for the shot. (Player 1 can then cut behind 5 for a secondary shooting option.)

The same objective can also be achieved without disturbing the inside rotation by having the weak side wing receive 5's screen (Figure 3–55), or by having 3 cut across the lane to receive 2's screen instead of 5, as shown in Figure 3–56.

CONCLUSION

Overloading patterns are extremely versatile; in fact, every player-to-player or zone offensive alignment either overloads initially or rotates into some type of overload as the pattern unfolds. Thus, overloads may be set up from any alignment—or, conversely, any alignment can be achieved from an overload.

The principles and movements involved in setting up, maintaining, and rotating overloads are easily learned by most players. The spreading action tends to maximize the potential of one-on-one confrontations and forces the defensive players to the limits of their zone coverage. Ball and player rotation often confuses or alters defensive matchups and yields desirable inside scoring opportunities.

Overload offenses are not a universal cure-all for a team's offensive difficulties, but they represent a style of attack that should not be overlooked.

4 Splitting Patterns

Not to discover weakness is
The artifice of strength.
                    Emily Dickinson
                    No. 1054 (1865), st. 1

BASIC SPLITTING PATTERNS

Baseball great Wee Willie Keeler had a succinct explanation for his success as a hitter in the major leagues: "I hit 'em where they ain't." The same philosophy underlies the use of splitting patterns against zone defenses.

Every zone defense has openings, or *seams*, which define the boundaries of each player's responsibilities. A splitting pattern is one in which the players set up offensively in the areas between the defensive players, then cut into, or set screens along, the seams of the zone. From the basic splitting alignments, a team may send cutters through the zones, set screens in or around the zone, or freeze the defense by penetrating between defensive players on the dribble.

Splitting patterns can be effective in their basic form, without such embellishments as the penetrating dribble into the seam, screening, or sending cutters through the zone—but only against teams whose zone defensive coverage is extremely unsophisticated. Without the offensive embellishments, any of the zone defenses shown in Figures 4–1 through 4–5 can rotate rather simply into matchups that leave the offense with nowhere to go.

False Splitting Patterns. Another problem sometimes encountered is that of false splitting patterns, or offensive alignments that only seem to split the defense, but in reality permit the defense to match up without altering their basic coverage.

90 Zone Offenses for Women's Basketball

Figure 4-1 Splitting the 2–1–2 or 2–3 Zone Defense.

Figure 4-2 Splitting the 1–3–1 Zone Defense.

Splitting Patterns 91

Figure 4-3 Splitting the 1–2–2 Zone Defense.

Figure 4-4 Splitting the 3–2 Zone Defense.

92 Zone Offenses for Women's Basketball

Figure 4-5 Splitting the 1–1–3 Zone Defense.

Few coaches, or teams, are so unsophisticated as to continue to allow the offense to freeze five, or even four, defensive players in their basic positions until the offense achieves whatever high-percentage shot it wishes. Often, in fact, coaches use defensive alignments that lure the offense into using patterns that apparently split the defense, but actually set up matchup zone coverage that freezes the *offense* rather than the defense.

For example, if Team A sets up in a 1–1–3 zone defense, many coaches will elect to set up 2–1–2 offensively in order to get the shot from the corner of the free-throw line. However, if X_1 follows the dribbler as shown in Figure 4–6, X_2 covers 2, and X_3 moves up to guard the high post, the defense is now matched up with the offense, and offensive penetration is very unlikely to succeed.

Or take another example which, although technically not a false splitting pattern, exemplifies the problem confronting teams using offensive splitting patterns. Probably the easiest zone defense in which to match up with the offense is the 1–3–1 zone. If Team A sets up in a 1–3–1 zone defense, the offense will likely split the zone by setting up 2–1–2. However, the defense can match up easily by X_3's sliding up to cover 1, X_5 moving over to guard 5, X_2 dropping back to cover 4, and X_1 picking up 2 as shown in Figure 4–7.

The mere fact that a team is deploying a matchup zone does not

Splitting Patterns 93

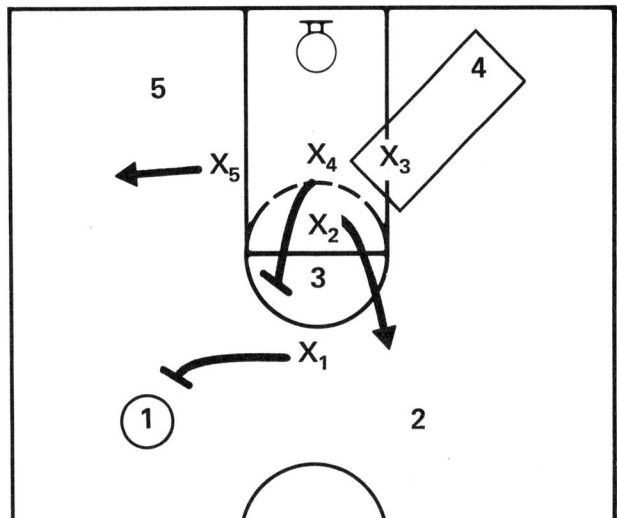

Figure 4-6 False Splitting Pattern Against 1–1–3 Zone Defense.

Figure 4-7 Matching Up from 1–3–1 Zone Defense.

mean that the offensive team cannot, or should not, set up to split the defense; it does mean, however, that splitting by itself will be ineffective after the matchup occurs, because the zone is being played as if it were player-to-player defense. Once a team matches up in a zone defense, there is no longer anything left to split. A team may send cutters through the lane, either toward or away from the ball, or use overloads to combat the matchups, but it will not split a matchup zone defense.

Thus, the splitting pattern must be accompanied by other movements designed to move the defense or confuse the matchups. The two ways to attack matchups are to change the matchups or to change the areas in which the matchups occur.

The first movement in confusing the defense is the ballhandler's penetrating dribble between (or into) the defensive guards. (See Figure 4–8.) Such movement freezes the defensive player(s) in their positions and delays adjustment to the offensive pattern. Once one or more outside defensive players are frozen, the advantage swings to the offense unless the defensive team is smart enough to match up quickly—and few players are capable of spotting such matchup situations in the heat of the game, especially after the dribbler has begun penetrating between two outside guards.

Freezing Two Defensive Players. The most common use of the penetrating movement occurs when the opponents are in an even-front

Figure 4-8 Freezing Two Defensive Players.

Splitting Patterns 95

Figures 4-9, 4-10 Freezing One Defensive Player.

(i.e., 2–3 or 2–1–2) zone defense. As shown in Figure 4–8, the offense has already begun the splitting pattern by setting up 1–2–2 against the 2–3 zone,[1] and point guard 1 has begun testing the outside defenders by dribbling toward a point directly between them.

The presence of two offensive players inside at the low post positions freezes the three inside defenders as well, since they cannot move to cover either wing until they know which wing is going to receive 1's pass.

Unless they have been coached to defense the pattern otherwise, most players will challenge the dribbler from both outside defensive positions, thereby facilitating the pass to either wing.

The defenders may choose to play toward one wing as shown in Figures 4–9 and 4–10, particularly in cases where one of the wings is a better shooter than the other. In such cases, point guard 1 may dribble toward either wing, with the wing on that side sliding away from the ball, to free a teammate for an open shot.

SPLITTING THE EVEN-FRONT ZONE DEFENSES

An even-front zone defense is one in which two defenders set up outside. The 2–1–2 and 2–3 zone defenses are among the most common zone defenses, with the 2–2–1 zone defense occurring less frequently. The "V" offense is a splitting pattern for 2–1–2 and 2–3 zone defenses, but the most common splitting alignments against even-front zones are 1–2–2 and 1–3–1. Both alignments can be effective in attacking the even-front zones, but the 1–2–2 alignment is more likely to achieve the pass into the free-throw lane.

Player 5's movement to the middle of the lane, combined with 4's cut across the baseline behind the defense, tends to free 2 or 3 for the 10–12 foot shot, or 4 for the corner shot.

Other methods of splitting the even-front zones have been discussed elsewhere.

The rotation of 3, 4, and 5 tends to confuse the defensive coverage, especially when X_1 and X_2 attempt to trap the ballhandler. Player X_3 must cover 5's cut into the lane, which leaves X_4 to cover both 2 and 4—if 1 can make the pass!

Screening from a 1–3–1 Splitting Alignment. In Figure 4–12, 3 screens X_1 as 1 dribbles toward the left side of the court. At the same time, 4 screens X_5 and rolls out of the lane to the corner, and 5 screens X_3 and rolls to the weak side of the court. These three screens should free 1 momentarily for the shot from the corner of the free-throw line, or 4 for

---

[1] The offense could also split either of the even-front zone defenses by setting up 1–3–1, or 1–2–2 with a double high post alignment. (See The "V" Offense, Chapter 5.)

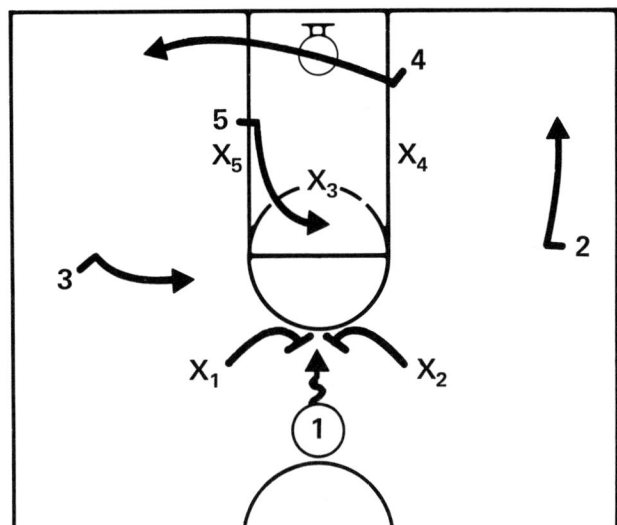

Figure 4-11 Splitting the 2–1–2 or 2–3 Zone Defenses.

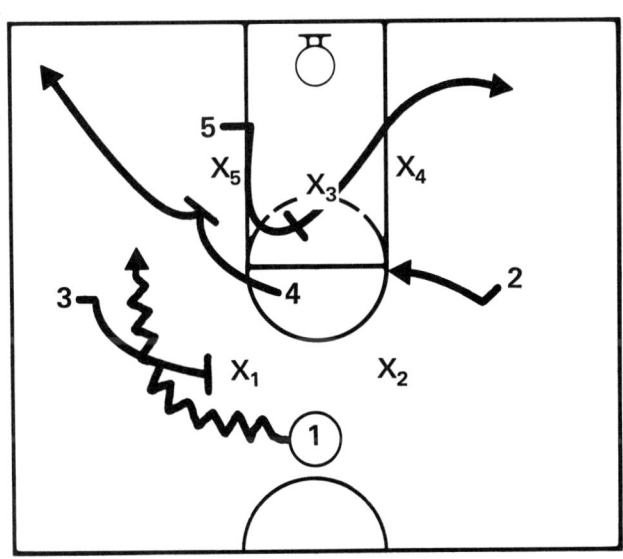

Figure 4-12 Screening for 1 from 1–3–1 Splitting Pattern Against 2–3 Zone Defense.

the corner shot. The rotation could be accomplished by having 3 step out to the top of the circle for 1's pass, 2 screening the outside defensive guard on her side of the court, 5 screening X_3, and 4 screening X_4, as shown in Figure 4–13.

Thus, after the initial screening movement 4 and 5 merely screen inside and switch sides of the lane; and 1, 2, and 3 take turns screening outside and dribbling around the screen.

Figure 4–14 depicts screens by 3 and 4 designed to free 5 for the

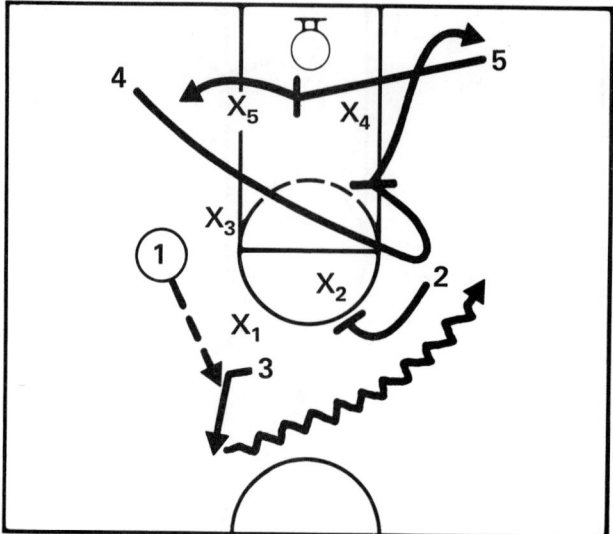

Figure 4-13 Rotation from 1–3–1 Screening Pattern (continued from Figure 3–53). Player 1 passes to 3, who dribbles around 2's screen on X_2. Player 4, cutting to high post, drops low to screen X_4, then slides away to the base line. Player 5 screens X_5, then clears to weak side. The offense is trying to isolate 3 and 4 on X_4.

Figure 4-14 Screening For 5 From 1–3–1 Splitting Pattern Against 2–3 Zone Defense. As 1 dribbles toward X_1, 4 slides inside, screens X_3 momentarily, then clears to the corner; 3 screens inside for 5 sliding outside; and 2 moves to the low weak side opening.

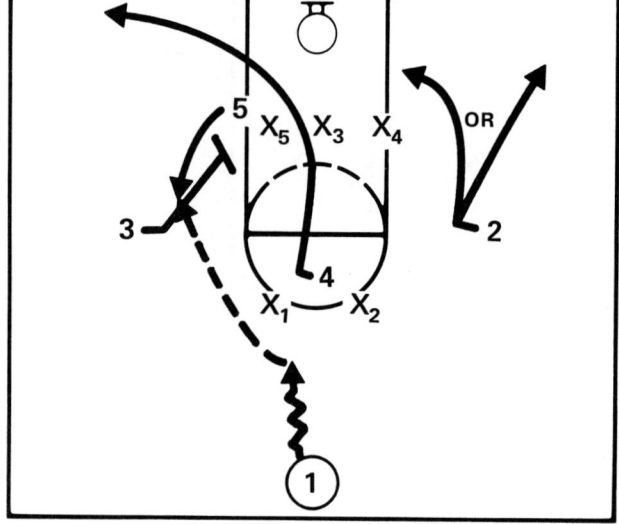

12–15 foot shot from the corner of the free-throw lane. Player 1 dribbles into the outside guards and passes to either 5 or 4, depending upon inside coverage. Rotation involves 1 breaking to the top of the circle for a return pass from 5, then dribbling toward X_2 as 2 and 3 screen inside for 4 cutting across the lane. (See Figure 4–15.)

A variation of the previous patterns is for wing 3 to screen X_1 as in Figure 4–14, but 2 cuts behind the defense to the ball side corner. Player 4 screens X_5 and rolls to low post, thus setting up the overload with 1, 2, and 4. (See Figure 4–16.)

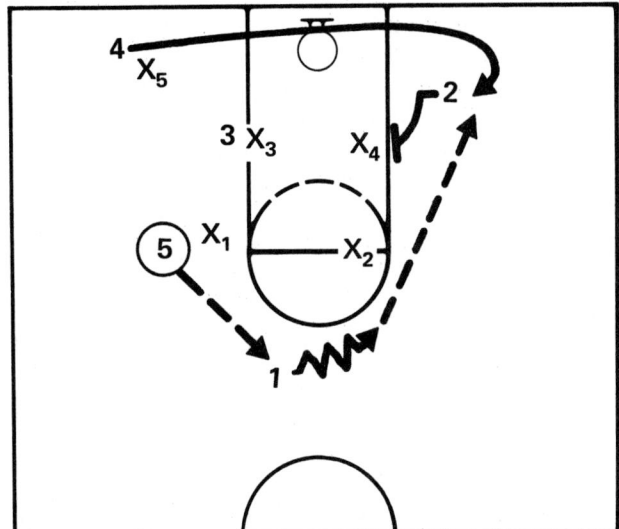

Figure 4-15 Rotation from 1–3–1 Splitting Pattern.

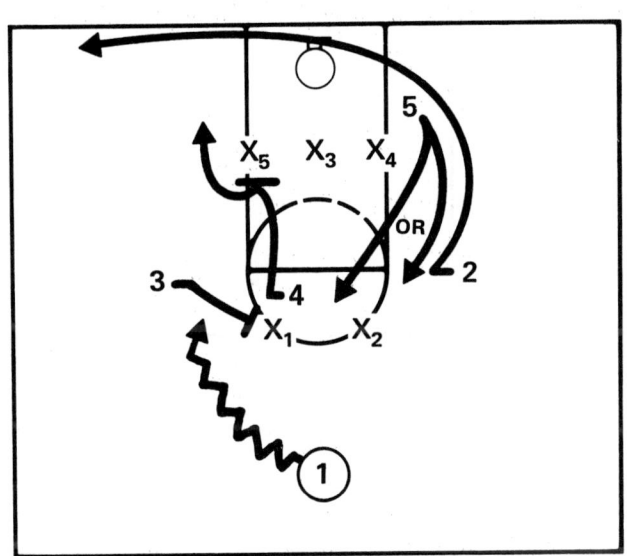

Figure 4-16 Variation of Screening Pattern From 1–3–1 Splitting Alignment.

Splitting the Odd-Front Zone Defenses. One wonders why more teams do not use the odd-front zones—the 1–3–1, the 1–2–2, the 1–1–3, and the 3–2 zone defenses—since they are far more difficult to split than the even-front zone defenses. Even when a team is able to split an odd-front zone, the outside shots afforded by the splitting are less desirable than those afforded by the even-front zones.

For example, if a team sets up in a 2–1–2 zone defense, the offense may set up 1–2–2 or 1–3–1, with the wings set up at a 45 degree angle to the basket. At such an angle, the backboard may be used to the fullest in shooting. On the other hand, when a team sets up 2–1–2 offensively against an even-front zone, the shooting angle decreases to 55–60 degrees outside, and the corner alignment yields one of the most difficult shooting angles in basketball.

In splitting the 1–3–1 zone defense, cuts and slides through, around, and behind the zone will increase the offense's scoring possibilities. Typical 2–1–2 splitting and screening patterns with cuts are shown in Figures 4–17 through 4–26.

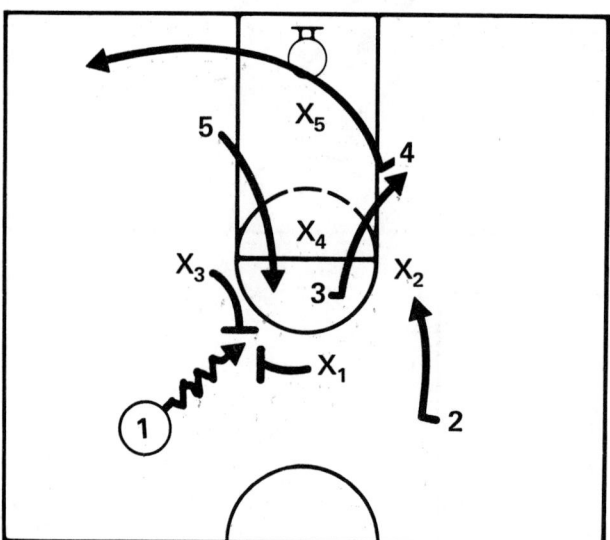

Figure 4-17 Splitting the 1–3–1 Zone Defense. Player 1 penetrates between X_1 and X_3. Player 5 slides into the opening in the lane, 3 cuts low on weak side, 4 cuts to ball side corner, and 2 moves into shooting position in case X_2 drops low to cover 4's cut.

Figure 4-18 Cutter Pattern from Splitting Alignment Against 2–3 Zone Defense. Player 5 cuts outside for 1's pass. Player 1 cuts through to weak side. Player 3 slides low, 4 cuts to the ball side corner, and 2 fills 1's spot.

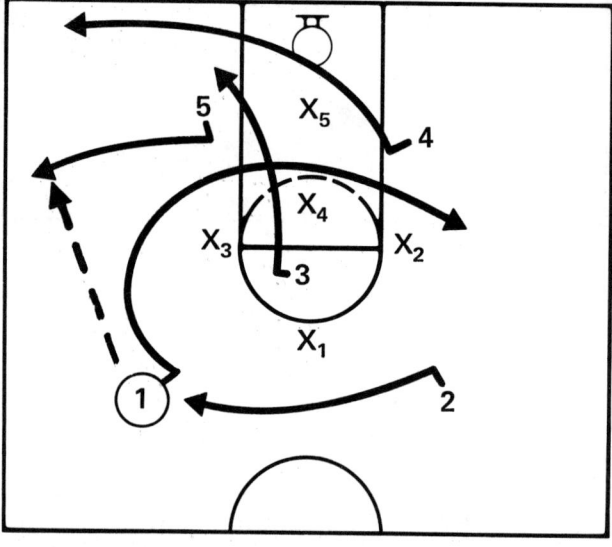

Of the set plays against 1–3–1 zone defenses, Figures 4–20, 4–21, 4–24, 4–25, and 4–26 involve the penetrating dribble by the ballhandler. The object of penetration is, of course, to free one or more offensive players players other than the ballhandler for a short jump shot or one-on-one confrontation inside. In Figure 4–21, 2 and 5 are the intended shooters; in Figure 4–24, 1 is the primary shooter, with 2 and 4 secondary shooters; and in Figure 4–25, 1 is again the designated shooter, with 2 and 3 cutting to the outside openings. Figures 4–11 through 4–16 feature 5 screening inside

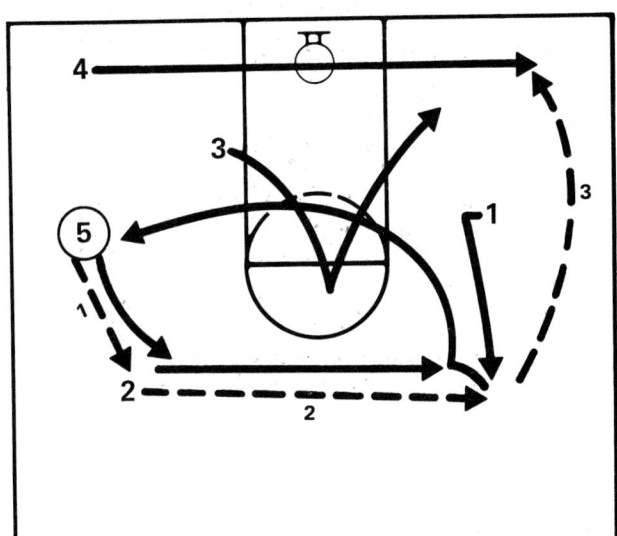

Figure 4-19 Rotation in Cutter Pattern Against 1–3–1 Zone Defense.

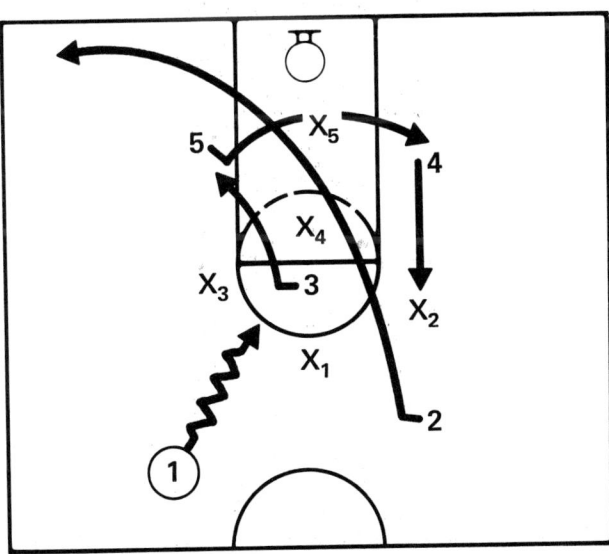

Figure 4-20 Splitting the 1–3–1 Zone Defense.

102 Zone Offenses for Women's Basketball

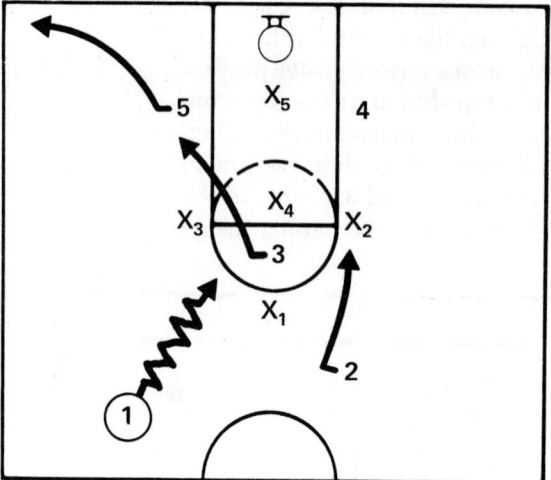

Figure 4-21 Splitting the 1–3–1 Zone Defense Without Cutter.

Figure 4-22 Screening for the Shot for 5 from the Free-Throw Line.

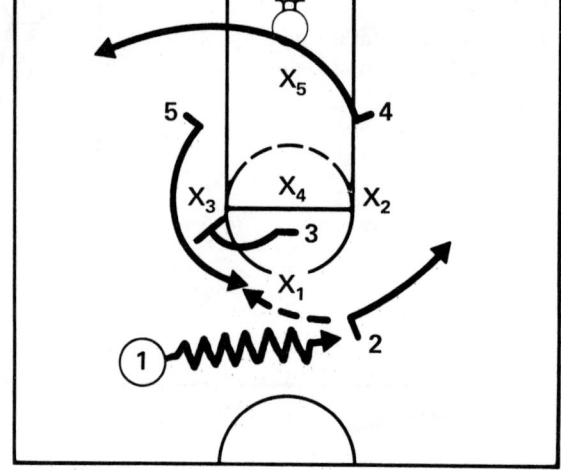

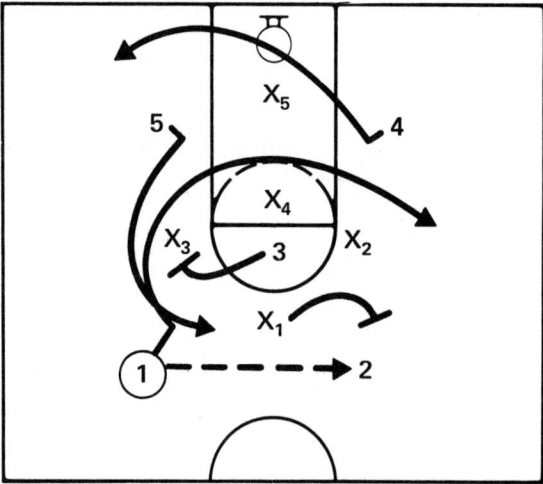

Figure 4-23 Variation of Free-Throw Line Screening Pattern.

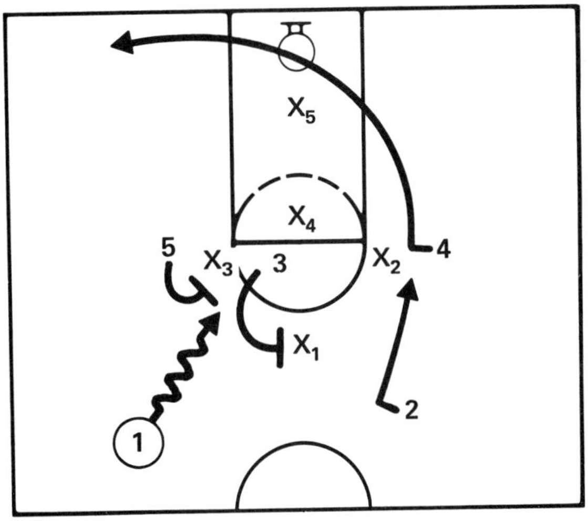

Splitting Patterns 103

Figure 4-24 Screening for 1 from 2–1–2 Offense.

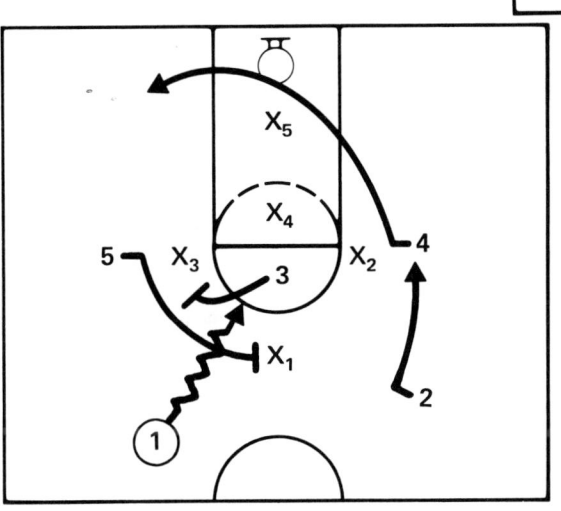

Figure 4-25 Variation of Screen For 1.

Figure 4-26 Inside Screen for 4.

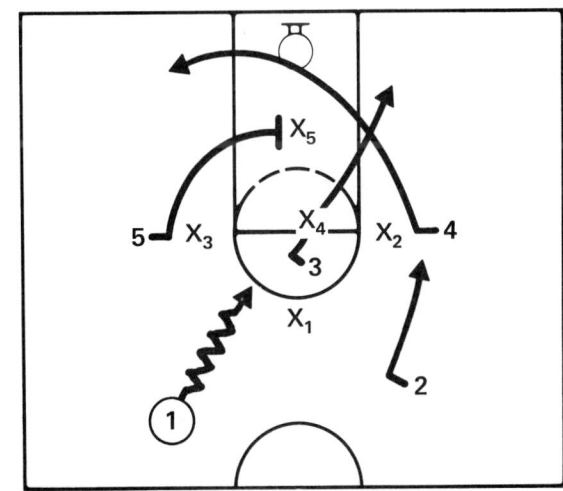

for 4 cutting across the lane and behind the defense.

In Figure 4–22, 1 dribbles across the top of the circle, attempting to lure the defensive point guard away from the screen being set by high post 3 for 5. Player 2 moves away from the ball, and 4 cuts across the lane in case the defenders move up to defense the screen.

Figure 4–23 depicts a variation of the same play, but instead of dribbling across the top of the circle, 1 passes to 2 and circles through the defense to the outside opening on 2's side of the court as 3 screens for 5.

SPLITTING PATTERNS AGAINST ODD-FRONT ZONE DEFENSES: THE 1-2-2 ZONE DEFENSE

As explained previously (and shown in Figure 4–6), the 1–1–3 zone defense cannot be split—at least, not by the conventional method of setting two guards outside in a 2–1–2 alignment. The defense will merely slide into a 2–3 alignment, which may or may not be to the offense's advantage.

A 1–2–2 alignment is equally conducive to matching up. (In Figure 4–27, if the high post player were at low post, the defender at high post would move to cover the wing pass, and the weak side inside defender would move out to cover the weak side wing.) In fact, the best alignment to attack the 1–1–3 zone defense is the 1–3–1: if the high post defender tries to cover the wing passes, those players can slide farther toward the baseline for the open shot, although it is doubtful that the defender at high

Figure 4-27 Attacking the 1–1–3 Zone Defense.

post could adequately cover either wing pass even without offensive movement.

It is important to understand why teams would want to use a 1-1-3 zone defense. The only feasible reason is to adequately defend against a team with two extraordinarily strong inside offensive players, and thus force the outside shot while keeping four players inside to rebound. Addi-

Figure 4-28 Setting Up an Overload Against 1-1-3 Zone Defense.

Figure 4-29 Setting Up an Overload Against 1-1-3 Zone Defense.

106 Zone Offenses for Women's Basketball

tionally, the three inside defenders may double-team either the ball side offensive player or the better of the two offensive threats, single-guarding the other player.

Why, then, would the players set up in 1–1–3 rather than 2–3? Probably to deny the offense the opportunity to penetrate between the outside guards, although the "1–1" alignment is frozen just as surely as the "2" alignment.

Whatever the case, the 1–3–1 offensive alignment tends to cause the

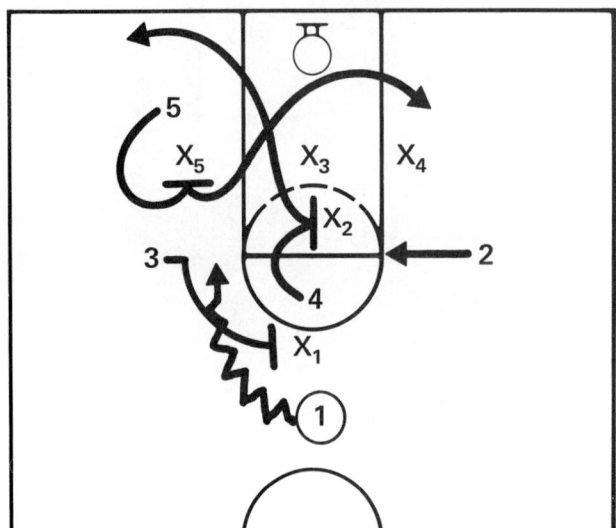

Figure 4-30 Screening For 1 Against 1–1–3 Zone Defense.

Figure 4-31 Attacking the 1–1–3 Zone Defense, Pass-and-Cut Variation.

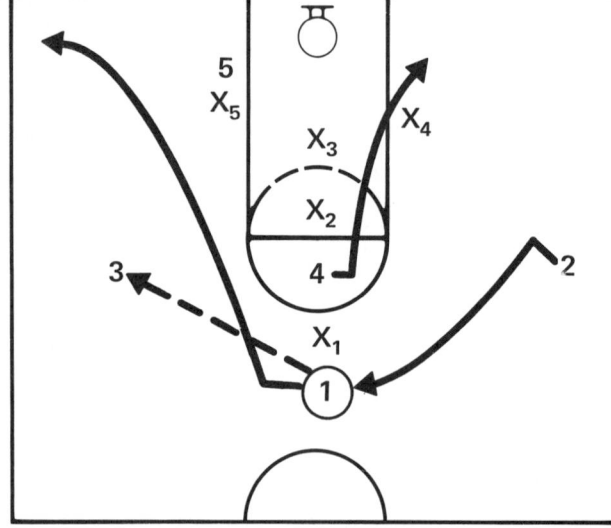

1–1–3 zone defense more trouble than even-front alignments.

Since the defense's primary goal is to double-team the inside player on the ball side of the court, they will likely keep the other player in the "3" alignment inside if 4 either sets up at, or cuts to, low post opposite the ball, as shown in Figure 4–29.

When the ballhandler dribbles to the wing (Figure 4–29) or passes to the wing and cuts to the ball side corner (Figure 4–31), the defense will not be able to deal with the overload without abandoning their earlier coverage.

SPLITTING PATTERNS AGAINST ODD-FRONT ZONE DEFENSES: THE 1-2-2 ZONE DEFENSE

The 1–2–2, or "jug" defense, has few natural weaknesses. As a coach, I've run the 1–2–2 zone for years, and the primary reason is that I've had more trouble running offensive patterns against a 1–2–2 alignment than any other zone defense, with the possible exception of a 1–3–1 matchup zone.

I finally decided that, if I couldn't beat them, I might as well join them.

The 1–2–2 alignment covers the low post positions well, and more than adequately provides coverage of the corners, wing, and point. The only apparent area of weakness is the high post and middle of the lane, but we've generally dealt with the problem by either: (1) sinking our point guard back to defend the high post, or (2) going farther out than usual to guard 1, and thus forcing the lob pass to the high post.

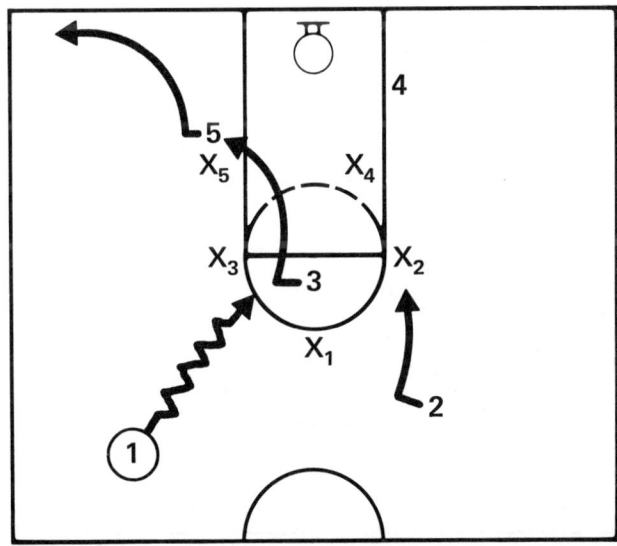

Figures 4-32, 4-33, 4-34, 4-35, 4-36, 4-37 Splitting Patterns Against the 1–2–2 Zone Defense.

108 Zone Offenses for Women's Basketball

Typical splitting and screening patterns against a 1–2–2 zone defense are shown in Figures 4–32 through 4–37.

Figures 4–32, 4–33, and 4–34 depict cutting patterns against the 1–2–2 zone defense, whereas Figures 4–35, 4–36, and 4–37 involve one or more screens to free offensive players. In the cutting patterns, 1 attempts to freeze one or both outside guards on one side of the court as another offensive player cuts into the middle of the lane to confuse the defensive coverage. Meanwhile, other players move to the open perimeters of the

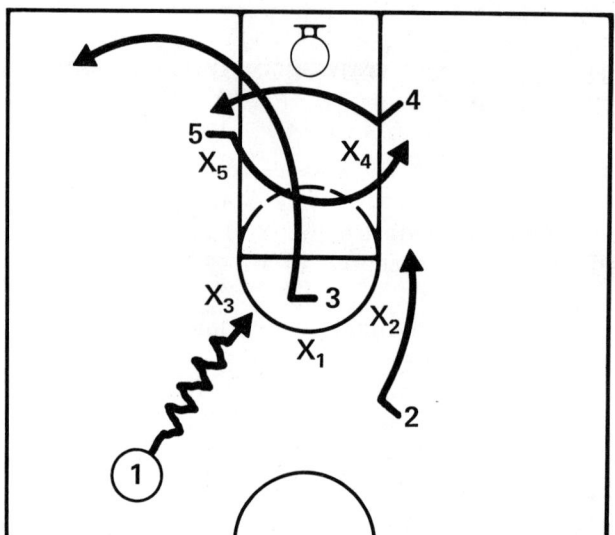

Figure 4-33.

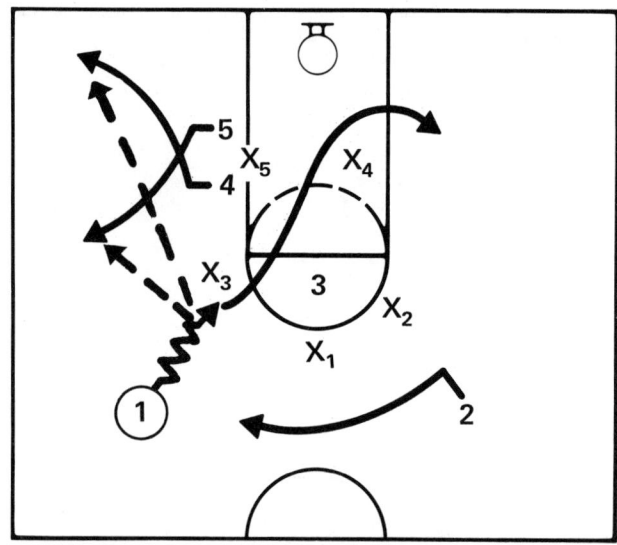

Figure 4-34.

zone: 2 to high post at the opposite corner of the lane, and other players to the ball side corner and weak side low post.

The screening patterns also involve 1's penetrating dribble to force either the matchup or the trap with the outside guard(s) on that side of the court and screens on the ball side to free players for corner shots or short jumpers. In Figure 4–35, 5 screens for 4 cutting across the lane behind the defense. Figures 4–36 and 4–37 show an inside stack alignment, with 3 the primary receiver in Figure 4–36 as 5 slides outside and 4 screens the

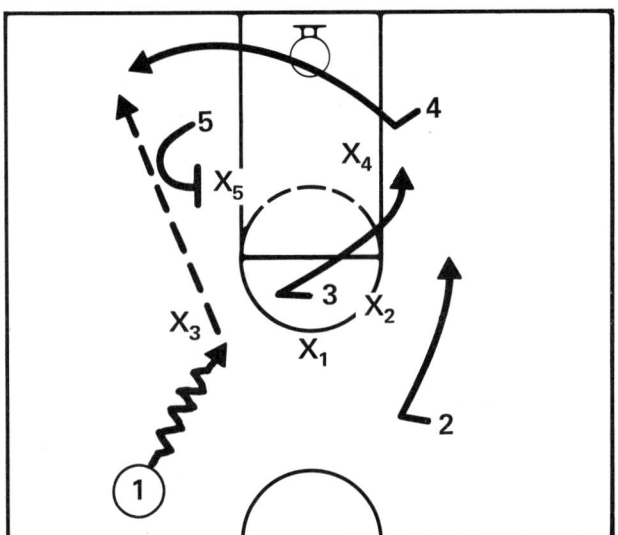

Figure 4-35.

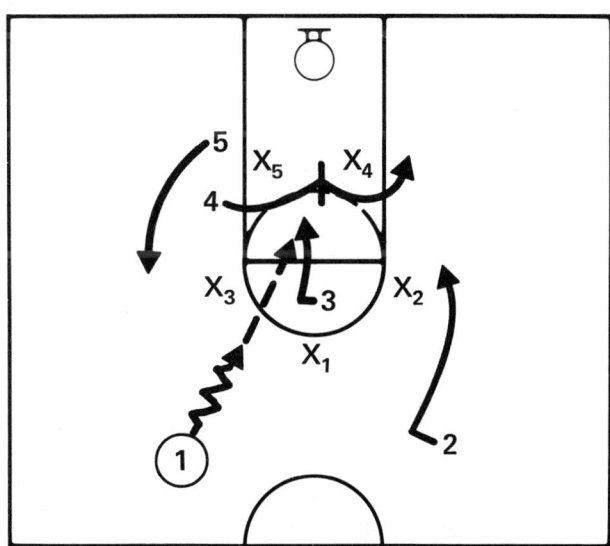

Figure 4-36.

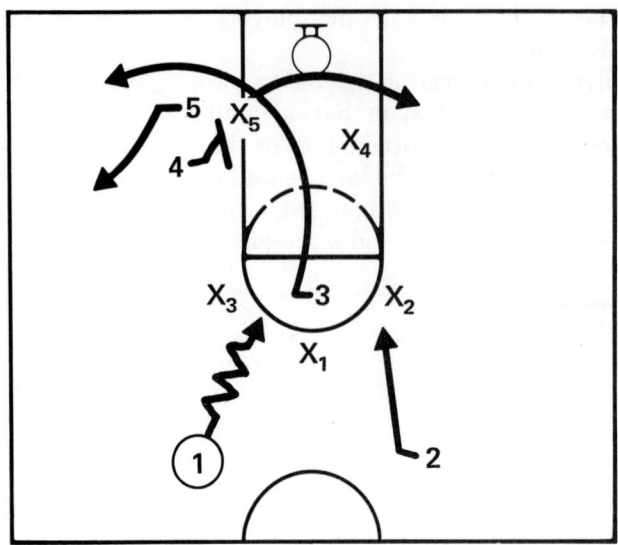

Figure 4-37.

opposite inside defender; and in Figure 4–37, with 4 screening for 5 and clearing across the lane as 3 cuts to the ball side low post or corner.

The 1–2–2 zone defense can be used in matchup form to keep four players inside for rebounding purposes (Figure 4–38), or it can be used to double-team the ball side low post player. (See Figure 4–39.) The offensive team should be alert to the inside single- or double-guarding strategy in order to determine whether to attack the 1–2–2 from inside or outside. Figures 4–32 through 4–37 are designed to attack the 1–2–2 as it is used in matching up with the offense.

However, a further consideration must be taken into account concerning double-teaming the ball side low post; some teams will send the defensive point guard inside to double-team at low post when the ball is passed to the corner. In such cases, the ball side corner of the free-throw lane will invariably be open (Figure 4–40), since the defender at the wing will likely be slow in dropping back to cover the high post position. But even if the wing defender covers the high post position, the ballhandler may move toward the basket for a return pass from the corner for the open shot. In effect, then, double-teaming inside creates a two-on-one advantage somewhere for the offense, whether it is the wing and point players on the ball side of the court or the point and weak side player away from the ball.

We can see in these types of coverage the strategy of all zone defenses: to give up something, but as little as possible, in order to either protect a weakness or attack an offensive strength. In the first case, single-guarding the low post inside, the defense is attempting to use player-to-player defense within their zone coverage, dropping slightly away from

Splitting Patterns 111

Figure 4-38 Single-Guarding, or Matching Up, in 1–2–2 Zone Defense, Ball at Wing.

Figure 4-39 Double-Teaming the Ball side Low Post in 1–2–2 Zone Defense.

Figure 4-40 X_1 Double-Teaming Inside in 1-2-2 Zone Defense, Ball in Corner.

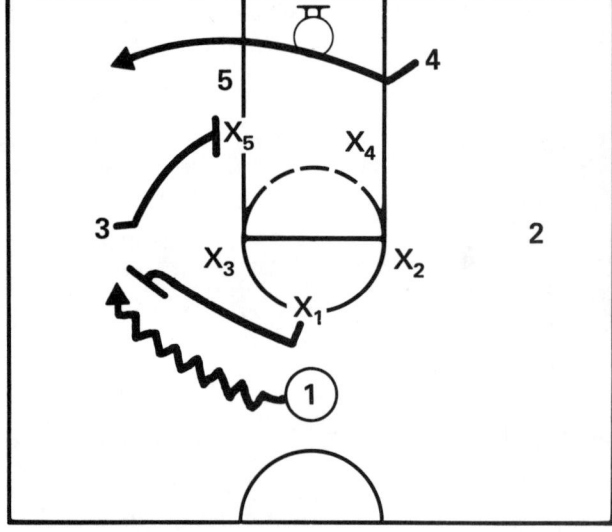

Figure 4-41 Double Screen for 4 Against 1-2-2 Zone Defense.

players without the ball for rebounding purposes, but not so far away as to permit open shots or to give the offensive team the advantage.

In the second case, double-teaming inside, the advantage swings even more greatly to the offense than before—if they are capable of attacking the rest of the defense! In reality, however, the advantage existed prior to the double-teaming, or else the team would be in a matchup alignment and single-guarding the low post position.

Against defensive double-teaming, then, player movement and ball rotation provide the best means for attacking *all* zone defenses.

In Figure 4–41, wing 3 moves inside to set a double screen with 5 for 4 cutting across the lane behind the defense as point guard 1 dribbles left. This set play attacks the 1–2–2 zone whether the defense matches up or double-teams inside.

SPLITTING PATTERNS AGAINST ODD-FRONT ZONE DEFENSES: THE 3-2 ZONE DEFENSE

Like the 1–1–3 zone defense, the 3–2 zone is deceptive and illusory. Obviously designed to stop teams with outside shooting proficiency, the 3–2 alignment also adapts easily to inside coverage, since the usual method of setting up the 3–2 zone defense involves bringing out the "1" player in a 2–1–2 zone defense to stop penetration by the point guard. Of course, the 3–2 wasn't designed to be used in this manner, but the effect is the same: offensive teams tend to spread their alignment when confronted with a 3–2 zone defense, forgetting about penetrating on the dribble in splitting the defense.

Possibly the best offense against a 3–2 zone defense is the 2–3 baseline screening offense described in Chapter 5 or variations such as the high 2–3 set plays shown in Figures 4–42, 4–43, and 4–44.

It should be noted that 1's dribble toward X_1 tends to freeze X_3 in position as well, since X_3's dropping back merely allows 1 to continue dribbling toward X_2 and thus freeze X_1 and X_2 as in attacking a 2–1–2 zone defense.

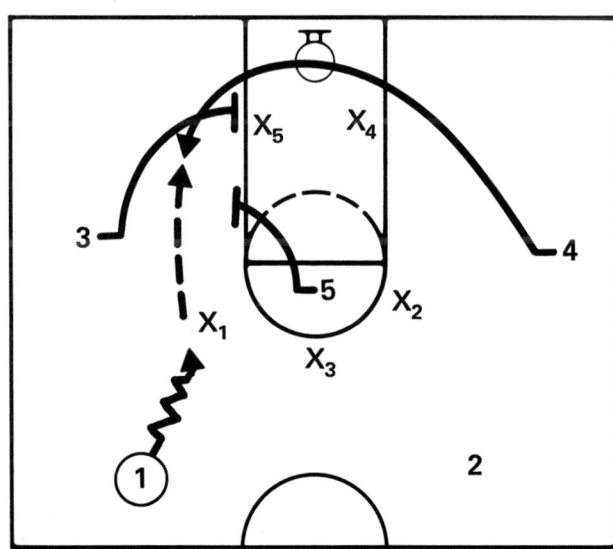

Figure 4-42 Double Screen for 4 Against 3–2 Zone Defense.

114 Zone Offenses for Women's Basketball

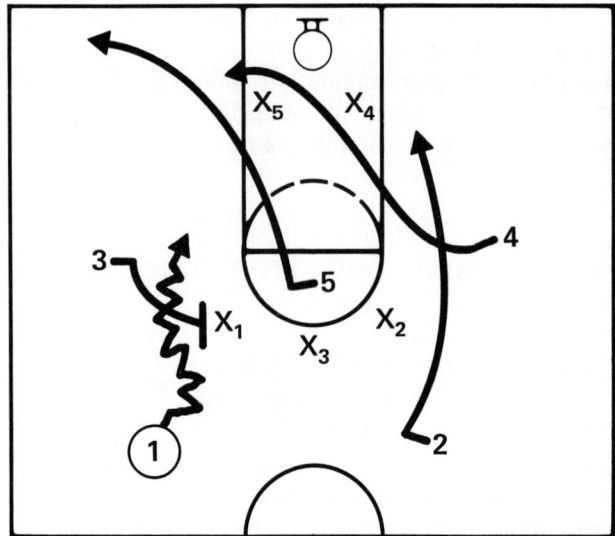

Figure 4-43 Screen for 1 Against 3–2 Zone Defense.

Figure 4-44 Splitting the 3–2 Zone Defense.

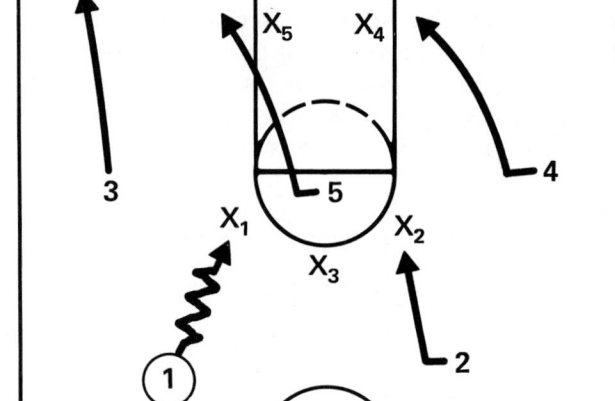

    If X_3 drops back to guard 5 cutting into the lane as shown in Figure 4-44, X_5 will have to either abandon 5 to guard the wing pass to 3 sliding toward the corner—an undesirable alternative for the defense, since 5 has inside position on X_3, and X_4 must maintain coverage of 4 cutting toward the basket—or give 3 the outside shot. Neither alternative promises much relief from the offensive pressure afforded by 1's dribble and 5's cut.

CONCLUSION

Every basketball team uses splitting patterns to combat zone defenses. However, few teams really explore the range of offensive possibilities available from the splitting alignment. Without offensive embellishments such as screening inside or along the perimeter of the zone, or cutting into the lane to freeze inside defenders, the defensive players are likely to match up, and thus destroy much of the effectiveness of the splitting concept.

In order to take advantage of the splitting alignment, a team must have at least one player capable of penetrating the zone's seam and passing to an open teammate when the defenders along the seam are frozen in their positions. If the offensive team has no players capable of dribbling into two defenders and passing off without losing control of the ball, outside screens can still free the ballhandler, but the resulting patterns will never be as effective as those in which the ballhandler herself challenges the defense.

Thus, coaches desiring to derive maximum benefit from splitting alignments against zone defenses should drill their ballhandlers in the skills necessary to dribble the ball into the defensive players and pass by (not over) their arms to teammates. Almost without exception, lob passes drain zone offenses—especially splitting patterns—of their effectiveness as surely as if the players were wearing handcuffs and leg chains.

A coach must also be aware of alignments which apparently split the defense but actually permit the defense to match up; and of even- and odd-front defenses, together with the offensive alignments and patterns that yield optimal scoring opportunities against each, even when defensive rotation threatens to spoil the success of the splitting pattern. Splitting patterns can be used effectively in attacking zone defenses, but only when the coach and players are aware of the nuances of zone defensive coverage that can and cannot successfully be attacked by offensive penetration.

5 Special Zone Offenses and Techniques

But who is to guard the guards themselves?
Juvenal
Satires, VI, 1. 347

The term *special offenses* is perhaps a bit of a misnomer for this chapter, since it consists largely of patterns and techniques that do not fit neatly into the chapters on overloads or splitting patterns. The offenses are "special" only in the sense that they either: (1) attack specific zone defensive alignments or coverages, or (2) use unusual alignments or approaches to combat regular zone defenses.

A 2-3 BASELINE SCREENING OFFENSE

Although bearing a superficial resemblance to an overload alignment, the 2-3 baseline screening offense is technically closer to being a splitting pattern against odd-front defenses than an overload. However, since the splitting aspect is only incidental to the more important task of getting the ball to the baseline or the corner, it is included in the present chapter rather than in Chapters 3 or 4.

The baseline screening offense is most effective when inside players 3, 4, and 5, are adept at screening and can hit the short 8–10 foot shot. In Figure 5–1, as 1 passes to 2, low post 4 cuts across the lane and behind 3's screen to receive a pass from 2. Player 5 slides toward weak side low post.

Rotation consists of 4's passing out to 2, who passes on to 1, with low post 3 cutting across the lane and behind 5's inside screen to receive 1's pass. (See Figure 5–2.)

The pattern can be simplified further by using only *one* cutter, in

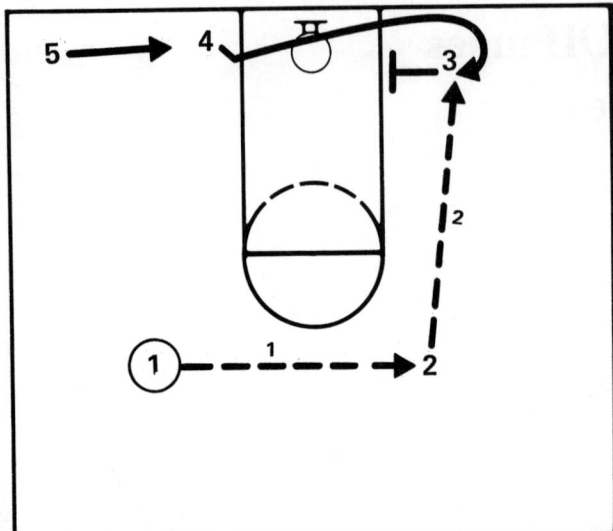

Figure 5-1 2–3 Baseline Screening Offense, Basic Movements.

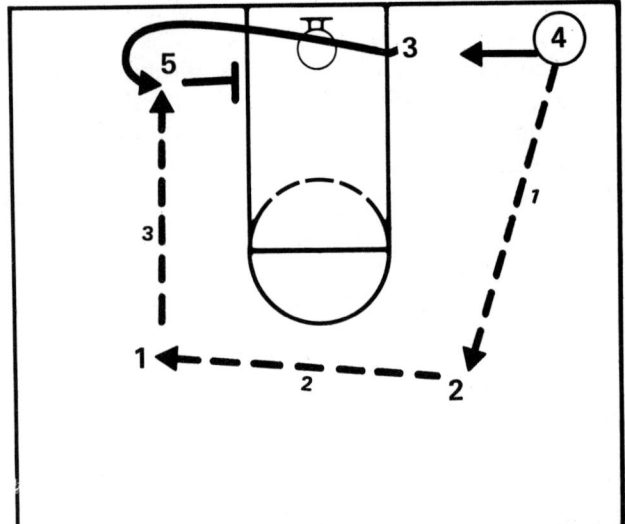

Figure 5-2 2–3 Baseline Screening Offense, Rotation.

situations in which a team has only one baseline or corner shooter. In such cases, low posts 5 and 3 merely maintain their positions as screeners for 4 on either side of the lane. Thus, the best shooter handles the ball from the baseline position most of the time, an especially desirable practice when a team has only one outstanding offensive player.

The weakness of this approach may be found in the extra time required for 4 to cut from corner to corner; still, the same weakness is found in *all* zone offensive patterns featuring a single cutter from corner to cor-

Special Zone Offenses and Techniques 119

ner, and the prevalence of such patterns indicates that the time allotment is not too great to preclude its use.

Concerning play of the outside guards, the only real consideration is that dribbling should be held to a minimum except when possibilities for penetration arise.

Further continuity may be added to the pattern by sending 1 through the lane and rotating 4 and 2 around to receive 3's pass. (Figure 5–3.)

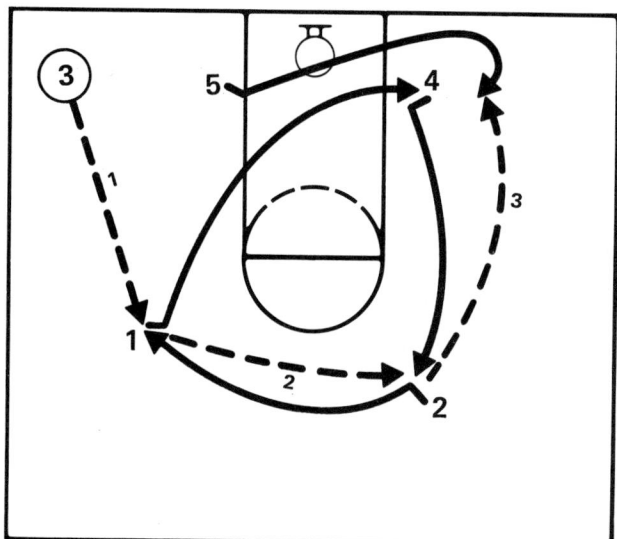

Figure 5-3 Variation of Continuity For 2–3 Baseline Screening Offense.

Figure 5-4 Alternate Method of Setting Up the Baseline Screen.

120 Zone Offenses for Women's Basketball

A splendid alternate method of setting up the baseline movement is shown in Figure 5-4. Operating from a 2-1-2 alignment, the high post player cuts toward the corner away from the ball as the ballhandler passes to the other guard. The pass receiver then returns the ball to her in order to pass to the cutter, who by now is cutting behind the baseline screen. The rest of the pattern is the same as that shown in Figure 5-2.

The 2-3 baseline screening offense is effective as a splitting offense against odd-front zone defenses, but it can also be used to attack matchup zones as well, although ball rotation is sometimes difficult. When the outside defensive guard stays outside, the cutter has ample room to operate one-on-one from the corner without fear of double-teaming from an outside guard.

THE "V" OFFENSE

The "V" offense is actually a 1-2-2 offense designed to attack even-front zone defenses through a double high post alignment. (See Figures 5-5 through 5-8.)

Basically, the "V" offensive pattern consists of point guard's (25)

Figures 5-5, 5-6, 5-7, 5-8 The "V" Offense.

Special Zone Offenses and Techniques 121

Figure 5-6.

Figure 5-7.

Figure 5-8.

penetrating dribble between the outside defensive guards to freeze them, then passing to either 32 or 3 at high post. If 32 receives the pass, 3 cuts into the lane. Since X_{10} has to cover 32—if X_{55} covers 32, 12 along the baseline will have an open layup—3 will have the layup or 3–6 foot shot, as shown in Figures 5–5 through 5–8.

The first defensive adjustment is likely to be X_{55} or X_5's moving up to cover the cutter into the lane when the ball is passed to 32 or 3. In such cases, the pass to the corner will almost certainly be open, and 32 will be open sliding to low post when X_{55} covers 12. The possibility also exists that 3 will be open cutting across to high post on the ball side of the court.

A more realistic defensive adjustment is for the opponents to shift into a 1–2–2 zone alignment. Such adjustment by the defense will cause the offense no end of difficulty in its basic pattern, since the matchup at once eliminates the point guard's penetration, the high post's shot, the weak side high post's cut through the lane, and the corner shot.

Is the "V" pattern thwarted when the defense shifts to 1–2–2 coverage? Not necessarily. First, the offense may be disguised as something else—for example, a low 1–4 offense with double low post and two corner players, or a high 1–4 alignment with double high post and two wings. In the former case, the low posts cut to high post for the point guard's pass; and in the latter case, the wings cut to the corners to freeze the inside defensive forwards.

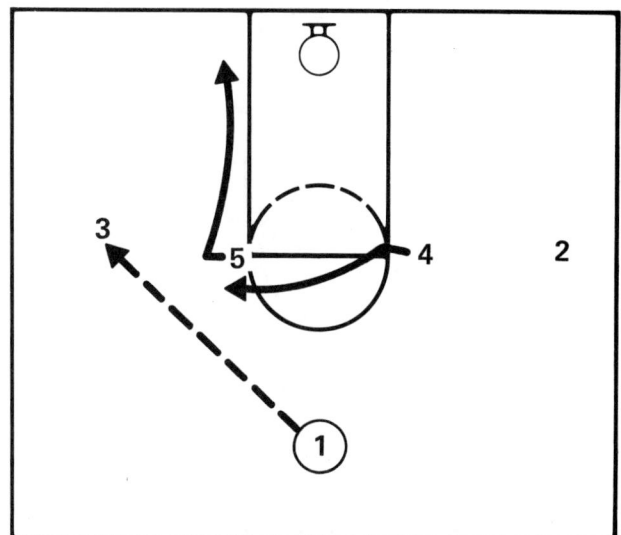

Figure 5-9 Setting Up the Multiple Overload from 1–4 Instead of the "V" Offense.

The advantage of such movements is that the opponents never know when to shift into 1–2–2 coverage and when to stay in their original 2–1–2 or 2–3 zones. For example, in using the high 1–4 alignment, 32 can slide to ball side low post, with 3 cutting to ball side high post as 25 passes to 12, and the offense is then in the multiple overload rotation alignment shown is Figure 3–40. (See also Figure 5–9.)

The possibilities for movement and rotation have already been described, but the point to remember is that, while a team may or may not recognize and adjust to the "V" alignment, it will *not* be able to adjust to the "V" as well as the other possibilities.

A HIGH-LOW SCREENING OFFENSE

All too often, it seems, coaches inherit teams whose personnel consist of one more or less legitimate scoring threat and four players who couldn't put the ball in the hoop if they were sitting on top of the backboard dropping it toward the basket. Of course, the opponents quickly discover these personnel deficiencies, and the coach is then confronted with the awesome task of constructing a zone offense that will increase the possibility of getting the ball to the scorer despite overplaying, double-teaming, or combination defense.

The high-low screening offense shown in Figures 5–10 and 5–11 presents numerous opportunities for a team with only one good shooter (3 in the diagrams). In fact, the first movement, 4's cut to high post as 1 passes to 2, will often yield a high-percentage shot either at the corner of the free-throw lane for 4, or in the vicinity of the corner for 3.

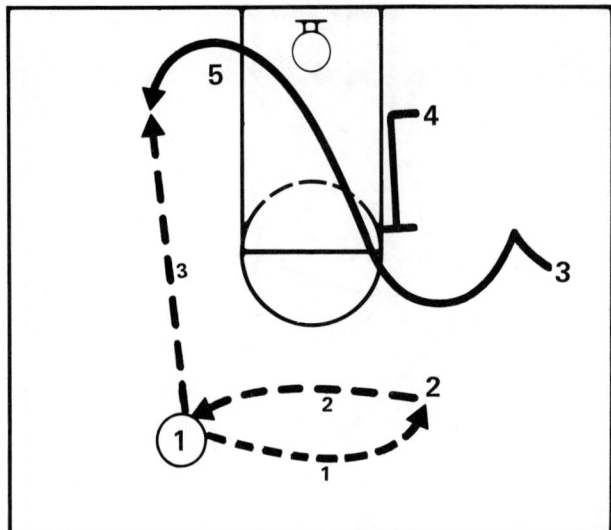

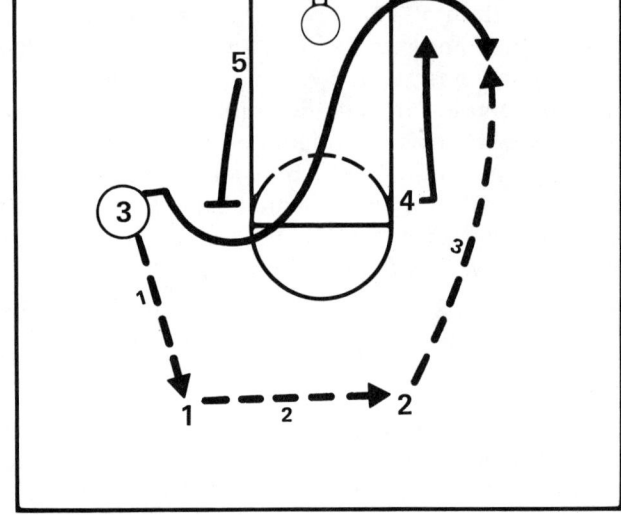

Figure 5-10 High-Low Screening Offense, First Movements.

Figure 5-11 High-Low Screening Offense, Rotation.

If 4's cut doesn't spring her (or 3) free, 3 cuts around 4's screen as 2 passes back to 1. Player 3 continues through the lane and, if she doesn't receive a pass from 1, cuts behind 5 at low post and continues outside. Player 4 returns to low post. Player 5 cuts to high post and, if open, receives 1's pass.

If 5 is covered, 1 passes to 2, and 3 cuts around 5 and continues through the lane.

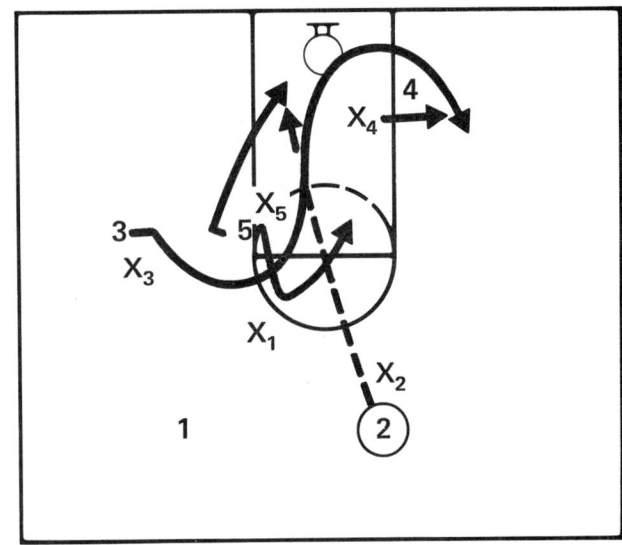

Figure 5-12 Inside Pass to 5 When the Defense Switches, High-Low Screening Offense.

If the inside defenders switch as shown in Figure 5-12—which they undoubtedly will, since switching is almost always automatic in zone defense—5 may be open for the inside pass from 2.

Personnel Requirements. Although hardly a foolproof zone offense, the high-low screening pattern will likely ease a team's personnel problems. Players 1 and 2 do not have to be superlative ballhandlers since they remain largely in the same outside areas of the court throughout the pattern, but it is helpful (though not imperative) for them to be able to make the outside shot when their defensive guards drop back to increase inside defensive coverage. (It is suggested that if the outside defensive guards move further outside to disrupt the pattern, 1 and 2 merely drop back toward midcourt to spread the defensive coverage.)

Players 4 and 5 likewise require few skills to execute their patterns. Their movements to high and low post require little practice except in terms of timing, and even their screens need not be of expert quality if 3 knows how to use them to free herself for a pass from 1 or 2. All 4 and 5 really need to know is the automatic of the offense—the movement to the basket when 3 cuts into and across the lane.

WEAK SIDE SCREENING OFFENSE

This continuity pattern is easy to learn, uses cutters toward and away from the ball side of the court (including a screen on the weak side), and provides outside rotation to change both the matchups and the areas in which openings arise in the defense. Additionally, the screening position may be used to hide a fundamentally weak offensive player, or to attack the defense when the players relax their coverage of 3's weak side cuts to overplay the rest of the pattern.

Player 1 passes to wing 5 and moves to the top of the circle. Player 3 moves to weak side high post and screens for 2, who cuts to the ball side corner behind 3. (See Figure 5-13.) Ball rotation consists of 5 passing to 1, who relays the ball to 4 as 3 goes weak side again to screen for 5. Player 5

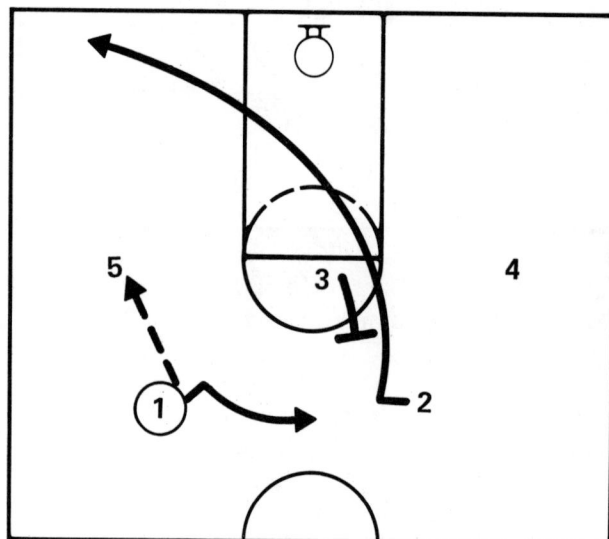

Figure 5-13 Weak Side Screening Offense, First Movements.

Figure 5-14 Weak Side Screening Offense, Rotation.

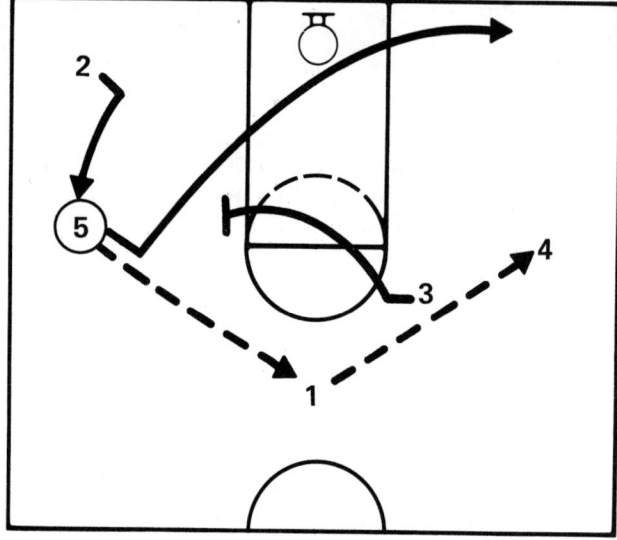

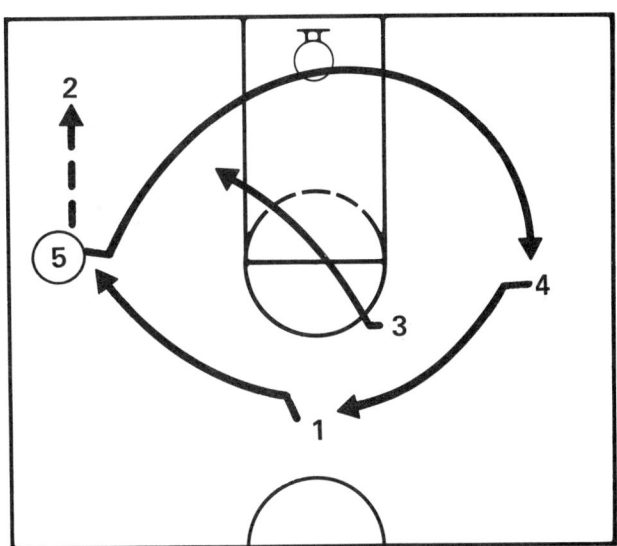

Figure 5-15 Single Cutter Movement in Weak Side Screening Offense.

cuts into and across the lane to the ball side corner. Player 2 moves out to 5's wing position, and the offense is ready to be run to the other side of the court again. (See Figure 5-14.)

Whenever the ball is passed to the corner, the passer cuts through the lane, and the outside players rotate around toward the ball in the familiar single-cutter-through pattern. (See Figure 5-15.) The screening pattern is then ready to be repeated.

The weakness of the weak side screening offense is found in the difficulty sometimes encountered in passing the ball from the wing to the point when 1 is overguarded. In such cases, the offense must resort to automatics such as 1's cutting backdoor to the basket for the pass, going one-on-one or two-on-two, or 3's cutting to the ball side to receive a pass or set up splitting the post.

KEYING IN A ZONE OFFENSE

I remember well my first encounter a few years ago with keying offenses. I had gone to Millen, Georgia, to scout an opponent of the Jenkins Co. Eaglettes, and I happened to stay and watch the boys' game afterwards. Since the possibility existed that our boys' team might play the Jenkins Co. boys in an upcoming Christmas tournament, I decided to prepare a scouting report on the Eagles for our boys' coach.

The first time Jenkins Co. brought the ball downcourt on offense, I diagrammed their 1–3–1 alignment, recorded the players' numbers at their positions, and recorded as many of the multiple cuts as I could remember. My diagrams were incomplete, but I wasn't worried at the time: I'd just get the rest of it next time they came downcourt.

Next time downcourt, however, the Eagles set up in a 1-2-2 offensive alignment, and their cuts were different. I assumed that they were running a series of set plays, or freelancing.

As the game wore on, however, the Jenkins Co. boys continued to show different alignments and cuts, and the realization began to dawn on me that something was going on for which I was totally unprepared. Nobody, not even the pros, ran that many different set plays, and their patterns were too organized to be freelance. I wondered how the players knew where to set up and where to cut to, since they never called plays or adjusted their alignments. It was almost as if they set up wherever they wished and made random cuts from those positions.

I didn't figure out what they were doing that night, nor for the next four times I watched them play. Still, I was too proud to ask Coach Mac Morrison how he did it.

Much later, I decided that they were doing two things: (1) disguising their pattern by constantly changing alignments, and (2) keying their cuts to the movements of one or more of the players. I'm still not sure I've figured out Coach Morrison's zone offense—it differs in several respects from the keying offense presented in this book—but it doesn't really matter. The point is that, because I didn't know what I was seeing, I was totally unprepared to deal with the offense. I was relieved that I didn't have to prepare my girls' team to defend against it.

One of the greatest problems in attacking zone defenses is the predictability of most zone offensive patterns. After the offensive team runs through its patterns a few times, the defense usually learns which movements and shooting options are most hazardous to them, and they often are able to counter with defensive adjustments that negate many (or all) of the advantages of the particular offensive pattern being used.

Many coaches yearn for a zone offensive technique in which the offense works for certain shots from certain areas of the court as before, but does so in such a manner that their intentions are hidden or disguised by "keyed" movements that are not easily detected by the defense.

There is such an offense. It is based on recognition of court positions, multiple cuts toward and away from the ball, and keyed movements. It is not an easy offense to learn, but its ever-changing appearance makes it equally difficult for the defense to solve. It can be run from any offensive alignment, thus compounding the defense's problems. In addition, scouting it will reveal nothing of value unless the scouting personnel recognizes the two vital features: the players' court positions *after cutting* and the keys that determine the offensive players' cuts to those positions.

Court Positions. The court positions are the same as those described previously: the point, the ball side wing, the high post at the center of the lane and cut to high post in the vicinity of the corner of the free-throw line (ball side), the low post, the corner, and the position between weak side low post and weak side wing occupied by the player cutting away from the ball.

Cutting Toward and Away from the Ball. The purpose of such cuts is obvious: the cuts toward the ball side force the defense to shift fully to guard the overload, and the cuts away from the ball facilitate ball rotation to provide the open weak side shot or add continuity to the offense.

Offensive Keys. An offensive *key* is a word, movement, pass, or signal by any offensive player that leads to, or directs, movements by other offensive players. For instance, an offensive key often encountered is that which takes the form of direct pass/bounce pass options. If the point guard uses a direct pass to the wing, she cuts away from the ball, and if she bounce-passes to the wing, she cuts behind the wing to receive the ball back and begin the pattern from that position.

In the particular keying zone offensive pattern being examined, the keys to offensive movement are afforded by the point guard and low post.

Point Guard Keys. The movements in Figures 5–16 and 5–17 are keyed by 1's dribbling to the wing position rather than passing the ball to 2. Notice that 5 slides to the corner from ball side in Figure 5–16 and criss-crosses to high post from weak side low post in Figure 5–17. The reason for this automatic movement that also has been used in patterns discussed elsewhere is that the weak side cut to high post is blind and therefore is

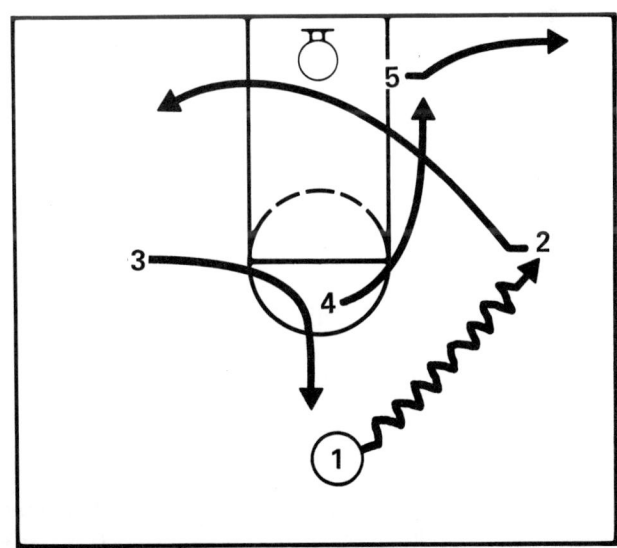

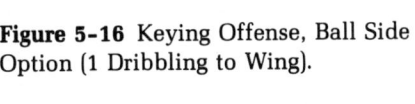

Figure 5-16 Keying Offense, Ball Side Option (1 Dribbling to Wing).

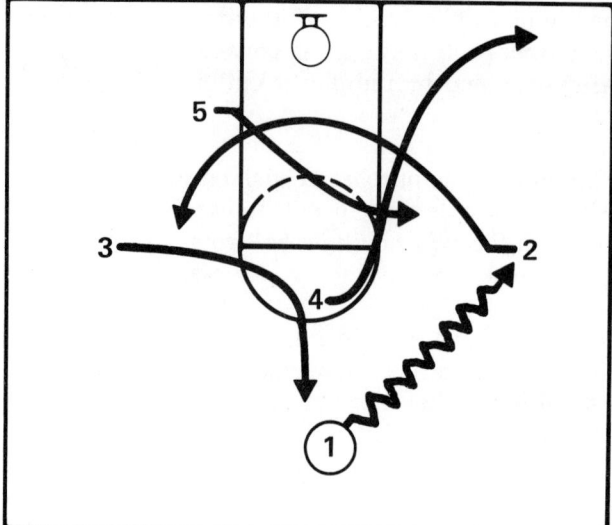

Figure 5-17 Keying Offense, Weak Side Option (1 Dribbling to Wing).

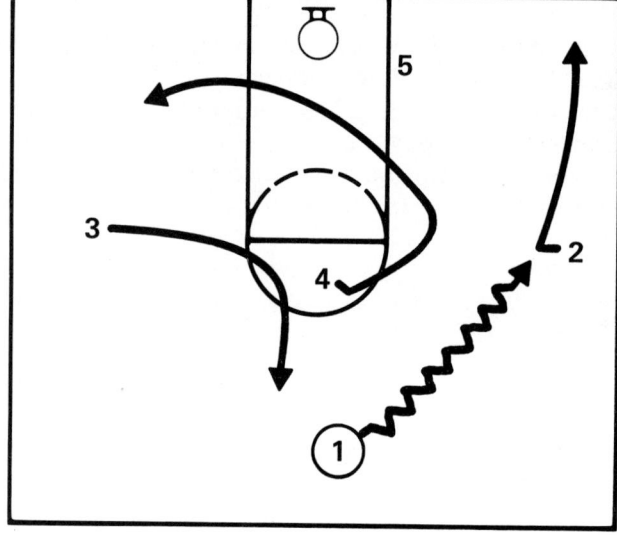

Figure 5-18 Player 2 Cuts to Corner As 1 Dribbles to Wing, Keying Offense.

more likely to achieve the pass to high post than when the defenders can see 5 sliding to high post.

When 1 dribbles to the wing position, 2 clears to the weak side and 3 moves toward the middle, then cuts outside to become the point guard in rotation.

An alternate method of setting the overload when 1 dribbles to the wing is for 2 to slide away from 1 to the corner. (See Figure 5–18.) However, it is doubtful that this pattern is any more effective than 5 or 4's corner cut and possibly is less effective because 4's slide requires less defensive movement inside to adjust to the pattern. (Player 4's sliding to high post before cutting away from the ball may help to confuse the defensive coverage.)

Low Post Keys. When the point guard passes to wing 2 rather than dribbling, low post 5 keys both her own and 4's movements. Player 3 cuts toward high post and slides high in every alignment and pattern, and 1 cuts away from the ball in every pattern except those in which she dribbles to the wing position.

The low post player has several options. On ball side, she may remain at low post (Figures 5-18 and 5-21), although her immobility may facilitate inside defensive coverage, or she may cut to the corner (Figure 5-19). As discussed elsewhere, 5's cut from ball side low post to ball side high post is generally unproductive because it occurs in full view of the defense. Therefore, it has been eliminated from lengthy consideration in analysis of this pattern.

At weak side low post, 5 may cut to the ball side corner (Figure 5-22), ball side low post (Figure 5-23), ball side high post (Figure 5-24), or even to the point guard position (Figure 5-25). In each case 5's movements key those of high post 4.

In Figure 5-19, 5's cut to the corner keys 4's sliding to the corner of the lane and dropping to low post. (Of course, 4 moves to the opening at high post before going low.) Figure 5-20 shows the kind of rotation pattern available in getting the ball back to 1 at weak side.

Figure 5-21 shows 4, realizing that ball side low post 5 is remaining

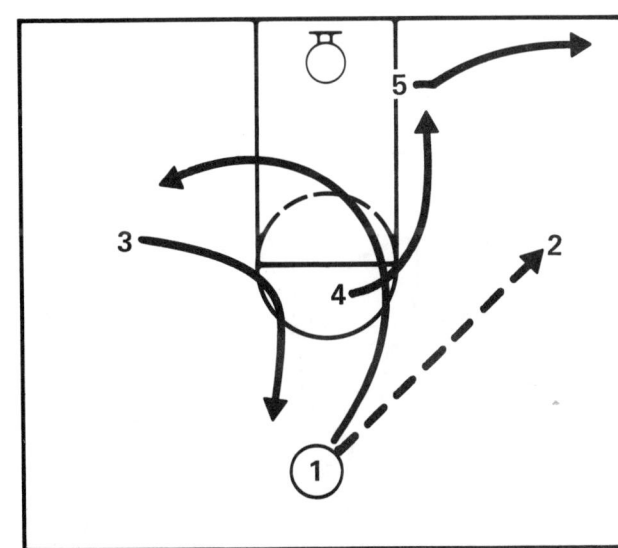

Figure 5-19 Strong Side Low Post Corner Cut.

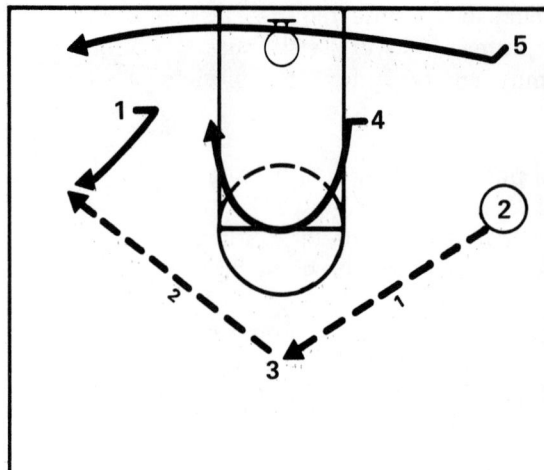

Figure 5-20 Rotation from Overload Established in Figure 5–19.

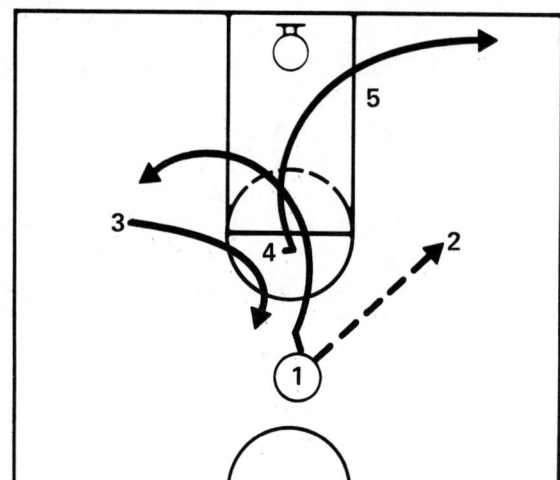

Figure 5-21 High Post Cut to Corner.

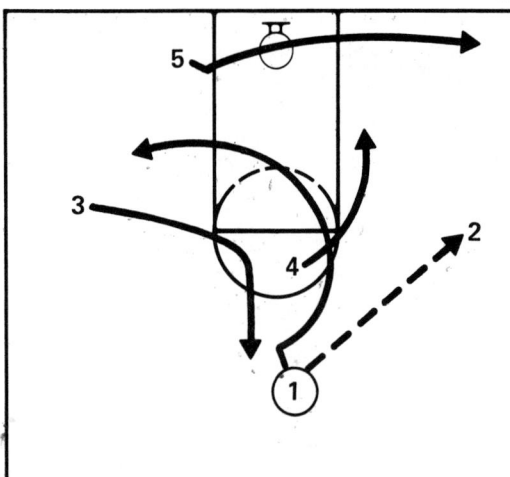

Figure 5-22 Weak Side Low Post Cut to Ball Side Corner.

Special Zone Offenses and Techniques   133

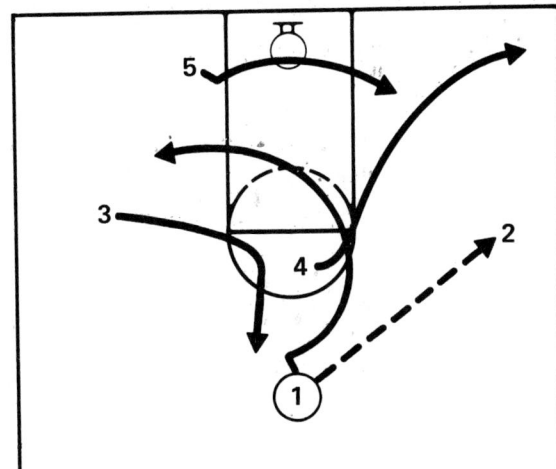

Figure 5-23 Weak Side Low Post Cut to Ball Side Low Post.

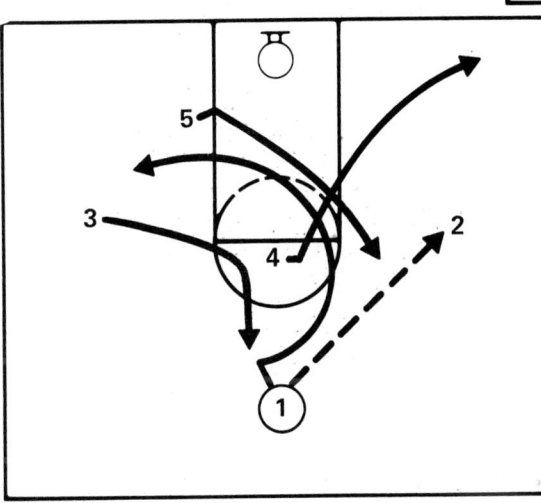

Figure 5-24 Weak Side Low Post Cut to High Post.

inside, cutting to the corner. (The cut may be either behind or in front of 5.) Player 5 then may or may not decide to cut to high post.

Figures 5-22 through 5-25 all involve weak side low post cuts. The coach may prefer weak side cuts to be keyed by the *high post* rather than by the low post for expediency and visual purposes. Whatever the case, the weak side cuts certainly provide greater diversity than keying on the ball side low post. If the high post slides low, as in Figures 5-22 and 5-24, the low post may cut to either weak side low post (Figure 5-23), ball side corner (Figure 5-22), or even to the point (Figure 5-25). The high post player may cut to the corner, as in Figure 5-24, in which case 5 may cut to either high post as shown, or merely slide across the lane to ball side low post.

Figure 5-25 Player 5 Delays Cut, Weak Side Wing to Ball Side Corner.

ATTACKING MATCHUP ZONE DEFENSES

Matchup zone defense is likely to be at the same time the best and the most difficult defense to execute in basketball. It is the best defense because it deploys either: (1) player-to-player principles from a zone alignment, or (2) zone principles from player-to-player coverage—either of which creates considerable problems for most teams offensively. By far its most effective usage is the former, with the defense setting up in zone coverage and matching whatever alignment the offense decides to use.

Whatever the case, a frequent result of matchup defense is offensive players standing around wondering what to do, especially when the focus of the offensive attack is on splitting the defense without inside or outside movement.

A second point to remember concerning matchup zones is that the defense is still playing its original defense regardless of its new alignment (e.g., from 1-3-1 or 1-2-2 to 2-1-2). *Coverage of cutters through the lane or toward or away from the ball is the same as in the original zone.* The zone can no longer be split, but overload patterns can be extremely effective in creating favorable matchups, or in determining where the matchups occur.

A third point concerning the matchups is that they change every time a cutter is sent through the lane and outside, or every time a screen forces defenders to switch. When the defense has to switch assignments constantly, the matchups tend to become confused, and the offense sometimes can create forward-on-guard or center-on-guard one-on-one matchups favorable to the offensive team.

Once the matchups have been established, the defensive players will maintain their positions as the single cutters make their cuts through the zone, with players dropping back slightly to cover the cutter, then moving back outside to cover the outside rotation.

Points to Consider in Dealing with Matchup Zone Defense

1. It is always difficult to attack a matchup zone defense, except with outstanding offensive players. Mediocre teams seldom use matchup defense. Besides, the opponents have already measured the risks involved, and their analysis has indicated that the initial matchups, at least, are in their favor. One attacks matchup zone defenses *very carefully.*

2. Matchup defense may be played either aggressively, by challenging all five offensive players and overplaying the passing lanes; or passively, by playing off the ball and challenging the offensive players only when they enter high-percentage scoring areas. The coach should attempt to analyze the defense's intentions before deciding upon the kind of patterns to run against the matchup.

3. Continuous or directed motion provides the best way to beat any matchup zone defense. (By directed motion we mean movement directed toward specific goals, as opposed to random movements.) For this reason, many coaches run their regular player-to-player offense when confronted with matchup zone defense, especially when their player-to-player offense is a continuity pattern. Continuity patterns provide continuous movements, cuts, screens, and player interchanges. Too, using a regular player-

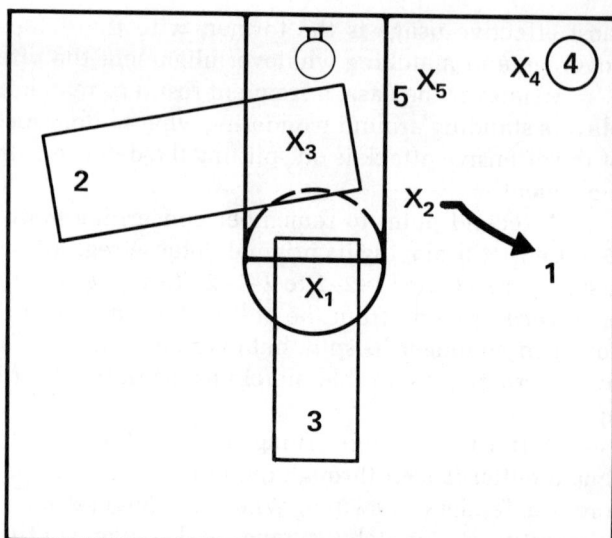

Figure 5-26 The New Matchups After Single-Cutter Movement.

to-player offense with which players are already familiar means that they will not have to learn a special offense for the sole purpose of combatting a matchup zone defense.

4. When the defensive players overplay the passing lanes and aggressively challenge the ball, one-on-one or two-on-two offensive maneuvers (e.g., backdoor cuts, pass-and-cut, and give-and-go) or a strong inside offensive game can overpower the matchups—*when* the offensive team is strong in those areas of the game!

5. To set up the inside game against aggressive outside coverage, spread the wings or intermediate wings and use screens or high–low post interchanges to free inside players for passes. "Passing game" offenses are ideally suited to aggressive matchup defense.

6. When a team matches up on defense, it generally initially sets the players in the desired matchups. Offensive maneuvers that alter those matchups are more likely to succeed than those in which the initial matchups remain intact. Cuts, screens, player rotation, and inside interchanges are all methods of changing the matchups. For example, if a small guard moves inside to screen for a tall forward moving outside, the defense can either give up the pass and shot or switch defensive assignments. Either way, the offense has taken a first step in combatting the matchups.

7. Forcing double coverage can free teammates for open perimeter shots when other methods fail to affect the matchup coverage. Figure 5–27 illustrates a common method of forcing double coverage against matchup zone defense.

The direction of the penetrating dribble is dictated by the direction

Special Zone Offenses and Techniques   137

Figure 5-27 Forcing Double-Coverage Against Matchup Zone Defense.

of the point defensive guard's overplaying. In Figure 5-27, the ballhandler is given the dribble to her left, so she dribbles in that direction, not really trying to avoid double-teaming by the player guarding the wing, but willing to go to the basket if the defensive pointguard fails to stop her. However, the double-team occurs as shown, and the wing slides away from the dribbler for the clear shot.

It should be noted that the double-teaming does not have to result from attempted penetration from the top of the circle, but can occur anywhere along the perimeter of the defense, and with any two outside offensive players.

Overload Offenses and Matchup Zone Defense. Overloading provides an excellent way of attacking the matchups, providing that two considerations are taken into account: first, the matchups must favor the offensive team; otherwise, the offense will bog down in inactivity and lack of movement. And second, ball rotation is often difficult against matchup zone defenses.

If the matchups favor the defense, overloads will be largely ineffectual except when the overload can revolve into matchups or positions more favorable to the offensive team. The revolving rotation overload offense described in Chapter 3 was designed to counteract such unfavorable defensive matchups.

Ball rotation is sometimes difficult to achieve when the defense plays its matchup coverage to stop the outside rotation rather than the inside cuts in a single-cutter offense. Of course, the offensive players must be aware of this change in coverage and attempt to pass to the cutters in order to force the defense back and open the outside area for player and ball rotation.

Cutter Patterns and Matchup Zone Defense. Practically any cutter pattern described in this book will suffice to change a team's original defensive matchups, except when the defense sets up in a given zone alignment and changes to player-to-player coverage. In such cases, however, player-to-player patterns probably will be more effective, anyway.

The cutter patterns may include any of the following: point to ball side or weak side corner, or to weak side wing; wing to wing or opposite corner; high post to corner, wing, or point; or low post to low post, high post, wing, or corner. Each of these movements forces the defense to alter its coverage and, when combined in some type of continuity pattern, increases the offensive team's chances of taking advantage of lapses in the coverage.

Screening and Matchup Zone Defense. Many teams that use matchup zone defense fail to take into account the effects of screening of the matchups. Where screens are concerned, switching is automatic in almost every zone defense (including matching up), and a team that uses screening as a regular part of its offense against matchup zones is likely to find ample opportunities to take advantage of offensive mismatches, or to spring players open for high-percentage shots.

Player Interchange and Matchup Zone Defense. Another way of accomplishing the same purpose as screening is to interchange players to create more favorable matchups. A point guard may pass to a wing and cut to the weak side wing, with the weak side wing moving to the point, or the low post or high–low post players may switch positions to effect such an interchange.

The point is that, since the defensive players are going to switch anyway, screening may be unnecessary.

ATTACKING THE TRAPPING ZONE DEFENSES

Trapping is an aggressive defensive maneuver in which two or more players not only guard the ballhandler, but also attempt to steal the ball or force turnovers or held balls. Trapping is distinguishable from double-teaming by the fact that trapping always involves the ball, whereas double-teaming often occurs inside as a means of keeping the ball away from a taller player.

Points to Consider in Dealing with Trapping Zone Defenses

1. The defensive players may or may not be tall, and they may or may not be extraordinarily quick, but they will always be aggressive. Trapping defense is so risky for the defensive team that it *must* be played aggressively to have any real chance of succeeding.

2. Passive offensive efforts will not work against trapping. Merely keeping the ball outside will not work; the defensive team *wants* the ball outside. They want to play the passing lanes and force lob passes that will give the defenders time to spring their traps.

There are three ways to attack trapping zones. The first method occurs before the traps are set, the second sometimes arises during the act of trapping, and the third occurs when the trap has failed to contain the ball or force a turnover.

A. *Attacking Before the Trap is Set.* The greatest ally of defensive players in the use of trapping defense is the element of surprise. In a typical trapping movement, a team carefully "lets" an offensive player dribble to the baseline with loose defensive coverage, then suddenly overguards her and forces her to reverse pivot into a trapping teammate, while at the same time cutting off passing lanes and harassing her into a

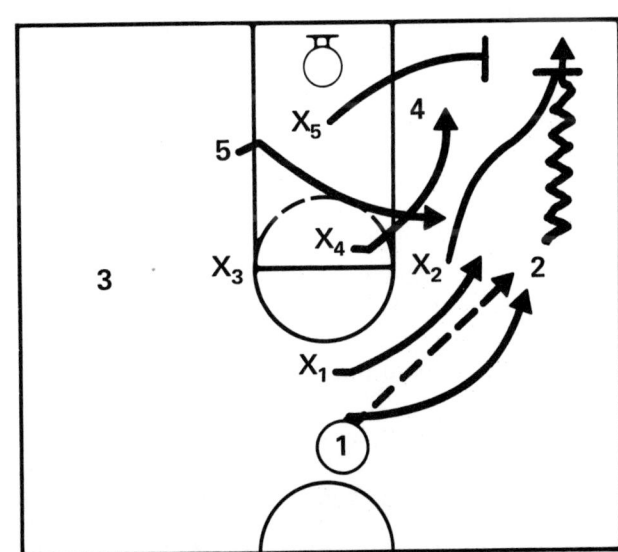

Figure 5-28 Typical Corner Trapping Movement.

bad pass or held ball. (See Figure 5–28.) The best way to avoid such traps, then, is to attack the defenders before they are prepared to spring the trap. And the best way to attack at this point is to force the defense to double-team the ballhandler when she is expecting it—or, more precisely, by dribbling toward a wing to force double-coverage, and then passing to a teammate in a manner similar to that shown in Figure 5–27. Trapping is generally less effective when the offensive team anticipates the traps and attacks before the defense is prepared to deal with the offensive thrust.

B. Attacking During the Trapping Movement. The key to reacting to a defensive trap is, first of all, knowing where the trap will be sprung. All teams tend to prefer certain areas of the court (e.g., the baseline or the point) to others for trapping. Knowing where the danger lies provides a good beginning in combatting the effectiveness of trapping defenses.

The second step in dealing with traps is knowing where the openings in the traps are likely to be found. Practically without exception, the openings occur in the areas diagonally opposite the ball—for example, from the ball side baseline to the weak side corner of the free-throw line, or from the ball side wing to the weak side corner or low post. It is a virtual certainty that all primary pass receivers will be covered when the trap is sprung. In Figure 5–29, the defenders are aligned as follows: two players trapping in the corner, one guarding 4 at low post, one guarding 5 cutting to high post, and the defensive point guard moving to the ball side wing position to cover the return pass to 1. Thus, *no one is left to guard the weak side high post area!* (The rapidity of the trapping movement and the presence of two players inside usually serve to negate the possibility of passing to the weak side low post.)

C. Attacking When the Trap Fails to Contain the Ball. When the defense has two players guarding a single offensive player and the trap fails, the offense has a momentary four-on-three advantage. It is imperative that the players be prepared to attack the defense before it recovers, or else they will be facing trapping situations throughout the game. If a team takes advantage of attacking situations before the defense recovers, the opponents may have to drop back into a more basic style of defense.

3. Spread the wings and pass the ball quickly. Spreading the offense will also spread the defense and, combined with quick, accurate passing, should serve to rob the defense of valuable time necessary to prepare the traps. When the defense double-teams, quick passing can yield open shots or layups while the defensive players are out of position to stop the rest of the offense.

4. Avoid reverse pivoting or picking up the dribble before checking the defense. Successful trapping contains separate elements of surprise, extreme defensive pressure on the ballhandler, and cutting off the passing lanes to the most likely pass receivers. Reverse pivoting while dribbling,

Special Zone Offenses and Techniques   141

Figures 5-29, 5-30 Diagonal Openings Against Trapping Defense.

and picking up the dribble prematurely are two of the easiest ways possible to aid the defense in successful trapping.

5. Attack the defense with diagonal passes to beat the traps. Suggested offensive alignments to beat the traps in the corner and at the wings are shown in Figures 5–29 and 5–30, with 25 the intended pass receiver in both diagrams.

It should be pointed out that the aforementioned coverages are always used from the wing or corner because the act of trapping requires that every primary passing lane be covered. The diagonal passes are not primary because, under normal conditions, it would take more than one pass to reach the player occupying that position.

OFFENSES AGAINST COMBINATION ZONE DEFENSES

Several types of strategy exist for combatting the combination zone defenses. First, a team may elect to leave the player outside and play to the other side of the court in an overload pattern, going to that player's side only sporadically when the coverage relaxes, or when favorable one-

Figure 5-31 Setting Up an Inside Game Against Box-and-One Combination Defense.

on-one situations arise. Some teams try to run their regular offensive patterns, relying on the players' overall offensive strength to overcome the advantages of the combination defense.

One strategy that often helps to free teammates for open shots is for the player receiving one-on-one coverage to move inside where an inside defender is already set up. This, in effect, forces two-on-one coverage on the defense or sets up an inside matchup with 30 and the player guarding her if the inside defensive player moves outside. (See Figure 5–31.)

Any offense that forces the rest of the defense to match up will work against combination defenses, if the matchups favor the offense. A major point that should be explained to the players, however, is that they should not try to force the ball to the player receiving player-to-player coverage, nor should that player force her shots or offensive movements whenever she gets the ball.

Possibly the best method of attacking the combination defenses is through the use of screens or criss-crosses, either as part of a regular zone offense (See also the various screening offenses in Chapters 4 and 5), or those found in player-to-player continuity patterns.

CONTROL OFFENSES: SLOWDOWNS, STALLS, AND FREEZES

Although generally lumped together under the single heading of control or delay offenses, slowdowns, stalls, and freezes represent separate and distinct tactics used for entirely different purposes. A *slowdown offense* may be described as "any offense characterized by extremely high-percentage shot selection"; that is, it reveals conscious effort on the part of the offensive team to work patiently for high-percentage shots from predetermined areas of the court. Thus, since any offense may be used for such purposes, it follows that the term *slowdown* (or *stall*, or *freeze*) *offense* is a misnomer. A slowdown offense is any offense used for slowdown purposes as described above.

In women's college basketball, the presence of a 30-second clock necessarily limits a coach's ability to control the tempo of the game by delaying, stalling, or freezing the ball. Generally, the best strategy for the college coach hoping to slow slightly the game's tempo is to run her regular zone offensive pattern with greater shot selectivity than usual. Care must be taken, however, not to become so engrossed in the pattern and protecting the ball that the clock is ignored. (Of course, circumstances may dictate that a team operate from a spread alignment, but then difficulty arises from the fact that the players must move into another alignment or pattern in order to set up a shot near the end of their thirty seconds of possession.)

Stalling offenses carry greater negative connotations than slowdowns. Stalling means that a team is consciously avoiding all but the highest percentage shots (usually layups), and the rest of the time is content to run the clock and retain ball possession. The distinction between delaying and stalling may be a bit hazy at this point, but it may help to consider slowdown offenses as regular offenses used for slightly irregular purposes, whereas stalling offenses generally occur from irregular, exaggeratedly spread alignments.

Also, teams engaged in stalling offenses tend to make fewer aggressive moves to spring players free for open shots than teams in delay offenses, and thus run the clock to a greater extent in the former case than in the latter. However, defensive adjustments to the stall sometimes result in increased high-percentage shots for the stalling team, and as long as they are getting scoring opportunities, they may not care about running the clock.

The distinction between *stalling* and *freezing* offenses is clearer: the stalling team will take the open shot, but the team that is really intent upon holding the ball at all costs (freezing the ball) will pass up almost all shots, regardless of their location. Alignments for freezing the ball vary from team to team, but all have in common the outside spread and players cutting (or staying) away from the ball.

Control Offense When a Team Is Behind. Generally, referees and fans alike frown upon slowdown tactics, especially when a team is behind. But without entering into a discussion of the virtues or ethics of the philosophy underlying such considerations, it should be recognized that the strategy exists for the coach (at the junior high and high school levels, at least) who wants or needs to bring an opponent out of its zone defense.

When a team is behind, the rules do not allow that team merely to hold the ball outside until the opponents come out to challenge the ball; in fact, the opponents do not have to come out of their zone at all, since the responsibility for forcing the action rests with the team that is behind. Thus, the trailing team is expected to advance the ball toward the basket in a more forceful manner than if it was merely protecting a lead. A deep freeze offense, such as a four-corner spread that keeps the ball outside beyond the ten-second line at midcourt without penetration, will not work.

Coaches seldom consider holding the ball when behind; after all, they reason, how will they catch up without scoring? However, other considerations may be taken into account, such as the fact that, when falling behind, calling a time out may not be enough to slow down an opponent's momentum; or that such a change in strategy may serve to confuse the opponents at a time when they are threatening to run away with a game.

To exemplify the arguments for and against holding the ball, consider the situation confronting a coaching acquaintance a few years ago:

We were playing [Team A], whose height, depth, speed and tournament experience was vastly superior to ours, although our records were about the same. It was a region semifinal game, with the winner heading for the state tournament and the loser eliminated from competition.

The early part of the game was close, to my everlasting surprise, but in the third quarter [Team A's] superiority began to take its toll, and they pulled away to a 9-point lead midway through the quarter. We called time out and decided to hold the ball for a while. For the next four minutes we held the ball without taking a single shot.

The opponents couldn't believe it! Their coach signaled them to stay back in their zone, of course, since we weren't likely to catch them when we weren't even trying to score.

Suddenly, our girl shot from the corner. She made it. The opponents came down and shot, missed, and somehow we got the rebound. We came downcourt and held the ball again, this time for only a minute before the same girl shot from the corner again. It went in again. Those were the first two times all night that they'd given us any kind of shot, inside or outside.

We lost the game by 5 points, and a lot of people said it was all my fault, that if we hadn't held the ball we'd have won. But I'm convinced that [Team A] would have beaten us by at least 15–20 points if we hadn't held the ball when we did. They were scoring every time they came down, and they weren't giving us anything at all at our end. People were howling for my scalp after the game, but it was the best job of coaching I've ever done.

Three strategies exist for delaying, stalling, or freezing when behind: running the regular zone offense, but setting up farther outside than normally; running a player-to-player continuity pattern or set plays; and running a control pattern that works the ball inside or to the corners.

Regular Zone Offensive Patterns as Control Offenses. Of the various slowdown strategies, perhaps the least effective is running the regular zone offensive pattern from wider positions on the court than those normally used in moving the ball around the court. Such tactics may be effective for a while, but the defensive team is usually quick to catch on and move outside to cut off the passing lanes, force lob passes, or create trapping situations—all without substantially weakening their inside coverage. Additionally, the change in strategy without changing the pattern tends to confuse the offensive players—especially young or inexperienced players—who are used to running the pattern to set up scoring opportunities.

There are exceptions, of course; still, a team must have the maturity and experience to handle the subtle negative connotations of holding the ball from a regular offensive pattern. Many coaches feel that it is easier for the players to adjust to an entirely different pattern when holding the ball or bringing a team out of its zone defense is desired.

146 Zone Offenses for Women's Basketball

Player-to-Player (Continuity) Patterns as Control Offenses. Player-to-player continuity patterns are not necessarily effective only as slowdown offenses. Indeed, many coaches use player-to-player offensive patterns against zone defenses as well as player-to-player defense. Player-to-player patterns can be used effectively against zone coverage in many instances, but the coach should take into account the fact that (1) they tend to combat zone matchups and bring teams out of sinking, or sagging, zone coverage; and (2) they require no transition to a player-to-player pattern if and when the defense changes to player-to-player coverage.

A Three-Player Control Offense. The offense shown in Figures 5–32 and 5–33 may be used as a regular offense, but it is included in this section because it adapts so well to use as a ball control offense. It provides inside movement to keep the defense from spreading its coverage, and the cut from the point to the corner keeps the ball in possession of the better ballhandlers for longer periods of time than normally. Also, the inside cut by wing 3 allows the coach to "hide" a player in the offense without substantially weakening the pattern's offensive thrust.

Player 1 passes to 3 and cuts to the ball side corner. Player 5 slides to low post in order to keep the defense deep, and 4 cuts behind her to high post. Player 2 fills 1's position at the top of the circle. Player 3 passes to 1 and cuts through the lane to the weak side wing. (See Figure 5–32.)

Rotation consists of 1 dribbling out to the wing and passing to 2, who relays the ball to 3 and cuts to the ball side corner. Player 4 cuts to ball side low post, and 5 cuts behind her to high post.

The only real area of weakness in the pattern appears when offen-

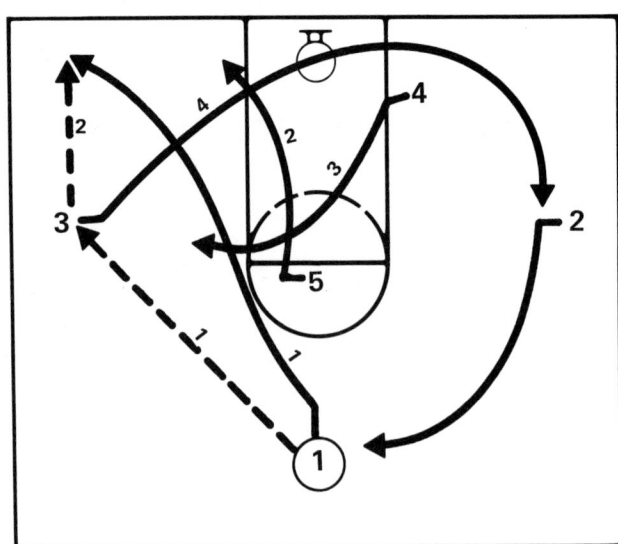

Figure 5-32 Three-Player Slowdown Offense, First Movements.

Special Zone Offenses and Techniques   147

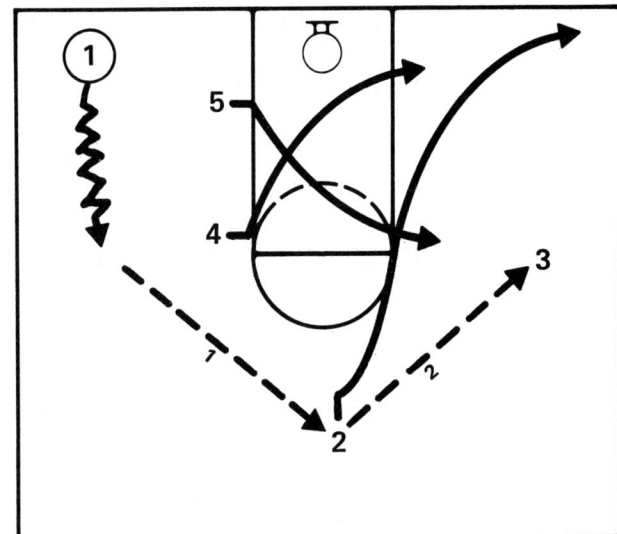

Figure 5-33 Three-Player Slowdown, Rotation.

sive players are unable to pass or dribble out of the corner. In such cases, however, other offensive tactics may prove more effective.

Control Offenses When a Team Is Ahead. Delay alignments, especially those used in deep freeze offenses, are as many and as varied as the number of teams that use them. However, three general alignments stand out from the rest in terms of usage and philosophy: the 3-2, the 2-1-2, and, to a lesser extent, the 1-2-2. From these alignments, a team may run anything from five-player stalls in which all five players assume ballhandling responsibilities more or less equally, to patterns in which one, two, or three players share the ballhandling duties.

On the high school level, the rules do not prohibit a team from stalling, delaying, or freezing the ball when ahead, except within the following guidelines:

1. No player on the offensive team may hold the ball or dribble in the midcourt area for more than five consecutive seconds without penetrating inside the midcourt area when guarded closely (i. e., within 6 feet) by a defensive player.

2. No team may hold the ball or dribble for more than ten consecutive seconds without penetrating inside the forecourt area except when the defensive players fail to move into defensive positions within 6 feet of the ball.

3. When a player dribbles from the midcourt into the front court, a new five-second count begins.

4. When a player starts her dribble in the front court, a new five-second count begins if she ends her dribble in the front court and then holds the ball. By inference, a player in the forecourt may hold the ball for four seconds, dribble for four more seconds, and then hold the ball for four seconds before the officials call a held ball.

The Five-Player Weave. When we refer to a five-player delay pattern, we mean one in which all five players are expected or required to handle the ball in turn. The oldest five-player delay pattern in existence, the five-player weave, is also possibly the most widespread in use. It is shown in Figure 5–34.

Player 1 passes to 2 (or 3) to begin the pattern. She then cuts down the lane for a possible return pass and slides to the weak side corner. Player 2 penetrates on the dribble, passes to 3, and cuts down the lane and away from the ball. Player 3 does the same, and 4 and 5 fill the positions vacated by 2 and 3.

Personnel requirements for the five-player weave are obvious: five players capable of protecting the ball and making the passes and cuts necessary to continue the pattern or combat defensive interference. Teams with only one or two, or even three, capable ballhandlers are likely to find the five-player weave inadequate for their needs.

A variation of the five-player weave, the corner screening (delay) offense, is shown in Figure 5–35. This pattern emphasizes corner screens to free players cutting outside and rolls to the basket by the screeners when the defenders switch.

After passing to either 4 or 5, 1 cuts backdoor to the basket or fakes

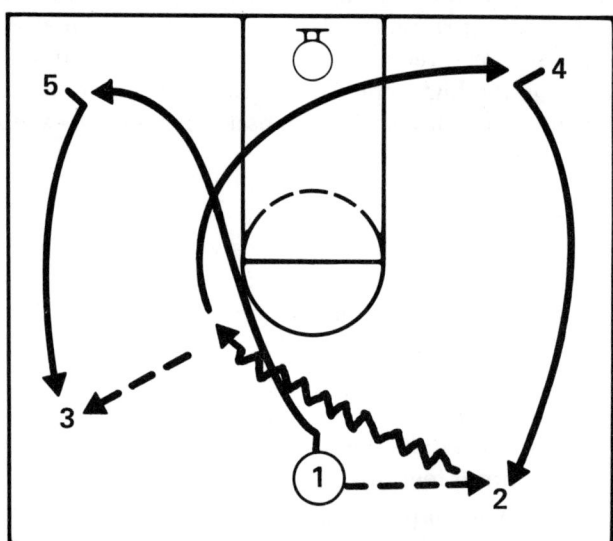

Figure 5-34 Five-Player Delay, Weave Pattern.

Special Zone Offenses and Techniques   149

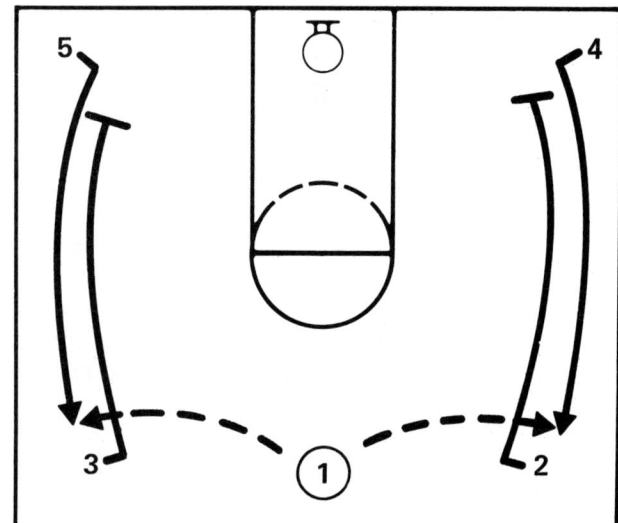

Figure 5-35 Corner Screening Offense, First Movements.

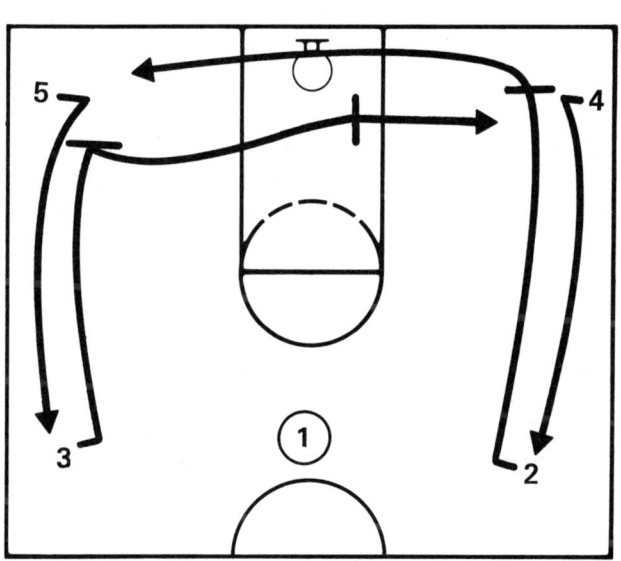

Figure 5-36 Corner Screening Offense, Outside Rotation Movements.

toward the basket and cuts outside to receive a return pass. The continuity is obvious: 5 and 4 cut to the corners, screen for 3 and 2, and roll toward the basket, returning to the corners if they fail to receive 1's pass.

The basic pattern can be extended further, and thus provides added scoring options and movement, by having the screeners cut across the lane instead of circling back to the corners. One of the cutters across the lane may be designated to screen for the other cutter, as shown in Figure 5–36, in effect creating an outside rotation pattern to which the defense will continually have to adjust.

Player 1's movements are the same in both patterns. Of course, 1 should be encouraged to drive whenever opportunities arise, and otherwise use aggressive movements to create scoring opportunities and keep the defense honest. Other players with or without the ball should be prepared to break the pattern whenever the defense overadjusts its coverage.

Four-Player Delay Pattern. When one offensive player's ball-handling skills are so meager that she is considered a liability to the success of the entire pattern, the obvious answer is a four-player pattern. However, the equally obvious question which then arises is: What do you do with the extra player? There are only four corners in the half-court, and if the weakest ballhandler is merely placed in a baseline corner, with the offense geared toward the other side of the court, the defense will likely respond by sagging off her to increase coverage of the middle.

One suggestion is to use her in 3's position as shown in Figure 5–36, but instead of 4's screening for her outside cut on the other side of the court, 4 remains outside and 3 cuts back across the lane to screen for 5 cutting across the lane. In other words, after her initial screen for 5 in the corner, 3 becomes a baseline screener on both sides of the court, without cutting at all. (See Figure 5–37.)

Just as 4 remains outside as 3 cuts to her side of the court, 2 will remain outside when 3 reaches the corner on her side. Because one player at a time remains stationary when 3 cuts from corner to corner, the offense actually involves only three players at a time. Some people consider the pattern a three-player delay, but since rotation involves all four players besides 1, the "four-player" appellation is not a misnomer.

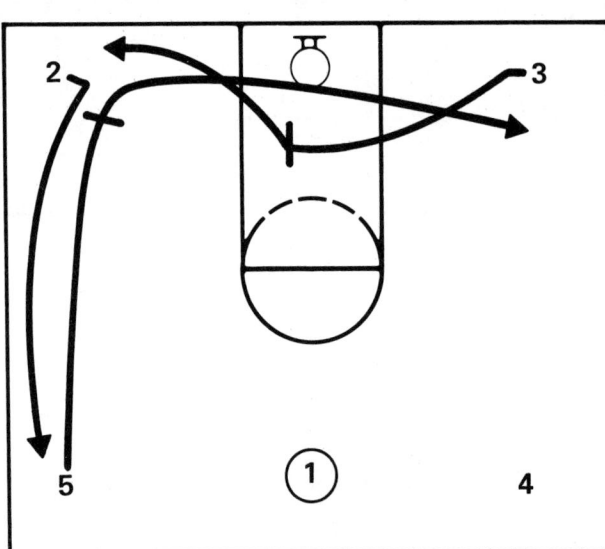

Figure 5-37 Player 3 as Baseline Screener in Four-Player Delay.

Special Zone Offenses and Techniques 151

Three-Player Delay Patterns. Although many three-player patterns exist, the most popular is the Figure 8, or three-player weave pattern. (See Figures 5-38, 5-39, and 5-40.) The "weave," as it is popularly known, requires three good ballhandlers, which tends to limit its effectiveness. On the other hand, it permits the offensive team to hide *two* players with limited ballhandling skills, and its movements and positions are easily learned by players on all levels.

Figures 5-38, 5-39, 5-40 Three-Player Outside Weave Pattern.

Figure 5-39.

Figure 5-40.

Diagrams cannot accurately portray the weave movements. Player 25's dribble should not necessarily be toward 30 (or 3) as shown in Figures 5–38, 5–39, and 5–40—at least, not in intent—but should be a semipenetrating dribble that veers off when the penetration is stopped. Such movement will also help younger players to remember that the ballhandler always moves *inside* and passes *outside* to the cutter, rather than the reverse.

Some coaches teach their cutters to meet the ball rather than waiting for the dribbler to come all the way to the sideline. This negates some of the danger of the defense's trapping the ballhandler. Players should also be taught to use backdoor cuts and fakes to free themselves when defenders overguard to deny the passes to the cutters.

When using the weave with young players, especially on teams with only one good ballhandler, it is advisable to have the dribbler start to her left, left-handed, and reverse pivot before reaching 3, in order to be able to dribble back across the court right-handed before passing off.

Three-Player Weave with High Post. The first high post alignment that comes to mind regarding delay or control offenses is that which sometimes is seen accompanying an outside weave pattern. Most coaches avoid delay alignments featuring a high post player because it tends to congest the middle and facilitate double-teaming when an offensive player drives. Still, if a team has a good ballhandler at the high post, the offensive possibilities increase when the opponents move outside to defense the weave. Splitting the post (Figure 5–41), backdoor cuts (Figure 5–42), inside passes to the post with subsequent one-on-one movements

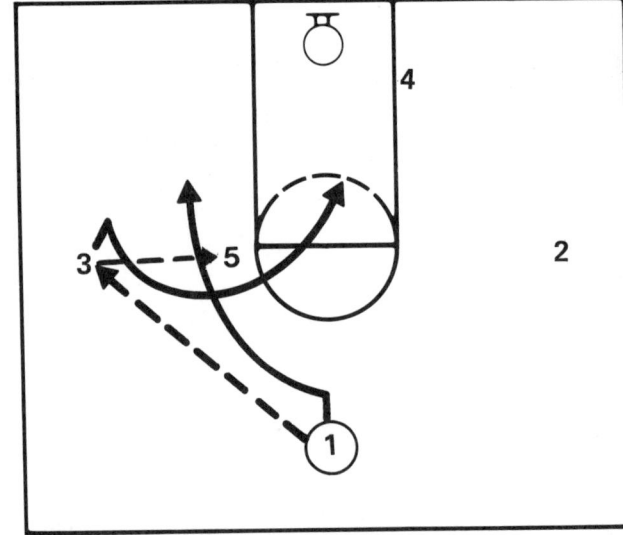

Figure 5-41 Splitting the Post from Weave Alignment.

Special Zone Offenses and Techniques 153

Figure 5-42 Backdoor Cut from Weave Alignment with High Post.

(Figure 5–43), or even a point pass-and-cut clear-out with the post cutting outside to fill the point position are some of the possibilities from the three-player weave alignment with a high post.

The outside weave alignment is also ideally suited for a high-low post interchange, especially in cases where both inside players are good ballhandlers or shooters from 15 feet. (See Figure 5–44.)

The movements shown in Figures 5–41 through 5–44 occur as the weave pattern unfolds; they do not arise from stationary positions as shown. Players 1, 2, and 3 should be aware that automatics such as those depicted in Figures 5–41, 5–42, and 5–44 arise in the course of defensive adjustment to the basic three-player weave movements. The movements in Figure 5–43 may be used as automatics but usually occur as planned movements designed to attack specific defensive weaknesses.

154 Zone Offenses for Women's Basketball

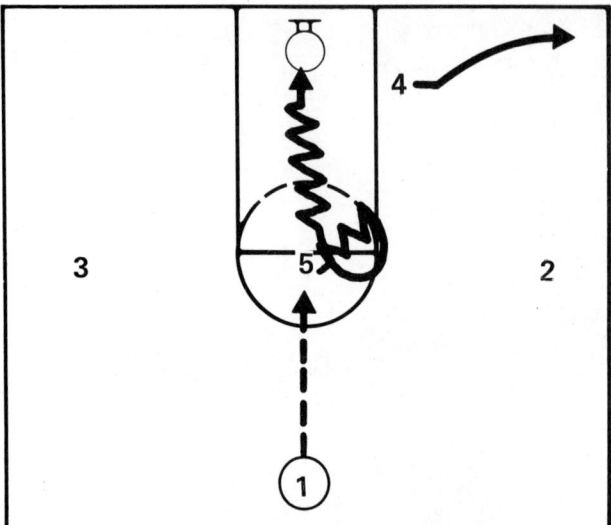

Figure 5-43 High Post One-on-One Movement from Weave Alignment.

Figure 5-44 High-Low Post Interchange from Weave Alignment.

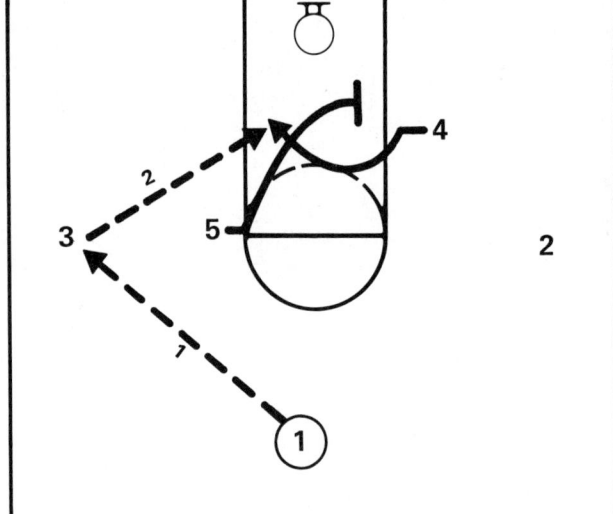

The high post's outside cut after 1's clear-out in Figure 5–45 can also be used as a five-player weave if 1 continues to the wing, 3 cuts to low post, and 4 moves to the high post position; or as a four-player weave, if 1 moves to the wing and 3 slides to high post. (See Figure 5–46.) In both cases, the weave pattern begins again with 5's dribble toward either wing.

The outside cut by 5 is almost always a valuable addition to any weave pattern—providing, of course, that the offensive player at the point clears out beforehand. If she is overguarded, 5 has the option of cutting toward the basket for a pass from the ballhandler and, since few defen-

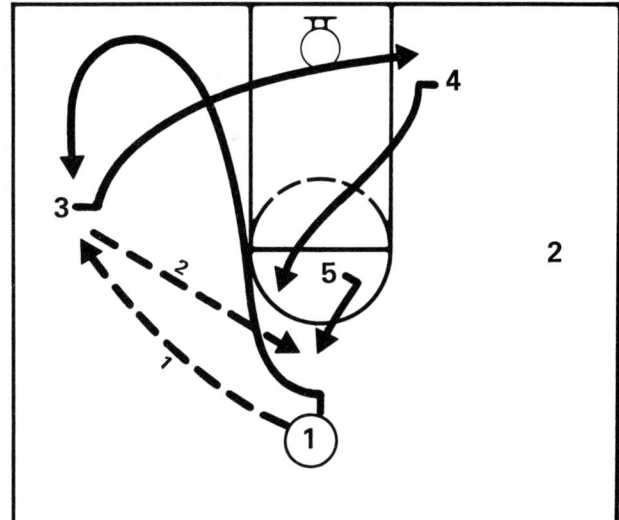

Figure 5-45 Five-Player Rotation from Three-Player Weave Alignment.

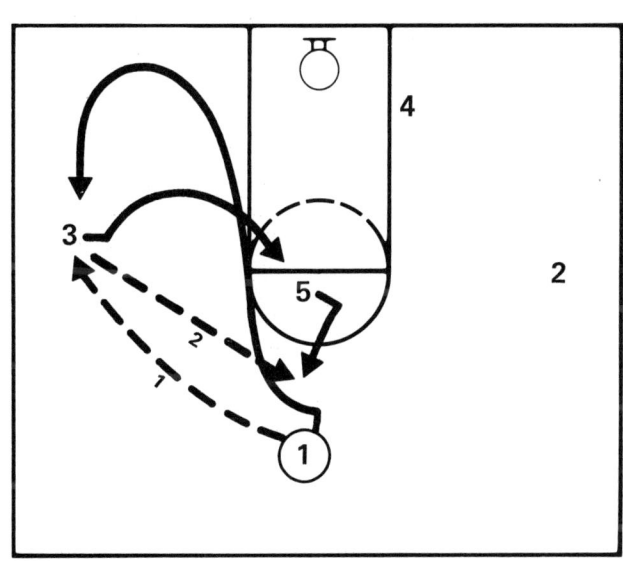

Figure 5-46 Four-Player Rotation from Three-Player Weave Alignment.

sive players will surrender such a potent scoring opportunity, 5 will almost always be open for the outside pass to continue the pattern.

CONCLUSION

Earlier, I discussed the conflicting philosophies of running one or two offensive patterns during the course of a game versus presenting as many different offensive looks as possible. While my answer may have appeared equivocal to some, one area in which I do not equivocate deals with the kind of zone offense I want my teams to run: *I want my offense to be different from those of the rest of the teams we play!* I want our opponents to have to prepare for my teams differently than they prepare for everyone else. This is for two reasons that are very important to me: first, the opponents may not have scouted us, in which case it should take them longer to figure out what we're trying to do than if we're using a conventional offense such as an elementary splitting pattern or single-cutter-through pattern with outside rotation. And second, our patterns may serve to draw the opponents out of their regular defense or style of coverage, and whenever a team is forced out of its regular defensive coverage, it is likely to make more mistakes than it would otherwise.

The offensive patterns described in Chapter 5 are "special," not only because they are used to attack the defense in specific alignments or situations, but also because they present unique problems for the defense beyond those found in simple splitting or overload rotation systems. With the single exception of the slowdown offenses, any of the patterns could be used as the basis for an entire system of set plays or continuity patterns, while at the same time providing a different look offensively.

In certain instances, offenses may be considered as "special" because of the personnel requirements to successfully execute the skills involved. For example, zone offenses based on movements keyed by one or more offensive players rank among the most difficult to defense of all zone offensive patterns, but the semifreelance aspects render such patterns beyond the skills of inexperienced players. Coaches should take into account the players' skills and experiential levels before adopting any of the "special" offenses as a regular offensive pattern.

6 Beating the Zone Presses

*The females of all species are most
dangerous when they appear to retreat.*
                                        Don Marquis

Perhaps the greatest single contribution of the turbulent years of the sixties to basketball was the widespread growth and use of full- and half-court pressing defenses. The development of these defenses—particularly the zone variations—created a myriad of new problems that plague coaches even today and probably will continue far into the future as well. Regardless of a team's style of play, it must be prepared to deal with a large variety of zone pressing alignments and strategies.

A coach once told me, "The first step in becoming a successful coach is learning to beat the opponents' presses. You can't score while the ball is in *their* half-court."[1] The defensive team using a full-court press will try to steal the ball, force an errant pass or turnover, or keep the offensive team in the defensive half-court for ten seconds. In any case, the defensive pressure will always be greater when a team is pressing than when they drop back into their regular defensive alignment at the other end of the court.

Zone Pressing Philosophy. Practically every zone pressing defense involves trapping. Trapping occurs quickly and aggressively, and a ballhandler unused or unprepared to deal with the double-teaming will likely panic and throw the ball away.

While the ballhandler is double-teamed, the other defensive players

---

[1] Joe Bell, coach at Milner High School in Milner, Georgia, between 1957–67. Coaching both boys' and girls' teams, Joe amassed a 415–125 won-lost record at Milner H.S. and was twice named "Coach of the Year" in Region 4–C.

will move into the primary passing lanes to intercept passes. This means that one or more offensive players will receive more or less loose coverage, but if the defensive double-teaming is aggressive enough, the ballhandler will have trouble finding her open teammates.

Most zone presses involve defensive players setting up in prescribed positions (zones), guarding offensive players as they enter their zones, and attempting to force the dribbler or ballhandler into unexpected double-teaming situations. This is not the only zone pressing strategy, as will be shown, but it is by far the most commonly encountered. Defeating such presses calls for alert, cautious ballhandling as well as a thorough recognition of the defense's zone pressing alignment and strategy.

CONSIDERATIONS IN COMBATTING ZONE PRESSES

1. Expect, and Look for, the Traps Before They're Set. Much of the effectiveness of zone presses arises from the element of surprise when the trap is sprung. For example, in Figure 6–1, inbounds passer 55 has passed the ball and is heading downcourt. The ballhandler, knowing 21 to be on the left side of the court, begins dribbling right-handed unconcernedly, covered loosely by her defender. Weak side defender X_{12}, who originally dropped back to cover cutter 55, moves up quickly to trap the dribbler. The ballhandler turns and passes toward 21, who was open originally. Now, however, X_{30} has moved into the passing lane to steal the pass.

It should be noted that, in the positions shown in Figure 6–1, a player is open in the half-court corner diagonally opposite the ballhandler. However, the defense is gambling that the dribbler will not be able to see her as she picks up her dribble and tries to protect the ball, while at the same time dribbling left-handed and searching frantically for a teammate around the waving arms and hands of her opponents reaching for the ball. In another, more composed situation, she might spot her open teammates, but she is aware that, even as the opponents' frenzied, helter-skelter double-teaming is harassing her out of her wits—she has no dribble left, remember—the referee is steadily counting toward a ten-second backcourt violation, too. If she doesn't pass immediately, she may never get rid of the ball!

That's the way it works. The player with the ball may be an extremely good ballhandler, but if the defender manages to turn her back into the middle and make her pick up her dribble, she is likely to wind up looking as silly as the most inexperienced novice in basketball. All because she didn't anticipate being trapped.

Do yourself (and your team) a favor. Include in your scouting reports information concerning how your opponents set up trapping situations in their press. And even if the opponents don't try to trap your ballhandler, she will still be more prepared to deal with the defense if she is looking for the trap. Forewarned is forearmed.

Figure 6-1 Turning the Dribbler.

2. Fast Break Whenever Possible. To be effective, pressing defenses must be played aggressively. Pressing is a risky strategy—especially the trapping zone presses—because the offensive team has numerical superiority heading downcourt with the ball whenever they evade the traps set for them by the defense. Successful fast breaking not only takes away most of the psychological edge of pressing, but it can serve to transfer the aggressive attitude and confidence to the offensive team as well. When the opponents' fast break against the press affords them layups or high-percentage shots, the defense will be forced to retreat into a more traditional or conservative coverage, or else abandon their press altogether.

In order to be effective against a pressing defense, fast breaking requires consideration of the following points:

A. The offensive team must get the ball into play quickly after baskets, since many pressing teams challenge the inbounds pass. Coaches often delegate responsibility for the inbounds pass to one player, who always retrieves the ball after scores, steps out of bounds, and passes to a teammate before the defense is organized. Care must be taken not to make the pass automatically, however; we lost a game two years ago because our experienced inbounds passer stepped out of bounds as usual, but failed to see a defensive player stepping in front of her intended receiver to steal the pass.

B. Regardless of whether or not a player is capable of making the long pass downcourt to a teammate, the fast breaking pattern should provide at least an illusion of such intentions. Otherwise, the defense will "cheat" toward the ballhandler and the short passes. If your players are capable of making such passes downcourt to teammates clearly ahead of the rest of the pack, go ahead and let them! Even if the passes are stolen once or twice, the maneuver will underscore your fast-breaking intentions, and it will keep the deep defensive players thinking in terms of retreating to stop the long passes rather than attacking the shorter passes near their own basket.

C. Ballhandlers should be taught not to dribble automatically upon receiving the inbounds pass. A ballhandler without a dribble is helpless, especially when the defensive team forces her to pick up her dribble. Players should be coached that dribbling becomes a necessity only when passing is less desirable. Most coaches prefer to pass the ball downcourt against zone presses, using a series of short, crisp passes to teammates cutting into the seams, or openings, in the defensive coverage.

Of course, circumstances may dictate that dribbling is preferable to passing in a given situation—you may be blessed with exceptionally fast, skilled dribblers whom you wish to handle the ball as much as possible in the fast break, and thus give them the option of dribbling as much as they see fit—but it is generally true that passing beats dribbling against zone presses.

D. Even when the fast-breaking pattern follows every prescribed rule of laning, *all five players should never fast break at the same time.* If they miss the shot—heaven forbid!—they'll have no one back to stop the opponents' fast break. And believe me, if all five of your players join in the fast break and lose the ball, even the slowest of opponents will fast break against you the other way! Perhaps it's just my conservative upbringing in basketball, but I doubt if I'd fast break with all five players even if the other team left the court entirely!

3. Spread the Offense. "If they press, sooner or later they're going to trap." If your players understand this fact, you can convince them that staying away from the ballhandler is the best way of ensuring that someone will be open for a pass when the trap is sprung.

Two defensive players are converging on the ball; at least two others are moving forward to cut off the most obvious (primary) passing lanes.

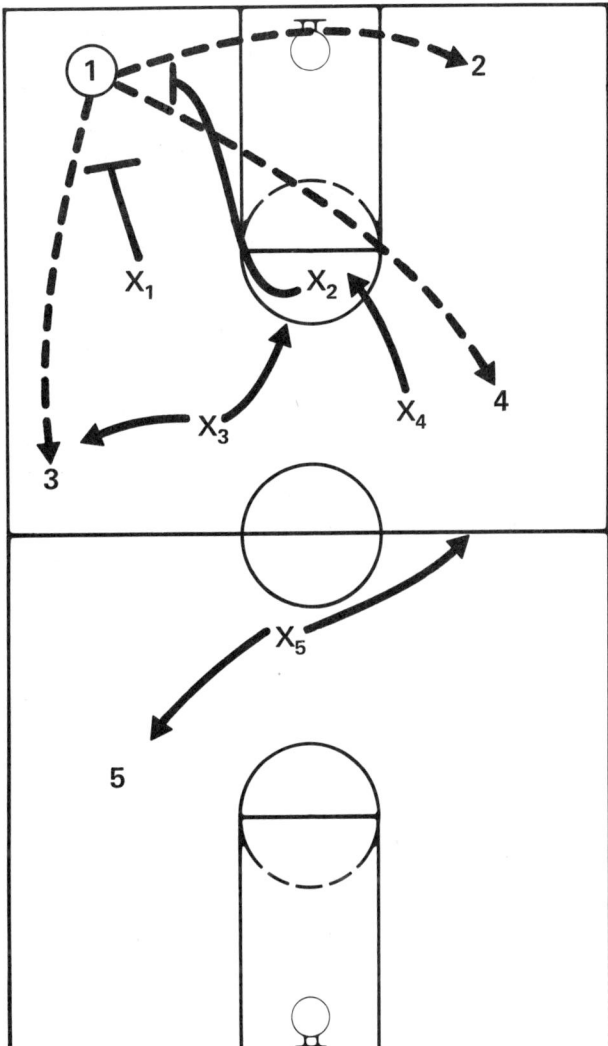

Figure 6-2 Typical Spreading Alignment Against Full-Court Press.

(They can't cut off *all* the passing lanes with only five players.) By spreading the offense in any of several methods similar to that shown in Figure 6-2, you will likely ensure that at least one primary passing lane remains open, if your ballhandler knows where to find it.

In Figure 6-2, if X_4 moves up to cover the pass to 2, X_5 will have to move up to guard 4. (And if X_5 moves up to guard 4, 5 will be open.) Admittedly, 5 is not exactly a primary receiver, but even if 1 fails to see her, 1 may be able to elude the double-team, in which case the offense will definitely have fast-breaking possibilities arising.

4. Look for Openings in the Defensive Coverage. Attack the middle of the court from the sides, or the sides from the middle. When two defensive players trap, the area between them is likely to provide fertile ground for cutting and passing. Passing over defensive players is risky, especially in their half-court. Lob passes should be avoided whenever possible.

5. Take the Ball to the Middle of the Court. Although hardly a prerequisite for beating the presses, taking the ball to the middle of the court is often advisable as a means of *splitting* a defense or even of spreading the defense from a diamond formation.

Each of the previous formations possesses certain advantages and disadvantages, but it should be noted that both are conducive to cutting and passing to the middle.

6. Keep a Player Back As a Safety Valve. Even when a team is not fast breaking, it should retain at least one player in the back court to help the ballhandler in case she gets in trouble. This "safety valve" player should move downcourt parallel to, or slightly behind (but always away from), the ballhandler.

7. Have Your Best Ballhandler Handling the Ball As Much As Possible. Such a statement appears obvious, but a surprisingly large number of coaches overlook this deterrent to ballhandling efficiency in beating the presses. A few years ago, I found myself wondering why opponents had begun to devastate my team with full-court presses. I finally realized that I was using my only superior ballhandler as a cutter to advance the ball downcourt, whereas the other players were incapable of getting the ball to her after she made her cut. The problem was easily resolved by bringing her back to the ballhandling position, cutting to receive the inbounds pass. With a bit more attention to detail on my part, however, the problem could have been avoided altogether.

ADVICE FOR BALLHANDLERS AGAINST ZONE PRESSES

All dribbling against zone presses should be for specific purposes. Don't start dribbling until you know where the defensive players are; and once you start, don't pick up your dribble until you know who you're going to pass to and are sure that she's open. Don't dribble any more than you have to. Most good teams dribble very little against zone presses, preferring short passes to cutters into the openings in the defensive coverage. Pass-and-cut patterns are often seen against pressing defenses.

Finally, and this point should be underscored and emphasized as strongly as possible, **don't force the ball downcourt!** The offensive team has ten seconds to get the ball across the half-court line; it doesn't have to occur in the first three or four seconds after the inbounds pass is made. Long or hurried passes may be necessary as defensive pressure increases, but they are never necessary in the first few seconds after the ball is passed inbounds. A ten-second back-court violation is preferable to an easy layup for the opponents as a result of a hurried pass.

THE INBOUNDS PASS

The defensive team has three options available concerning the inbounds pass: they can allow the pass to be made uncontested, they can guard the inbounds passer as well as the receivers, or they can have all five defensive players guarding the four offensive players inbounds. The coach hoping to defeat a full-court zone pressing defense should be aware of which type of coverage the defense is likely to use.

The Uncontested Throw-in. When the opponents permit the inbounds pass to be thrown in, it does not follow that their press coverage will be any less aggressive. All it means is that the trapping or intensified coverage probably will not occur until later, and in some other area of the court.

Uncontested throw-ins should never be taken for granted. It seems that, whenever a team expects the opponents to drop back and give them free bring-ins, a defender will slide forward unnoticed to steal the pass and score, or else the ballhandler will catch the inbounds pass and, in the same motion, turn and start dribbling downcourt, only to charge into a stationary defender who has moved into a close guarding position.

Contested Throw-ins—Guarding the Inbounds Passer. When the inbounds passer is guarded, as in a 1-2-2 full-court zone press, the offensive team generally has three problems: (1) avoiding getting the pass blocked or deflected, (2) working a player free to receive the inbounds pass, and (3) avoiding double-teaming of the pass receiver by the player guarding the inbounds passer.

A. *Passing Inbounds.* Faking helps: fake a high pass, then pass low (e.g., a bounce pass); or, fake the bounce pass and whip the ball by the defender's ear while her hands are low. Inbounds passers should try to avoid staring at potential receivers as they make their cuts: it's a dead giveaway as to where the pass is going. Also, they should be urged to stand away from the baseline.

Diagonal passes to one side or the other of the defender are generally preferable to lob passes over the defender. Lob passes are among the most overworked, overrated techniques in basketball, along with gratuitous, purposeless dribbling.

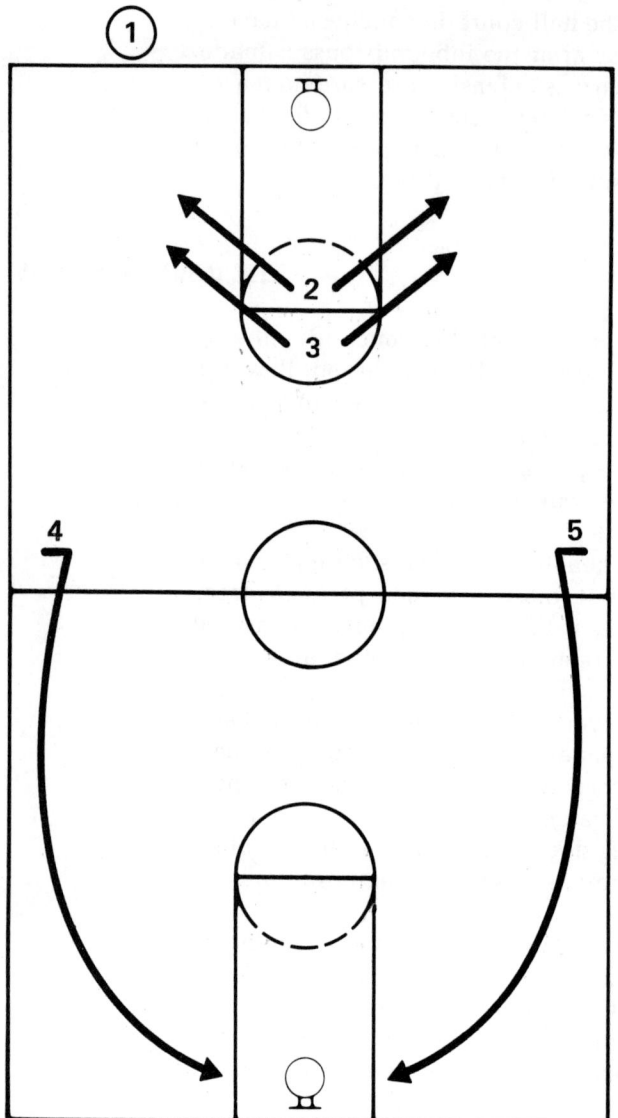

Figure 6-3 "One-Up, One-Back" Bring-in Alignment.

B. *Working a Player Free to Receive the Inbounds Pass.* The two most often encountered alignments used in breaking a player free to receive the inbounds pass are the "side-by-side" and "one-up, one-back" alignments shown in Figures 6–3 and 6–4.

In Figure 6–3, the cuts by 2 and 3 may be keyed by either the defensive coverage or by 2's movement: if 2 cuts to her left, 3 cuts right after brushing her defender off 2 in the process. (The same effect can be

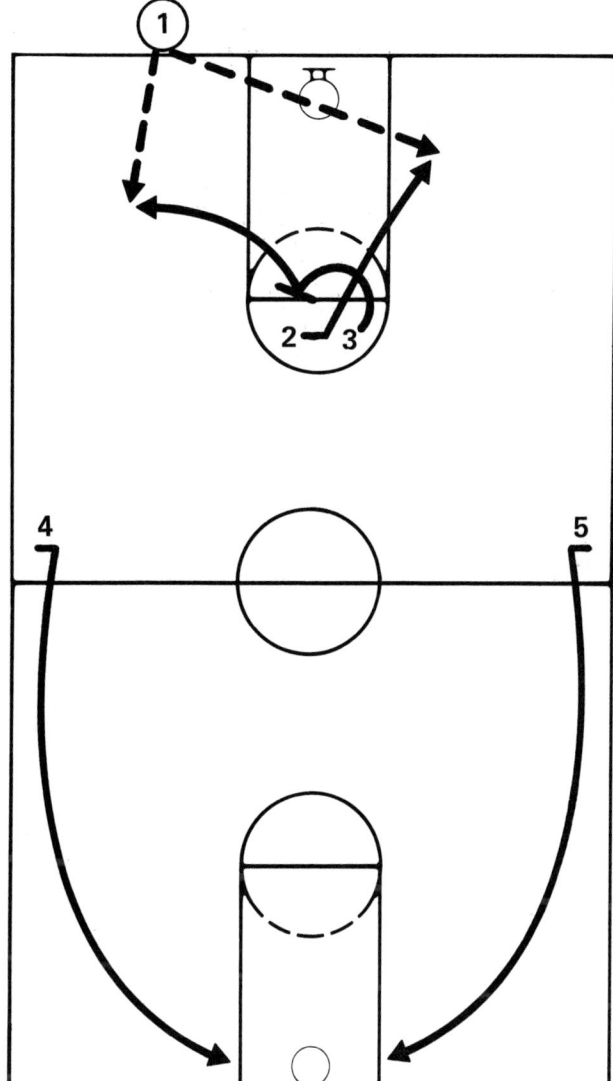

Figure 6-4 "Side-By-Side" Bring-in Alignment.

achieved by 2's pivoting either way to screen for 3, in a manner similar to that shown in Figure 6–4. In like manner, 2 and 3 may cut rather than screen from a "side-by-side" alignment.) Whether players screen or cut is a matter of preference and experience.

The screens of course may be set from wider alignments than those shown in Figures 6–3 and 6–4. However, the objection to wider alignments is that the time required to run the added distances, in addition to screening, cutting around the screen, and passing the ball inbounds may total more than the five seconds allowed to get the ball into play.

Sometimes the only pass the defense will allow is the long pass downcourt. It is an extremely risky maneuver, however, and should be tried only when other methods will not work. The offensive team should always fast break off this pass and in this situation. Two or three successful fast breaks will generally suffice to draw teams into more conventional defensive coverage in their presses.

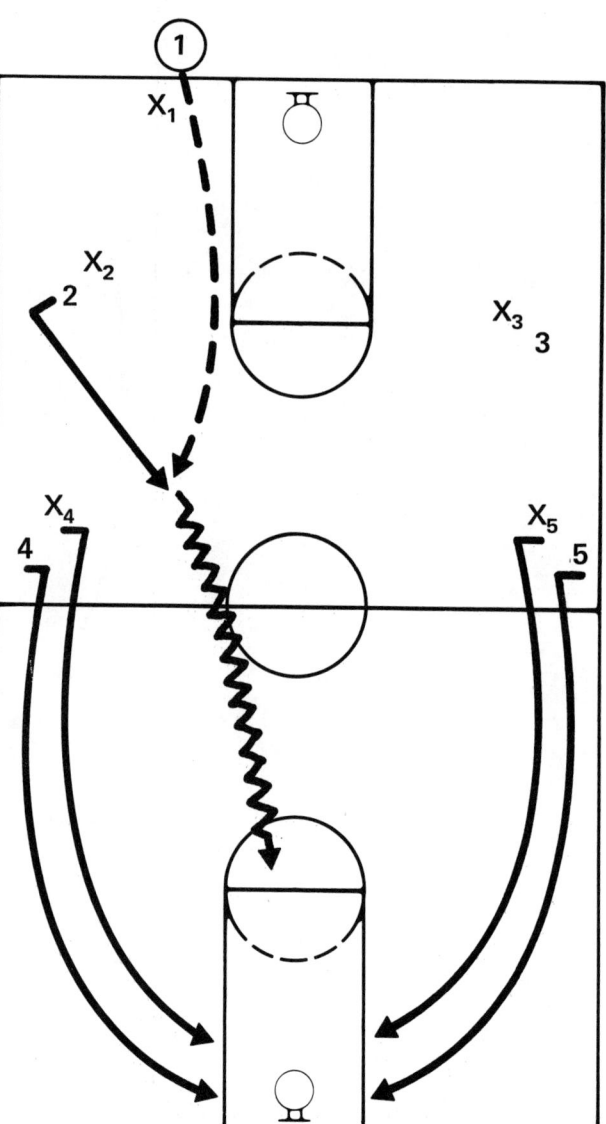

Figure 6-5 Lob Pass When 2 and 3 Are Fronted.

Avoiding Double-Teaming of the Pass Receiver. Many teams like to trap in their zone presses by having the defender who guards the inbounds passer (X_1 in Figure 6-6) trap the receiver immediately after the pass is thrown.

As can be seen in Figure 6-6, X_1 is in an excellent position to trap 3 with X_2, being only 3–4 steps from her when she catches the ball. This coverage is excellent for teams who like to trap immediately, before the receiver has time to dribble the ball or spot teammates open downcourt.

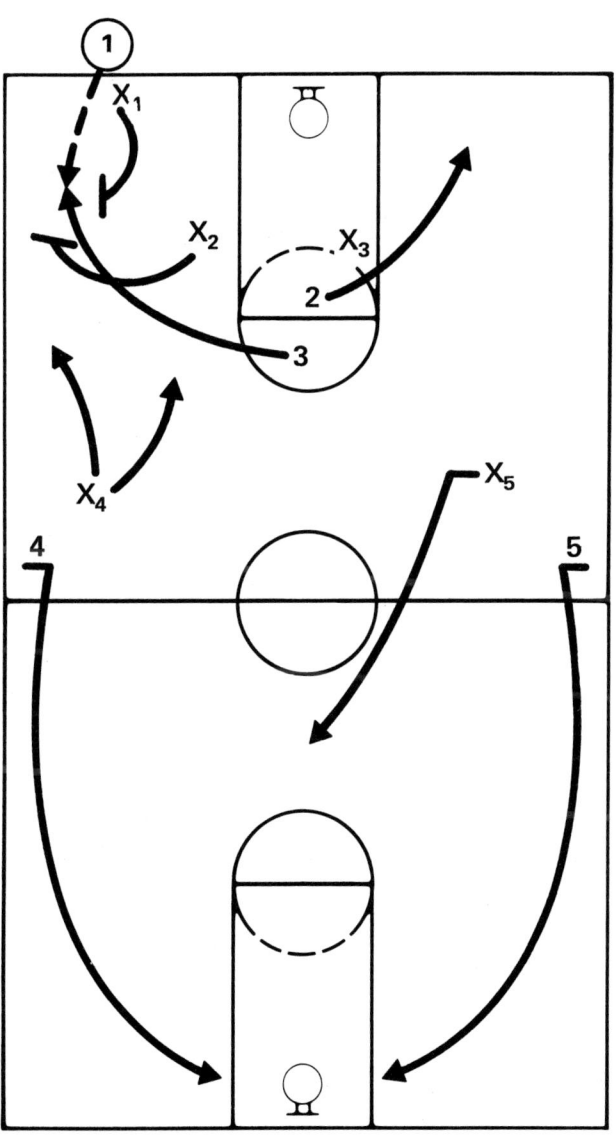

Figure 6-6 Double-Teaming the Pass Receiver. When 1 passes to cutter 3, X_1 and X_2 trap immediately. X_3 will probably cover 1's cut into the middle (not shown). X_1 may also follow the first part of 1's cut, then drop off to trap 3 with X_2.

168 Zone Offenses for Women's Basketball

The easiest way to combat this defensive strategy is to make a return pass to the inbounds passer immediately upon receiving the ball, as shown in Figure 6–7. (Her cut may be to the middle of the court as well as toward the sideline, of course.)

As with other offensive techniques dealing with trapping, success will depend to a large part on *anticipating the trapping movement by the defense, and knowing where it is likely to occur.*

Contested Throw-ins: Five Defensive Players Guarding Four Offensive Players Inbounds. When five defensive players guard the four inbounds offensive players on throw-ins, the offensive team must resort to desperate measures to get the ball inbounds. Since the defense is likely to double-team the best ballhandler and single-guard the other players, or else double-team the ball side offensive player and single-guard away from the ball, a simple maneuver such as that shown in Figure 6–8 may help in getting the ball inbounds.

Figure 6-7 Return Pass to the Inbounds Passer as a Means of Combatting Defensive Trapping.

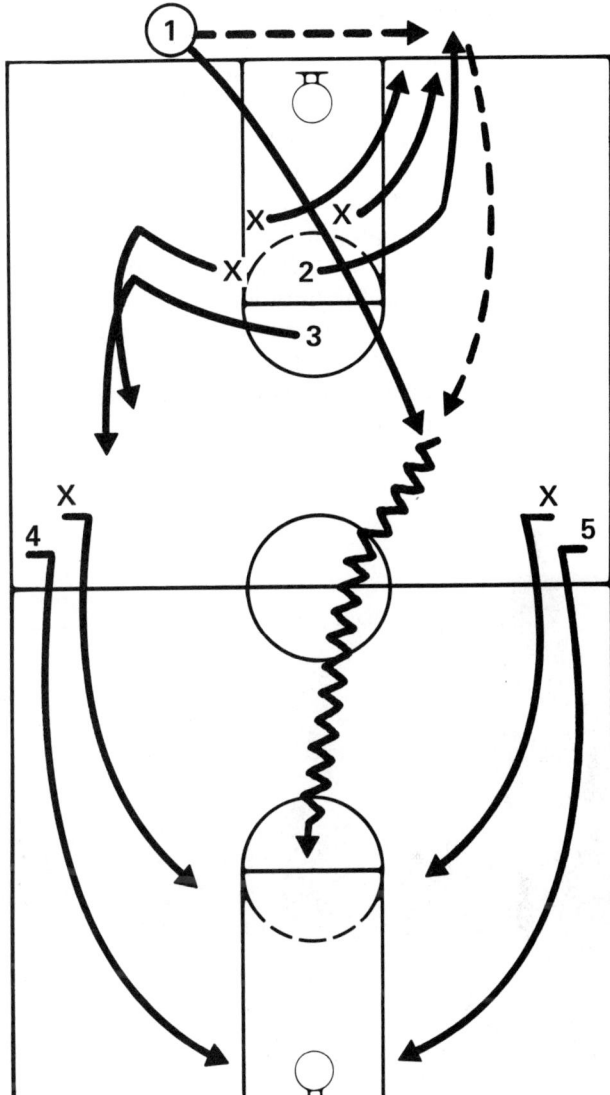

Figure 6-8 Inbounding the Ball Against Double Coverage of 2 (With 1 Unguarded). Players 2 and 3, covered in their initial cuts, are unable to get free. Player 2, double-teamed, continues out of bounds to receive 1's pass, and unguarded 1 cuts into the middle for 2's pass. (The defenders follow 2 to the sideline, but they cannot follow her out of bounds.)

Player 2 is double-teamed, 3 single-guarded. Player 1, the inbounds passer, is left unguarded for the bring-in. Player 2 cuts, then continues out of bounds for 1's pass. Player 3 has already cut toward 1's side of the court. After passing to 2, 1 cuts quickly down the middle of the court to receive 2's inbounds pass while the defensive coverage is confused. Player 1 should then be in position to lead the fast break, with 4 and 5 forming the wing lanes on either side of the court.

TRAPPING TECHNIQUES

Trapping Immediately. Many teams, whether guarding the inbounds passer or not, trap the receiver immediately rather than waiting for her to dribble or pass the ball.

The defensive players involved in the trapping may vary according to team needs and individual abilities, but the areas of the court where trapping usually occurs are predictable and invariable: with a single exception,[2] full-court pressing traps occur near the baseline in either corner, or at the middle, of the back court. (See Figures 6-9, 6-10, and 6-11.)

When the trap is sprung immediately, the defenders hope to frighten or intimidate the ballhandler into throwing the ball away. Indeed, such an occurrence is always a possibility, especially if the ballhandler isn't expecting to be trapped.

[2] Run-and-jump defense.

Figure 6-9 Corner Trapping, Full-Court Press.

Figure 6-10 Trapping in the Middle, Full-Court Press.

Figure 6-11 Corner Trapping, Full-Court Press.

COMBINATION PRESSES

Some full- and half-court presses combine player-to-player and zone defensive strategies. Such presses, known generally as *combination pressing defenses,* usually take the form of player-to-player coverage in which trapping is delayed until the ballhandler reaches a predetermined area of the court. The two most widely used combination presses are *delay trapping* and *run-and-jump defense.*

Delay Trapping. In delay trapping, the defensive players may set up in either zone or player-to-player coverage initially, but if they are in a zone defensive alignment they will match up with the offensive players until the trap is sprung. When the ballhandler is turned into the trap (see Figure 6-1), the other defensive players will immediately cut off the primary passing lanes, as in any trapping zone press. The advantages of such a defensive system are obvious: the player-to-player alignment tends to negate the quick passes that lead to fast breaking, and only the defenders know when or where the trap will be sprung. Thus, the element of surprise is almost sure to be with the defensive team. Splitting a player-to-player defense is an extremely unlikely possibility.

In Figures 6-12 and 6-13, the inbounds passer has cut down the middle of the court. Two offensive players are stationed downcourt along the sidelines to spread the defense, and a third player is acting as a safety valve, paralleling the ballhandler's progress downcourt.

When the trap is sprung, the defense will turn the dribbler toward the middle of the court, where she will then be dribbling left-handed and protecting the ball as the weak side defender slides across to trap her. The defenders at half-court will move into position to cut off the passing lanes in those areas. The deep defender will cover the long pass downcourt, playing slightly toward the ball side, the more likely target for a long pass.

The defensive team may delay its trapping, but the trapping will involve the dribbler's being forced to reverse pivot to her left, and thus to change from right- to left-handed dribbling as she is trapped from her blind side.

Delay trapping can be vastly superior to regular trapping from a zone press, due largely to the element of surprise. Delay trapping requires quick, aggressive defenders who thoroughly understand their pressing system. Thus, fast breaking may serve to confuse defensive coverage and alter the trapping arrangements.

Unfortunately, however, fast breaking is not always possible against delay trapping, especially when the defenders are highly skilled or the offensive team does not possess adequate ballhandling to control the defense. A second method of dealing with delayed trapping is to make sure that the offensive players are spread out on the court, with players

Beating the Zone Presses 173

Figures 6-12, 6-13 Delay Trapping.

174 Zone Offenses for Women's Basketball

in, or cutting into, the passing lanes as the ballhandler advances downcourt. (See Figure 6–14.)

Finally, pass-and-cut sequences—1 passing inbounds to 2 and cutting quickly down the middle of the court for a return pass, for instance—can serve to force the defensive players into retreating rather than attacking.

Run-and-Jump Defense. The so-called "run-and-jump defense" is similar to the delayed trapping technique except that, instead of double-

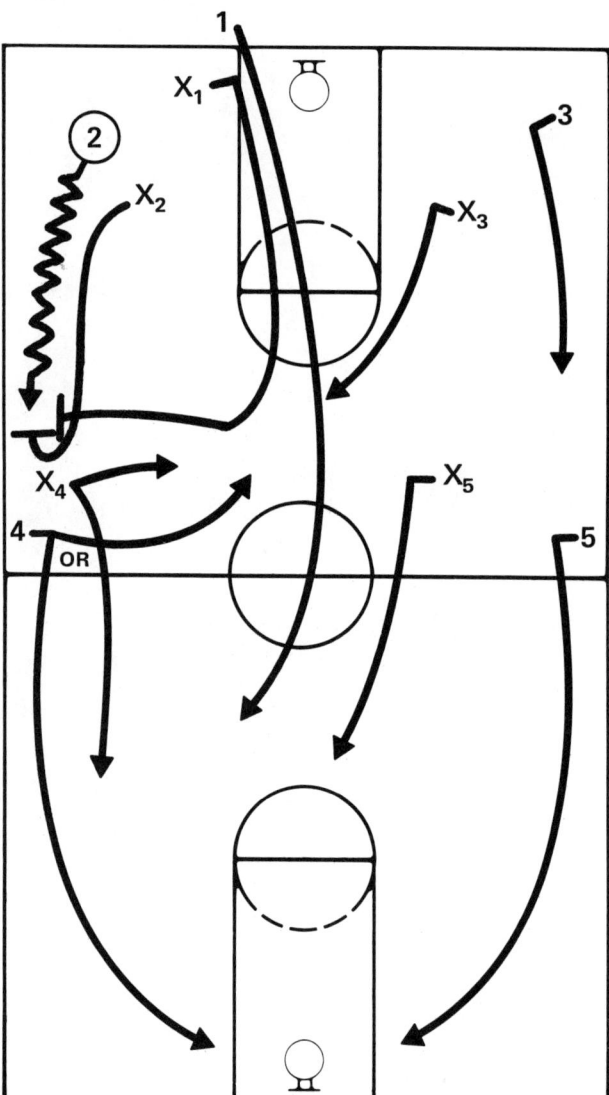

Figure 6-14 Spreading and Filling the Passing Lanes Against Delayed Trapping. The defense has player-to-player responsibilities as 2 begins her dribble along the sideline. As X_2 moves into position to stop 2's advance along the sideline, however, X_1 leaves 1 and traps 2. Either X_3 or X_4 may cover 1, and either X_4 or X_5 may cover 4, depending upon the players' skills and coaching preferences.

teaming the ballhandler, a defender turns the dribbler into a (defensive) teammate, then leaves to cover another offensive player as her other teammates cover the passing lanes. In Figure 6–15, X_2 allows 2 to dribble, influencing her toward the sideline, then jumps into position to turn her toward the middle of the court. Player X_1, who was loosely covering 1 as she cut down the middle, moves toward 2 and stops her dribble. Meanwhile, X_2, after turning 2, retreats quickly to cover 4; and X_3 and X_5 rotate into position to steal passes to 1 or 3. Player X_4 covers either the half-court corner away from the ball or 5 downcourt. (Coverage may vary from that

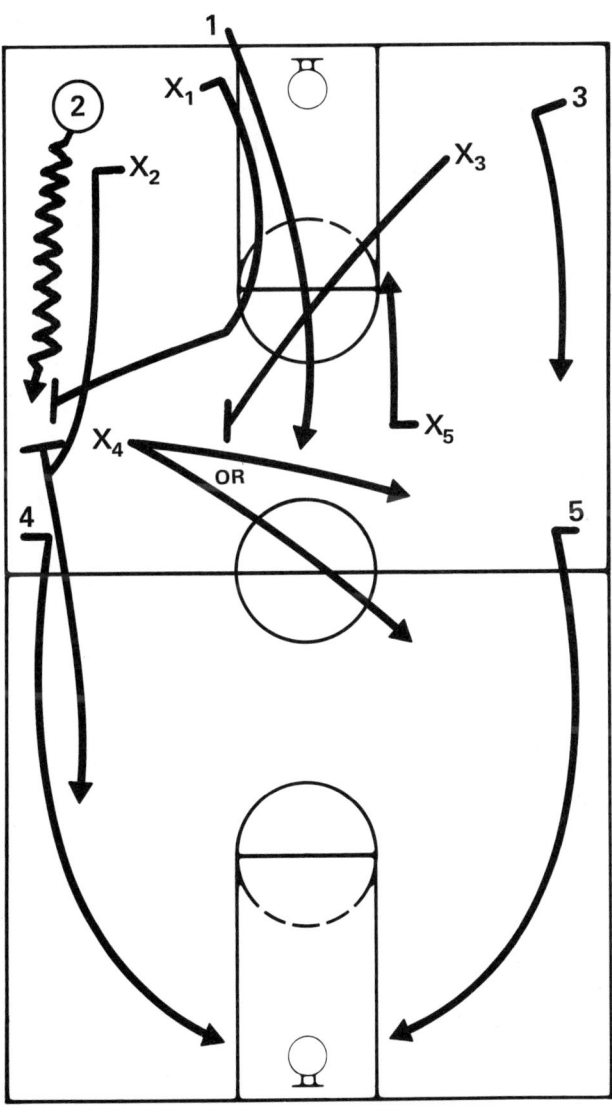

Figure 6-15 Run-and-Jump Defense. Switching in run-and-jump defense is exactly like the trapping involved in Figure 6–14. After 2 is stopped, though, X_2 will drop back to cover 4 deep, and the other defenders will pick up new player-to-player responsibilities: X_3 on 1, X_2 on 4, X_4 on 5, and X_5 on 3.

shown in Figure 6–15, of course, but the areas to be covered remain constant.[3])

The advantage of run-and-jump defense over traditional or delayed zone trapping is that the defensive team remains in player-to-player coverage, or at least matches up after switching defensive responsibilities.

Any of the techniques used to combat delayed trapping may be successful against run-and-jump defense. As with all offenses against pressing defenses, intelligent ballhandling and a knowledge of where the "run-and-jump" usually takes place (as well as the whereabouts of offensive teammates) is mandatory. Careful scouting will reveal the defensive team's preferences.

Start with the premise that every "run-and-jump" team prefers to maneuver the ballhandler toward a certain area of the court before setting their switching movement in action. One key to the movement is a gradual sliding away from her offensive player by the girl who switches with the "run-and-jump" player—X_1 in Figure 6–15, for example. If the ballhandler anticipates the switch, she may be able to reverse pivot quickly and thus freeze two defensive players (X_1 and X_2 in Figure 6–16) as she passes to a teammate before the defense can complete its switches.

Perhaps we should emphasize that the maneuver shown in Figure 6–16 is in no way a panacea for run-and-jump coverage. Player X_2 is in-

[3] In strictest usage, X_2 and X_4 would probably execute the "run-and-jump," with X_4 stopping 2 and X_2 picking up 4. Everyone else would be in player-to-player coverage.

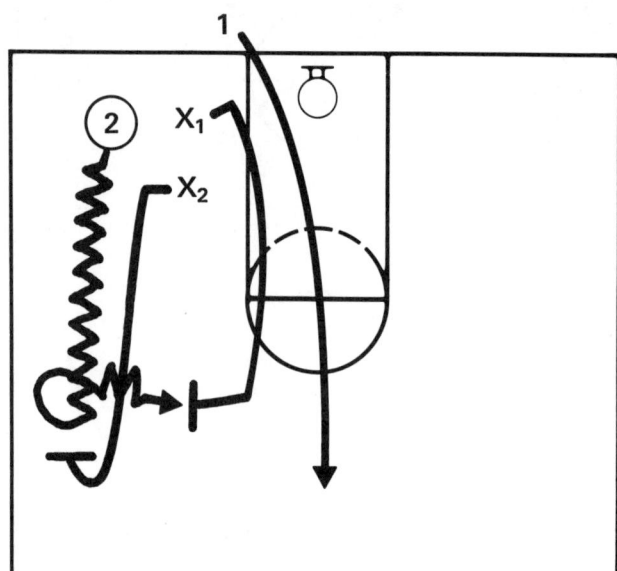

Figure 6-16 Combatting the Run-and-Jump Defense.

fluencing 2 toward the right sideline, and, although her defensive coverage is likely to be loose, she will surely attempt to stop 2 before she reaches half-court. The other methods described are likely to be more successful in combatting the run-and-jump, but the technique shown in Figure 6–16 should not be overlooked if the other methods fail.

Dribbling Through (or Around) the Trap. When either or both of the defensive players are slow in setting the trap, or lazy in their coverage, the ballhandler can sometimes dribble through or around the double-team and begin fast breaking downcourt. (See Figures 6–17 and 6–18.)

The purposes of dribbling against presses are two-fold: to attack the double-team before it is sufficiently organized to attack the dribbler, and to advance the ball downcourt when the passing lanes are shut off. In either case, dribbling may be sufficient to escape the double-team, but it is in no way mandatory for the dribbler to take the ball all the way downcourt on the ensuing fast break. Dribbling is, then, primarily a means of attacking the double-team rather than establishing the fast break. Whether the ballhandler dribbles through or around the double-team depends upon the coverage: since the defenders' trapping can stop only two of the three possible dribbling routes (i.e., the passing lanes shown in

Figure 6-17 Dribbling Around the Corner Trap.

178 Zone Offenses for Women's Basketball

Figure 6-18 Dribbling Through the Corner Trap.

Figures 6–20 and 6–21), the dribbler will take whichever route the defenders fail to stop.

In Figure 6–17, the defense has failed to overguard the ballhandler toward the sideline, and as a result the dribbler has taken that route in eluding the double-team. In Figure 6–18, one defender has covered the sideline dribble, but her partner has failed to move into position to trap the ballhandler by cutting off the area of penetration between them. Thus, the dribbler takes the line of least resistance and goes between the two defenders to break the press and set up a fast break.

One other method exists for attacking the full-court press by dribbling. It does not yield many fast breaks, but it can help a fundamentally weak team move the ball downcourt by reducing the effectiveness of the double-team. (See Figure 6–19.)

Player 12 inbounds the ball, cuts down the middle of the court, and continues to the ball-side half-court corner. Instead of avoiding the double-team, the ballhandler immediately dribbles toward X_{21}, in effect forcing the double-team. She then passes to either 12 or 32, whomever X_5 doesn't cover. The passes, especially to 12 in the ball-side half-court corner, are relatively difficult to make, since the ballhandler is dribbling to her left, and left-handed. However, one cannot always expect easy solutions to problems. If the defensive team's coverage is superior to the

Beating the Zone Presses   179

Figure 6-19 Forcing a Double-Team Against Full-Court Trapping Defense.

Figure 6-20 Passing Lanes with Ball Trapped in Corner.

Figure 6-21 Passing Lanes from the Middle of the Court.

ballhandler's skills, absolute answers are few and far between. (Perhaps we should note that the ballhandler can force the double-team anywhere on the court and not just in the manner shown in Figure 6–19. However, because the trapping tends to force the ballhandler to her left wherever the trap occurs, the movements are likely to be similar to those shown in Figure 6–19.)

Dribbling is most effective against the press when the defenders are slow or hesitant in trapping. It is least effective when the ballhandler is unskilled, upset, or slower than the defenders.

When trapping occurs at the center of the court, the primary passing lanes are broadened (Figures 6–20 and 6–21) with a resultant advantage in passing efficiency.

The reader should bear in mind that the primary passing lanes are also the primary dribbling lanes.

Once getting past the initial defensive pressure, the offensive team has a tremendous advantage over the defense—if, that is, it can continue to press its advantage by fast breaking.

PASSING TO BEAT THE PRESSES

There are two basic passing patterns against the zone presses, *weak side cutter patterns* and *pass-and-cut*.

The weak side cutter pattern shown in Figure 6–22 provides a devastating way of beating the zone presses and establishing a fast break. Player 1 passes to 2 and cuts down the ball side sideline. Player 3 cuts to

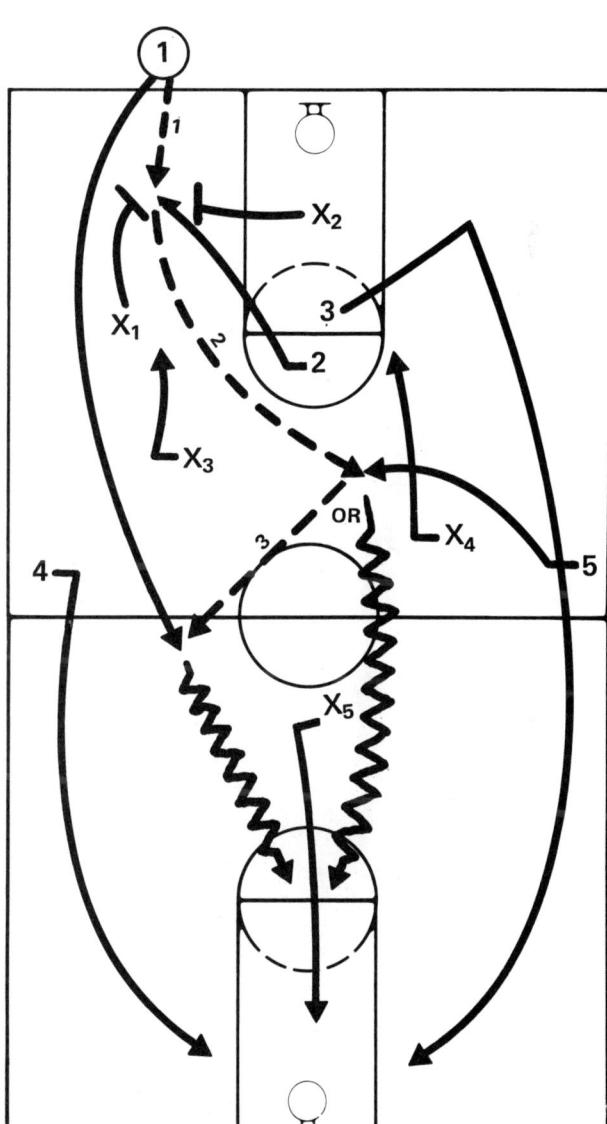

Figure 6-22 Weak Side Cutter Pattern Against Full-Court Zone Press.

the weak side corner and continues downcourt. As 2 catches the inbounds pass and pivots toward the center of the court, 5 cuts to the middle. Player 2 passes to 5, who turns and either passes to 1 or 3 cutting downcourt, or dribbles downcourt herself.

The beauty of the pattern lies in 5's cut, which comes from *behind* the defender in that area. If X_4 moves in to defense the pass to 5, 3 will be open, since X_1 and X_2 are trapping 2 and no one is left to cover the pass to 3. (If X_5 moves up to cover the pass to 1, 4 will be open for the long pass downcourt.) Since the trapping movement is by definition aggressive, the defensive players are moving forward toward the ball and their own basket, and the three passes shown in Figure 6–22, when thrown quickly and accurately, will yield a surprisingly large number of three-on-two and three-on-one fast breaks for the offensive team.

The most widely used pass-and-cut pattern involves the quick return pass to the inbounds passer. (See Figure 6–23.)

As shown in Figure 6–23, Player 12 passes inbounds and cuts down the center of the court for a return pass. (Her cut could also be made along the sideline.) This pattern works best when the defenders trap the receiver immediately.

After the pass-and-cut frees 12 to lead the fast break a few times, the

Figure 6-23 Pass-and-Cut After Inbounds Pass.

defense will likely delay trapping until 12 clears. In such cases, the ballhandler will then force the double-team, as shown in Figure 6–19, passing to the safety valve (whichever player occupies the baseline corner away from the ball).

Sometimes the defenders will try to trap 12 when she receives the return pass. When this occurs, the ballhandler may pass-and-cut herself to the opening, as shown in Figure 6–24. What happens, then, when the defense is able to shut off the return pass to 12, and then traps the inbounds pass receiver?

Player 12 cuts to the middle as before, and, failing to receive the return pass, clears to the ball side corner. If the defender in the ball side half-court corner fails to move up to cover 12, the ballhandler will pass to 12 and cut to the middle herself. At this point, either player may fill the middle lane in the fast break, depending upon which is the preferred ballhandler.

If the ball side defender near midcourt moves up to cover 12's cut to the ball side corner, only two defenders will be left to cover the offensive player away from the ball in the backcourt and the two players on either side of the court for long passes.

The pass-and-cut may also be effected from 2's cross-court pass to 3. (See Figure 6–25.) In fact, the pass-and-cut sequence may involve any two

Figure 6-24 Double Pass-and-Cut.

184 Zone Offenses for Women's Basketball

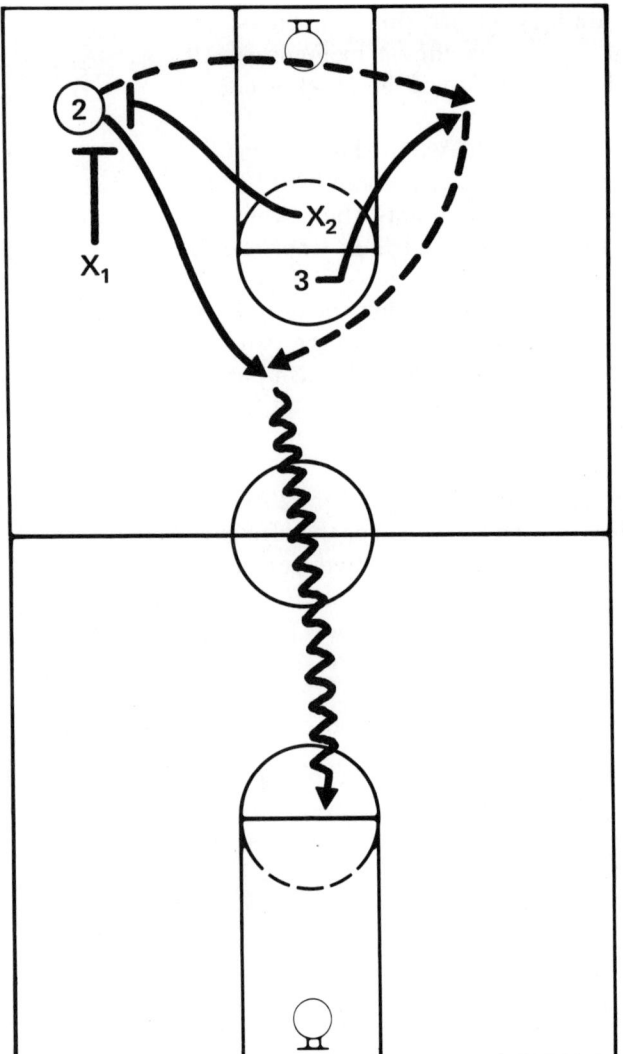

Figure 6-25 Pass-and-Cut After Crosscourt Pass.

offensive players passing to, and cutting from, practically any positions on the court. The strength of the pass-and-cut lies in the fact that it can help ensure the best ballhandler's doing most of the dribbling and ballhandling. Some teams use pass-and-cut sequences any time their best (or only) ballhandler has to pass the ball to a teammate.

FAST BREAKING

One of the easiest ways to beat a zone defense is to get your players downcourt before the opponents can get back downcourt to set up their zone coverage. Regardless of the opponents' skills or the kind of zone coverage they use, if they can't get back to stop your fast break, you're practically assured of having at least one high-percentage scoring opportunity.

Fast break basketball is exciting. Fans love it because the action is fast-paced and continuous, and players enjoy fast breaking because they score more points while shooting almost exclusively from high-percentage scoring areas. In fact, everyone loves fast breaking except opponents who have to try to stop it and coaches who fear the turnovers associated with high-speed basketball. At any rate, fast breaking isn't the offensive panacea it is sometimes purported to be—at least, not until a team assimilates all that fast breaking entails, including rigorous conditioning, running, and continuous drill in high-speed ballhandling.

Until 1976, I had always been a conservative coach offensively. While I thought I knew and appreciated the value of a fast breaking offense, I used the break in a manner I considered judicious. Running only when the lanes were open, the ballhandler was in position to advance the ball beyond the first line of defense, and a potential receiver was clearly beyond the defense. As a result, my teams' fast breaks were usually effective only after turnovers and steals. I alibied away our inability to fast break consistently by saying that our ballhandling wasn't good enough, or that we tended to take too many low-percentage shots off the break to make it worthwhile for us to try to fast break. In retrospect, I can see that it was my mistrust of the fast breaking philosophy itself that had denied us our share of fast break baskets.

In 1976, however, I inherited a relatively inexperienced team in which the tallest player was 5 feet 5 inches tall. (Our tallest starter was only 5 feet 4 inches!) We were quick, but I could see that our inside game was going to be nonexistent for all practical purposes. Our only chance to develop any kind of offensive consistency lay in fast breaking at every opportunity.

Regardless of the defensive style we adopted, it seemed that we were handicapped by our lack of height: trapping was out, because the ballhandlers could pass over our trapping players if they maintained low, balanced defensive stances, or dribble around them if they stood up to impede the ballhandlers' vision. Matching up was also impossible, it seemed, since the opponents would merely lob the ball inside to their tallest player. Practically every team on our schedule had at least one 6-foot player. We could double-team inside from a zone alignment, but in so doing we would surrender open shots from 12–15 feet, and even if we gave up those shots, we were almost certain to see the opponents playing volleyball inside with rebounds of missed shots against both zone and player-to-player defenses.

Offensively, we faced an even greater problem: no one on our team had ever made as high as 40 percent of her field goal attempts over an entire season (including layups), and our outside shooting was incredibly weak. Thus, we needed a defense that would enable us to regain ball possession without the opponents' taking a shot, and an offense that would ensure us high-percentage shots every time we got the ball. I had no idea where to find such an offense and defense until I attended a coaching clinic in Birmingham, Alabama, in October, 1976. Coaches Jerry Tarkanian of the University of Nevada at Las Vegas and "Lefty" Driesell of the University of Maryland were among the featured speakers, and their lectures seemed to be aimed directly at me.

Coach Tarkanian described his full-court pressure man-to-man (player-to-player) defense, in which his players hounded the ballhandler unmercifully and overguarded the potential pass receivers so that, when the ballhandler picked up his dribble, he had no one to pass to outside, and only backdoor passes available inside, if the offensive players were skilled enough to execute them. His system was, I realized, ideal for a situation like mine: it would vastly increase our chances of stealing the ball, since most of our opponents would look for the backdoor cut and pass only when it was so obvious that they couldn't fail to see it. And even if they made backdoor layups against us, it would hurt us no more than the lob passes inside they would have made against us if we were in a basic zone defense. Many teams play pressure player-to-player defense, but I suspected that our great speed and quickness would enable us to play it better than any of our opponents.

Offensively, Coaches Tarkanian and Driesell resolved many of my doubts concerning the fast break and its execution.

For example, I'd always stressed short, quick passes against zone pressing defenses, with dribbling used only as a last resort or against player-to-player coverage. Coach Driesell explained, however, that he preferred to have his fine ballhandler, Brad Davis, bring the ball down every time, whether by dribbling or by pass-and-cut patterns when he was unable to dribble. I'd noticed with distress that, whenever my best ballhandler was unable to bring the ball downcourt, we tended to get in trouble and throw the ball away needlessly.

Another technique stressed by both Tarkanian and Driesell was assigning lanes to each player and requiring them to fill the same lanes every time in fast breaking, regardless of where they were on the court when transition from defense to offense occurred. These assignments would, I feared, slow down our fast break and negate much of our speed. On the other hand, "laning" our fast break would help to ensure that our best shooters would be taking the shots, and our best ballhandlers handling the ball. After all, it does little good to have layup opportunities if the players taking the shots can't make the layups and the opponents are going to claim the rebounds. A layup is not a high-percentage shot for some players, and laning the fast break helps to ensure that better shooters are in position to take the shots.

The coaches drew a few diagrams to show how they organized their fast breaks, but such techniques can be taken from any of several coaching textbooks, including this one. The specifics, while important, are not nearly so valuable as the benefit to be derived from absorbing the philosophy underlying their fast-breaking systems. Fast breaking is in no way a cure for offensive ills, regardless of their nature or severity, nor is it a toy or gimmick to be practiced for fifteen minutes a day so a coach can say, "We're a fast breaking team." For teams under coaches such as Jerry Tarkanian and "Lefty" Driesell, fast breaking is a way of life, an irresistible, irreplaceable aspect of the game that affords them dimensions of play unknown to their opponents. Such teams practice their transition game endlessly, and in such a Spartan atmosphere, where the transition baskets that look so easy in games come as the result of countless hours of blood, sweat, and tears in practice, the fast break provides opportunities beyond the comprehension of more conservative, temperate coaches. For instance:

1. When used in conjunction with a pressure defense, whether zone or player-to-player, fast breaking helps to keep offensive and defensive pressure on the opponents everywhere on the court throughout the game. An adjunct to this is the corollary that fast breaking teams tend to handle the constant pressure of high-speed basketball better than teams who do not run: the players are more used to the high-speed ballhandling; instant transition from defense to offense and *vice versa;* and the fact that they generally run harder, longer, and faster in practice than do pattern-oriented teams tends to leave them in better shape physically in the latter stages of games than their opponents.

2. While teams that fast break constantly tend to commit more ballhandling errors than the average team, they also tend to force opponents into an even higher number of turnovers. Mental and physical mistakes are always a likelihood in high-speed basketball, but the team that is most used to handling the ball at high speeds will usually make less mistakes. Thus, fast breaking is not only a way of getting cheap baskets, but it can also serve to wear down the opponents physically and mentally. Our team won seventeen games and lost six in 1976–77, and in nine of the games we won, we were behind either at halftime or at the end of the third quarter. The expectations of our fans notwithstanding, we had great difficulty gaining a measure of control over our opponents even in our "easier" games, since our rebounding was poor at both ends of the court, our outside shooting was practically nonexistent, and our reserve strength only adequate at best.

On the other hand, we found that the constant offensive and defensive pressure usually got to our opponents sooner or later, either by key players' getting into foul trouble (tired players tend to foul more easily than when they're fresh); or by substitutions, which allowed our players to take advantage of mistakes made by fresh players unused to the high-speed transition game. It seemed that, even when the opponents' first team could combat our speed and aggressiveness, their substitutes were often confused and upset when confronted with our intense, unrelenting offensive and defensive pressure all over the court.

3. The fact that at least three of our players were always involved in the fast break meant that the defense was unable to double-team our high scorer, whose 18.6 ppg. average would otherwise have made her an obvious target for extra coverage. Whenever we took possession of the ball, however—even after our opponents' successful free-throws or field goals—it was always a foot race to the other end of the court, and the opponents' retreat back downcourt to our basket often resembled the Nazis' retreat from Russia in the winter of '42–'43 more than an organized defensive regrouping.

4. Perpetually fast breaking whenever we got the ball negated the opponents' attempts to press us. Admittedly, we had a fine ballhandler, but the threat of our fast breaking past the opponents' first line of defense—their players closest to *their* basket in the press—confused our opponents to a far greater extent than I'd experienced in previous years with teams that *didn't* fast break. Only one team all year pressed us full-court for an entire game, and we won that game 57–56. The games we lost were those in which: (1) the opponents never pressed us full-court, (2) their taller players never got in foul trouble, and (3) contact under the baskets was allowed to the extent that our players were unable to block out on defensive rebounds and thus failed to get the rebounds to start our fast break. Still, I shudder to think how many games we'd have won if we hadn't switched to the pressure defense and fast breaking—maybe six.

I turned to fast breaking only because the physical characteristics of my available personnel—extremely small, relatively inexperienced, incredibly quick—dictated a move in that direction. Yet I doubt that I'll ever return to my previous style of play in the future, even with slower teams. Learning to handle the ball at high speeds cannot but help to improve a team's performance, since the players will be better equipped to deal with fast breaking teams, and their patterned play will benefit from improved ballhandling as well. If players can handle the ball adequately when fast breaking, they are bound to see an improvement in their ballhandling at slower speeds.

The important point to remember is that the converse of this statement, that ballhandling at slower speeds will lead to improvement of high-speed ballhandling, is not true, although many people—including me—have assumed it to be so. The only way to improve ballhandling at high speeds is to practice high-speed ballhandling, and every coach should devote part of her practice to working on high-speed ballhandling drills, whether or not she plans for her team to run with the ball. In this respect, high-speed ballhandling is like mountain climbing: if you don't plan on doing it, you don't need to practice it, but if you ever find yourself in a situation where you have to do it, you'd *better* know how!

In preparing my players for fast breaking, I was surprised to discover that my traditional training methods, while rigorous, were not demanding enough to get my starters in shape to play thirty-two minutes of fast break basketball. Their endurance was adequate, but their effectiveness seemed to diminish in the latter stages of full-court scrimmages. I finally realized that it was their concentration and anticipation that was diminishing, and not their speed. They simply weren't used to playing for extended periods of time with both physical intensity and mental toughness. I found that I needed eight or nine players capable of short bursts of sustained effort if we were going to keep constant pressure on our opponents both defensively and offensively.[4]

Principles of Fast Breaking

A team may fast break against full-court pressure defense either by dribbling or by passing the ball. The ballhandling skills of available personnel will dictate which of the techniques a team will use in fast breaking against zone presses. The following guidelines may prove useful in considering the problems involved:

1. While it is virtually impossible to dribble too little against zone presses, players are often guilty of dribbling too much. Dribbling should be used to advance the ball downcourt when passing is clearly less desirable in a given situation.

When individual skills permit, passing is preferable to dribbling in establishing the fast break. In many cases, however, a team has only one or two ballhandlers with skills sufficient to move the ball downcourt at high speeds by either dribbling *or* passing, and in such cases, dribbling may represent the lesser of two evils for the offensive team.

2. Offensive players should constantly watch the dribbler and create an offensive triangle ahead of her. In Figure 6–19, for example, as the dribbler penetrates between the defenders, the inbounds passer and safety valve will follow the sideline lanes downcourt and fill the passing lanes diagonally ahead of the dribbler. On the other hand, the offensive triangle when the ball is brought up the sideline (see Figure 6–17) will consist of dribbler 2, 4 cutting to the weak side at half-court, and 3 cutting to the ball side corner.

3. Every fast break pattern should have a safety valve (an offensive

---

[4] Coach Jerry Tarkanian of UNLV suggests six–seven minutes as the maximum limits of players' ability to play at peak intensity at both ends of the court.

player purposely kept out of the fast break in case a sudden turnover permits the opponents to begin their own fast break). In Figure 6–17, inbounds passer 1 is the safety valve.

4. In fast breaking patterns featuring three offensive players, the ball should be taken down the middle of the court, with players other than the dribbler staying wide as they move downcourt. In two-player fast break patterns, however, both the ball and the players should stay wide of the middle of the court.

The two most important aspects of setting up the fast break are: aligning the players in such a manner that the best ballhandlers are in position to handle the ball beyond the first line of defensive players, and assigning lanes for each player to follow whenever the team fast breaks.

Aligning the Ballhandlers to Fast Break. Generally, a team will have either one or two ballhandlers it will prefer to handle the ball in the fast break. If one ballhandler is preferred, she should either be able to dribble around or through the double-team, pass-and-cut to receive a return pass, or cut from weak side in a manner similar to that shown in Figure 6–22. Serious problems arise when the team's only ballhandler passes the ball away and is unable to get it back. In such cases, not only does fast breaking become a remote possibility, but the offensive team is far less likely to beat pressing defenses.

Laning the Fast Break. The practice of assigning lanes to the players expected to be involved in fast breaking may seem incongruous to some, but it has definite merits which deserve consideration. First, although the laning will slow down the fast break slightly as players move into their lanes, it will provide greater efficiency in organizing the fast break, since there is no longer any question of who fills each of the passing lanes. Too, constant repetition of laning in practice drills as well as in games tends to further improve and simplify the fast break.

Some teams—ours among them—always send at least one offensive player downcourt beyond the ballhandler as soon as transition occurs, whether by defensive rebounds, stealing the ball, or opponents' scores. When a team relies on one outstanding ballhandler, it may send *two* offensive players down early.

Figures 6–26, 6–27, and 6–28 illustrate the objective of laning the fast break, namely, the repetition of movements into lanes by players other than the ballhandlers. In Figures 6–26, 6–27, and 6–28, defensive players X_1, X_2, and X_3 are the players involved in the fast break after transition, with X_3 serving as the primary ballhandler and X_2 as the first player downcourt. (We call this player our "streaker," for want of a better name. Her job is to streak downcourt in her lane as soon as we acquire possession of the ball, in order to force at least part of the opposing team to retreat.)

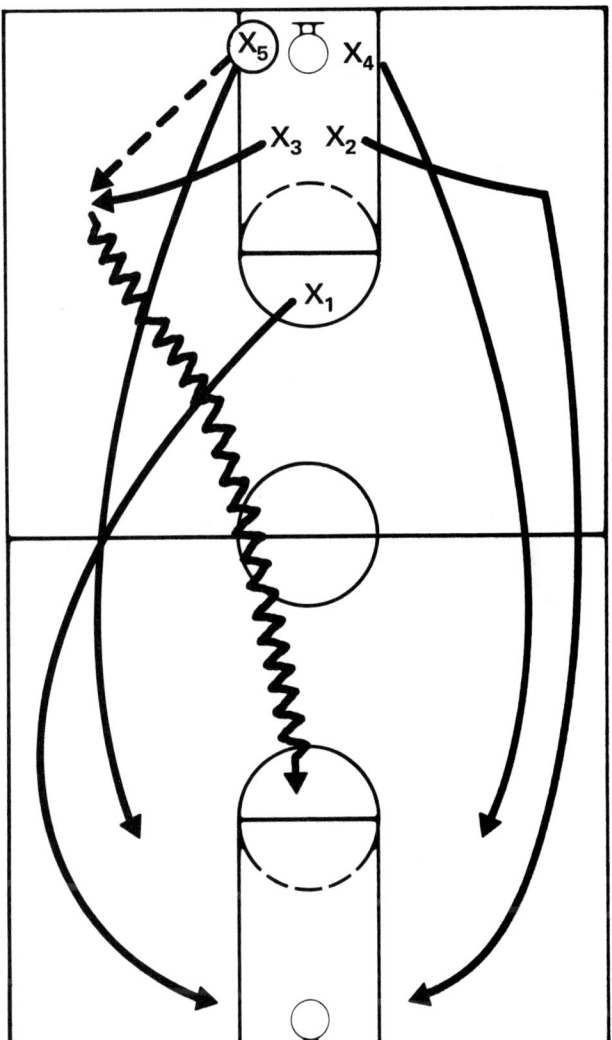

Figure 6-26 "Laning" the Fast Break After Rebound.

In Figure 6–26, X_5 has rebounded a missed shot. Players X_2 and X_3 move wide to the offensive wing positions, and when X_3 receives X_5's pass, she takes the ball to the middle and advances downcourt as X_2 fills the left-hand lane.

Figure 6–27 depicts the fast breaking sequence when a team prefers for its primary ballhandler—X_3 in the diagrams—to bring the ball downcourt regardless of where the rebound is taken. Of course, if the coach prefers for her secondary ballhandler to take the ball downcourt on occasion, X_3 will fill X_2's lane as X_2 dribbles to the middle and downcourt.

In Figure 6–28, the ball is at the wing, with the defense in zone

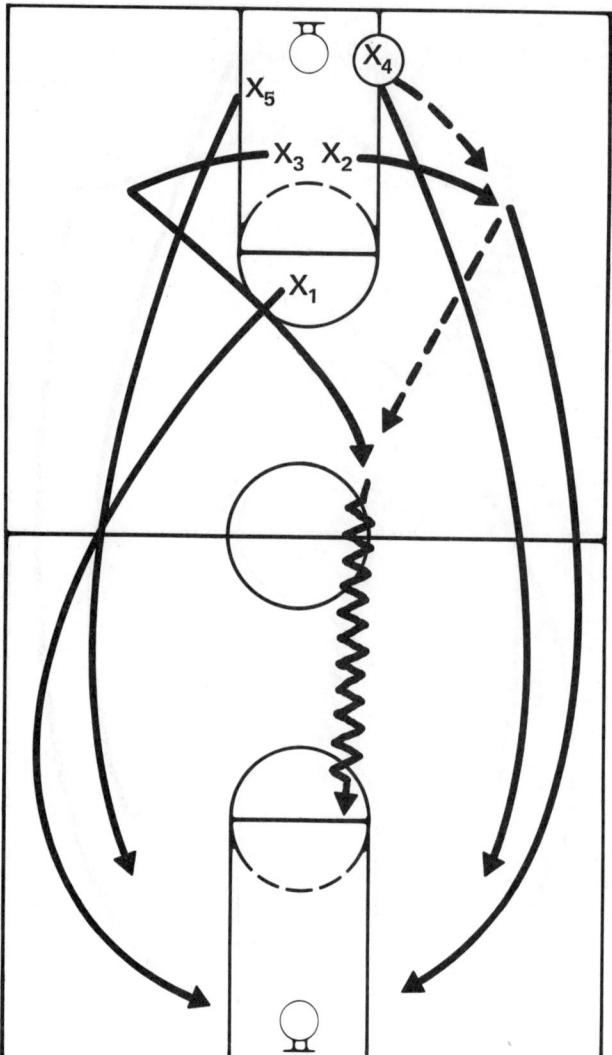

Figure 6-27 Outlet Pass to Start the Fast Break. Say 4 takes the defensive rebound. Then X_2 moves toward the sideline for the outlet pass and relays the ball to 3 in the middle. Other players fill the passing lanes ahead of, and behind, 3.

coverage. When the turnover occurs, X_2 passes to X_3, the primary ballhandler, and X_1 and X_2 fill the passing lanes. The sequence is, in fact, identical to those shown in Figures 6–26 and 6–27, and therein lies the value of laning the fast break: even if the positions of X_1, X_2, and X_3 were transposed or moved to other areas of the half-court (e.g., the corner, low post, etc.), *their responsibilities in fast breaking would remain the same!* Player X_3 would acquire the ball and move down the middle of the court, with X_1 and X_2 filling the same lanes along the sidelines regardless of their location on the court when transition occurred.

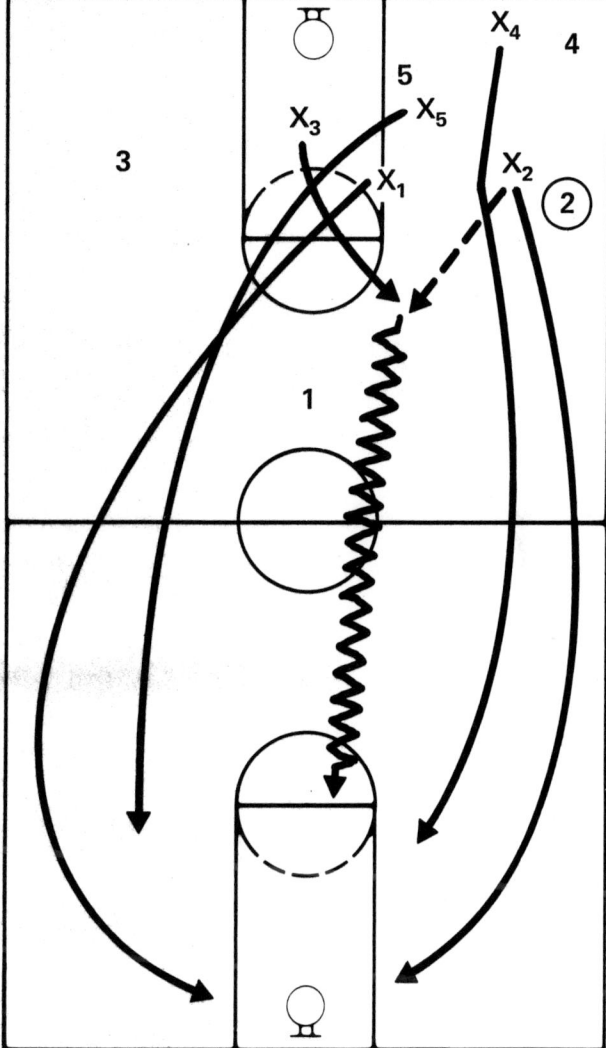

Figure 6-28 "Laning" the Fast Break After a Turnover. Say X_2 takes the ball away from 2 along the sideline. Player X_3, the primary ballhandler, cuts to receive X_2's pass. Player X_1 releases wide to fill one sideline passing lane, and X_2 fills the lane on the other side. (Of course, X_2 could be the ballhandler, with X_1 filling the left-hand passing lane and X_3 filling the right-hand lane.)

To return to Figure 6-27 for a moment, if X_3 were the only ballhandler when X_4 rebounded, X_2 would head downcourt without waiting for X_4's pass, and X_3 would move to X_4's side of the court to receive the outlet pass to start the fast break.

Another alternative sometimes used by teams with two ballhandlers of equal ability is to send both players to outlet passing areas as shown in Figure 6-29.

Player X_5 (circled) has claimed the rebound. As she pivots outside, X_3 cuts to the ball side sideline, and X_2 cuts to the area of the top of the cir-

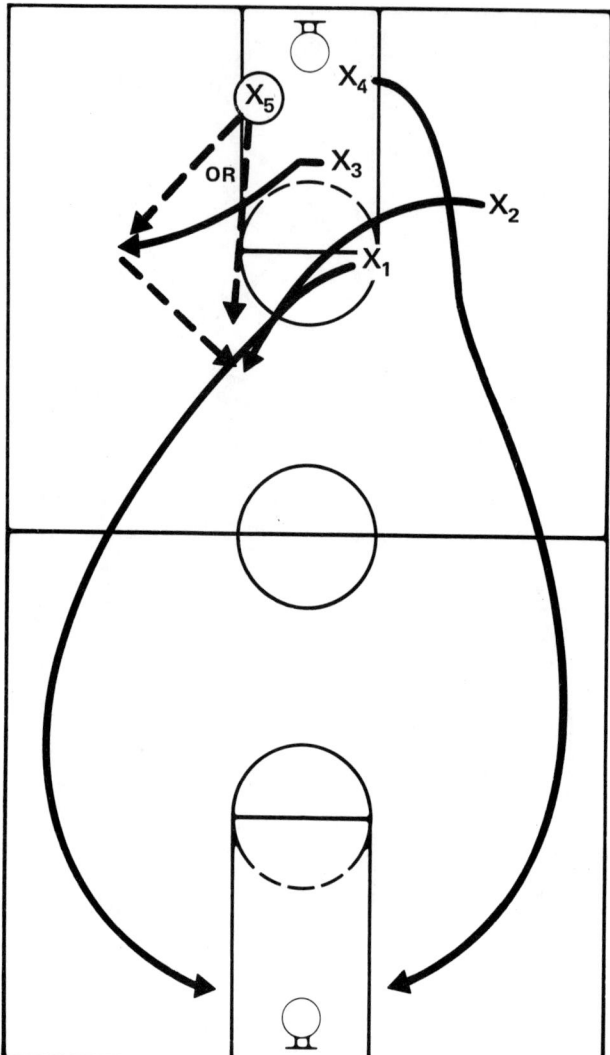

Figure 6-29 Two Outlet Pass Receivers After Defensive Rebound.

cle. Player X_5 can then pass to either X_3 or X_2 to start the fast break, and at that point either player may bring the ball downcourt, as shown in Figures 6–30 and 6–31.

Alternatives to Laning the Fast Break. As previously explained, the term *laning* refers to the act of sending specific players along previously designated routes in establishing the fast break. However, many teams, especially those with overall ballhandling excellence, prefer to operate spontaneously in establishing the fast break. That is, their players still

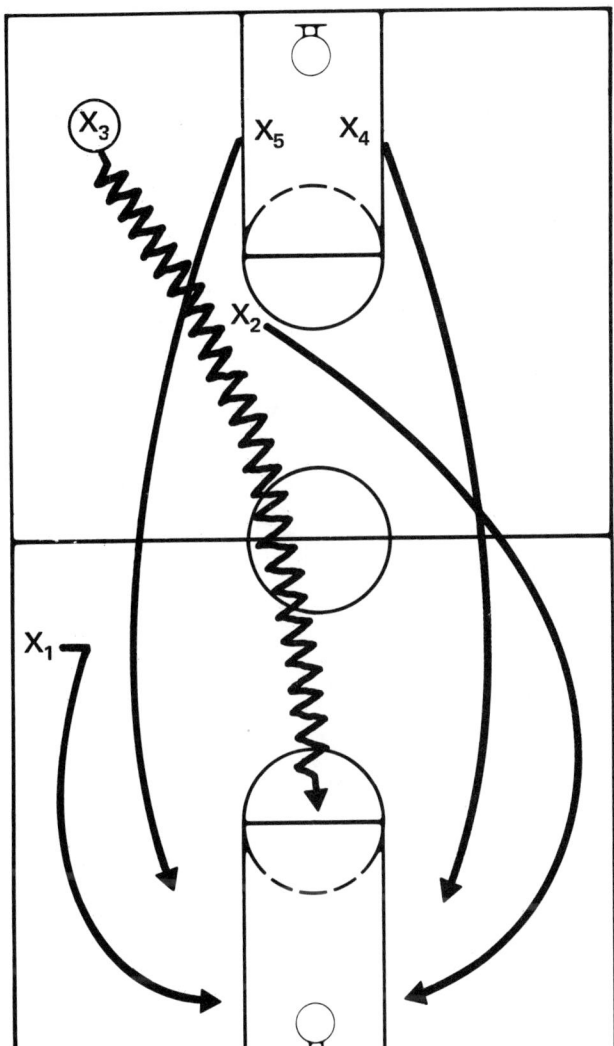

Figures 6-30, 6-31 Alternate Methods of Laning After Defensive Rebound and Outlet Pass.

"lane" their fast break, but only in the sense of filling the passing lanes as the ballhandler moves downcourt. The players involved in the fast break—ballhandlers, players cutting into and along the passing lanes, etc.—are those who first reach those positions.

The entire fast break need not be the product of random or haphazard positioning, however. Often, teams will designate their ballhandlers, while at the same time leaving the passing lanes open for unspecified cutters.

The first step in fast breaking after defensive rebounds is getting the

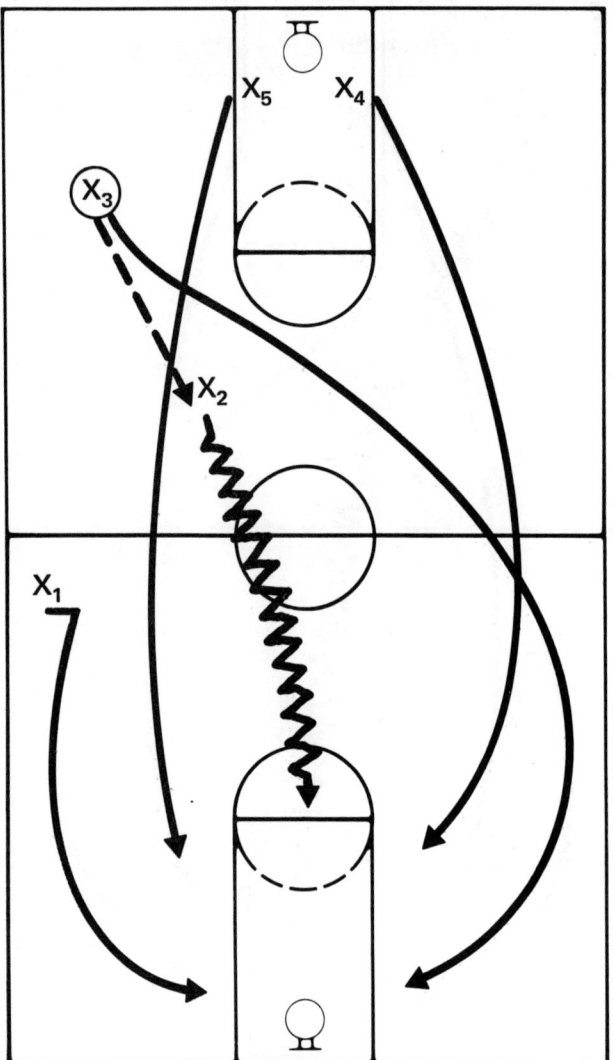

Figure 6-31.

ball to the ballhandler. When a team has one ballhandler, the best strategy is to send the intended ballhandler to the rebound, or to the open area at the top of the circle or near the sideline, depending upon the rebounder's ability to make the outlet pass.

Players should be taught to land in a low, balanced stance with their elbows wide to protect the ball after rebounding, then pivot to the outside of the court and either make the pass immediately or dribble once or twice as they search for the outlet pass receiver. With inexperienced players, the designated ballhandler should go to the ball, whether at the baseline or sideline, calling the rebounder by name as she tries to free herself for the outlet pass. (See Figure 6–32.) The greater the rebounder's ballhandling ability, the farther away the ballhandler can be to receive the ball and start the fast break. (See Figures 6–33 and 6–34.) The pass may be made without dribbling, of course, but inexperienced players are usually better off clearing toward the sideline by dribbling before passing.

Player 3's movements in Figures 6–32, 6–33, and 6–34 indicate the

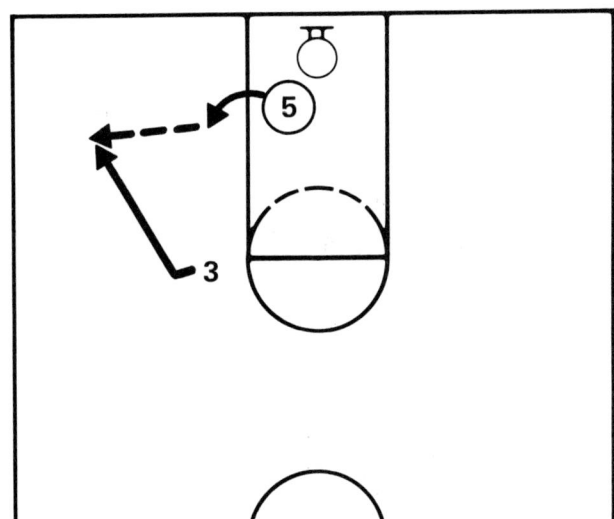

Figure 6-32 Cutting to the Rebounder.

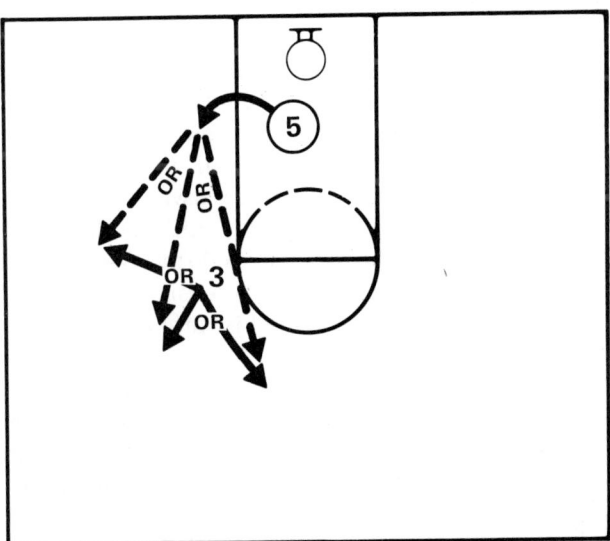

Figure 6-33 Cutting Outside.

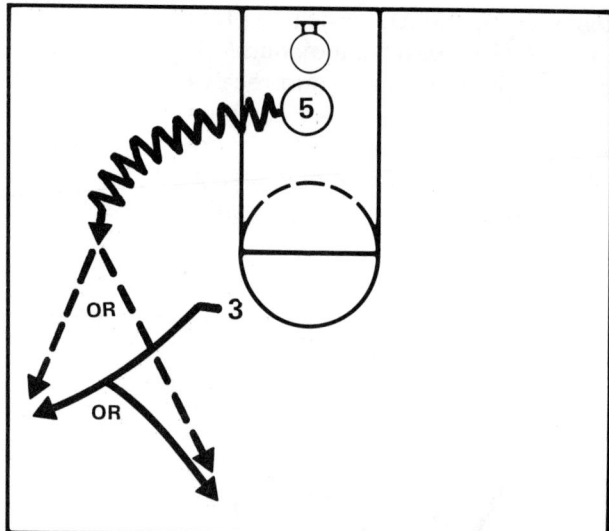

Figure 6-34 Cutting Downcourt.

rebounder's increasing ability to move the ball downcourt. As can be seen, the distance toward the baseline that the intended ballhandler will have to cut depends upon the rebounder's ability to move the ball downcourt by dribbling or passing.

When the rebound is taken on the side of the court away from the designated ballhandler, the suggested cuts are the same as those in Figures 6-32, 6-33, and 6-34, except that they occur on the other side of the court. Rebounders should be discouraged from dribbling across the lane in clearing for two reasons: first, the lane is usually filled with players from both teams, and dribbling into the crowd increases the likelihood of defensive trapping and subsequent turnovers; and second, the time required to clear across the lane before making the outlet pass will allow the defensive players to drop back downcourt.

In like manner, and for the same reasons, the designated ballhandler should not cut toward the baseline away from the ball, nor should she delay her cut. Unless instructed otherwise, ballhandlers away from the rebounder intending to fast break should avoid waiting until the defensive players clear the lane to cut and receive the outlet pass. Why? Because the defenders' clearing movements will be toward their defensive basket, and they will thus have all five players back to stop the fast break by the time the ballhandler receives the outlet pass.

Of course, *any* player may cut outside to receive the outlet pass. Generally, however, teams designate no more than *two* targets for outlet passes. These two receivers may be on opposite sides of the court, as in Figure 6-26, or they may both cut to the same side of the court, as shown in Figure 6-29.

Bringing the Ball Downcourt. Although teams have occasionally used a series of quick, short passes (or a single long pass) to move the ball the length of the court in fast breaking, such passes generally are used to advance the ball past the first line of defensive coverage, beyond which dribbling becomes less hazardous. Whereas inexperienced players sometimes are incapable of using their peripheral vision while involved in a series of passes, dribbling allows the other offensive players to look around more freely without fear of sudden, unexpected passes and without sacrificing speed for passing accuracy.

At times, the ballhandler will find an open teammate beyond any of the defensive players. A good question to ask in determining whether or not she should attempt the pass is, *Can she reach her teammate with the pass without the ball's bouncing?* If she cannot, she should not attempt the pass, regardless of her passing accuracy. If she can't reach her teammate without the pass becoming a bounce pass, she is too far away to make the pass, and she should continue dribbling until she reaches a point where she can throw the ball all the way to her receiver.

Another point to consider is that baseball-type passes should never be made by a dribbling player. (Indeed, many coaches feel that baseball passes should never be made at all.) It is virtually impossible for a player

Figure 6-35 Establishing the Three-Player Fast Break Lanes.

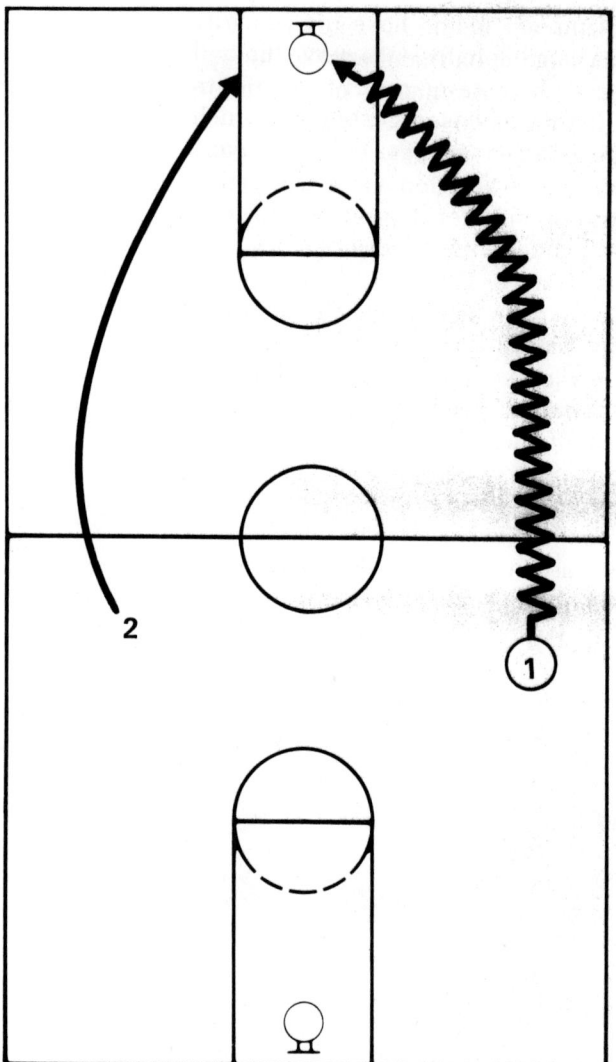

Figure 6-36 Establishing the Two-Player Fast Break Lanes.

to stop, catch the ball, and throw the long baseball pass downcourt without committing a traveling violation.

Whether a coach is going to allow baseball passes to be thrown from out of bounds is a different matter, depending upon whether or not the passer possesses sufficient strength and accuracy to make the pass and whether or not the coach is willing to risk such long passes. Many coaches feel that court-length passes result in too many turnovers to be worthwhile. However, if a team possesses a player with sufficient strength and skill to complete such passes, they can provide added dimensions to both fast breaking and beating the presses.

When the offensive team clearly establishes control of the ball beyond the first line of defensive resistance, the ballhandler(s) should attempt to determine the number and location of teammates included in the fast break. This is done by glancing quickly from side to side, or by using peripheral vision, as the ball is advanced downcourt. This analysis should tell the ballhandler whether she should dribble the ball to the middle of the court (Figure 6-35) or straight to the basket (Figure 6-36).

Finishing the Fast Break: Two, Three, and Four-Player Patterns. Important as is the process of locating one's teammates in forming the fast break, it is perhaps even more important to identify the opponents involved in stopping the fast break and to position oneself on the court accordingly.

When players fail to follow the proper routes downcourt when leading the fast break, the defenders are able to cover the passing lanes with less effort and greater success. For example, if the ballhandler is coached merely to "dribble down the middle of the court" in fast breaking, two-on-one patterns will be less likely to be successful than when the defender's coverage is spread to the maximum. (See Figures 6-37 and 6-38.)

In Figure 6-37, the angle of the dribbler's pass to her teammate is

Figure 6-37 Incorrect Spreading, Two-on-One Fast Break.

Figure 6-38 Correct Spreading, Two-on-One Fast Break.

more acute, and thus is far more difficult, than that shown in Figure 6-38 where the offensive players are farther apart. The outside shot may be open in either pattern, of course, but the pass inside is made with greater facility when the offensive players are somewhere between 15-20 feet apart when they cross the free-throw line.

With the defender at the center of the free-throw lane in both situations, the dribbler's passing angle is reduced considerably, and defensive coverage possibilities are thus similarly improved, when the dribbler brings the ball down the middle of the court.

Once proper laning is established, the next problem confronting the dribbler is deciding whether to shoot or to pass the ball. This decision will depend to a degree upon the quality of the defender's performance, but it will also depend upon the dribbler's ability to apply offensive pressure to the single defender. A first step in this direction lies in understanding the options available to the person playing defense. She may attempt to either: (1) block the shot, (2) block the pass, (3) fake blocking the shot and block the pass, (4) fake blocking the pass and block the shot, or (5) draw a charging foul by stepping into the shooter's path.

How does the ballhandler know what the defender is going to do? She doesn't. On the other hand, the defender doesn't know what the dribbler is going to do, either. The defender's plan, then, is to force the action as early as possible and make the dribbler commit herself to either shooting or passing. Either way, the defender will try to stay near the middle of the lane in order to avoid committing herself while the dribbler has time to alter her intentions.

Young, inexperienced ballhandlers are probably best served by being taught to "take the shot whenever possible." Passing the ball is a more natural impulse for most players than shooting, and if players are not urged to shoot, they may be susceptible to turnovers as they attempt to pass when unguarded. They run the risk of being fouled if they shoot the layup, whereas a turnover as a result of attempting to pass the ball nets them nothing. Besides, a player who goes up to shoot may be able to pass off to her teammate at the last moment, whereas the player whose sole intention in going to the basket is passing the ball will be unlikely to make the shot if forced into that alternative at the last moment. Put simply, young or inexperienced players are more likely to attack the defender in two-on-one fast break situations by taking the shot than by attempting to pass the ball.

As skills increase, however, the process is not so clearly defined. Superior ballhandlers can practically ensure themselves an open shot or successful pass in two-on-one fast breaks by using head, body, or ball fakes. When the ballhandler is clearly in control of herself and the ball as she nears the basket, the defender will not commit herself to covering one player or the other for fear of surrendering an uncontested layup if she misinterprets the dribbler's intentions.

For players who are too inexperienced to do more than react to the defensive player's movements, as opposed to aggressively attacking the defender herself, we try to teach them to *slide* toward the defender in at least their last two dribbles toward the basket. By sliding forward in a "step-together, step-together" fashion, the dribbler will be able to pick up the ball almost instantaneously in a balanced stance. Her forward momentum toward the basket will thus be slowed, but her ball control will be improved by sliding. And of the two factors in fast breaking, ball control is far more important than speed: all the speed in the world won't help a team's fast break if the ballhandlers can't pass, or if shooters are unable to put the ball in the basket!

Along with sliding, we teach our young players to watch the defender's feet, and when she takes a single step toward the dribbler to catch the ball and pass to the teammate cutting to the basket. Admittedly, we usually lose the ball when the defender fakes covering the dribbler and drops back to cut off the passing lane; but on the other hand, few young girls are skilled or knowledgeable enough on defense to execute such maneuvers. Generally, when the defender steps toward the ballhandler, she does so with the intention of guarding her.

Finally, we teach our younger ballhandlers to stop on both feet before passing the ball. This helps to ensure that they do not penetrate too close to the defender on the dribble, in which case they will not be able to pass to their open teammate.

Faking. Faking is an advanced skill. However, when a ballhandler is capable of catching the ball at the end of her dribble, faking a pass to her teammate and going up for the shot without pausing, she will seldom find her shot blocked or her progress to the basket impeded by the defender. In order to be effective, the fake must look as much like a real pass as possible: the dribbler should look at the player she apparently wants to pass to, extend her arms (and the ball) fully, and at the last moment turn to the basket and shoot while the defender is leaning away from her and toward her teammate.

The converse of this fake is more difficult: to dribble past the point of no return, go up as if to shoot (eyes on the basket, bringing the ball up into shooting position), and then, as the defender raises her hands to block the shot, suddenly bring the ball down and pass sharply beneath the defender's raised hands to her teammate.

Three-on-Two Fast Break. Because three players rather than two are potential ballhandlers, three-player fast breaks often prove more difficult to operate than two-player fast breaks. In practically every case, the two defenders will be aligned one-up, one-back (Figures 6–39 and 6–40) as opposed to side-by-side (Figure 6–41). At least, they *should* be.

In Figure 6–41, which defensive player assumes responsibility for stopping the dribbler? Both? Neither? And, assuming that one player stops the dribbler, how does the other player cover the cutters to the basket? Any number of solutions may be devised, but none is as satisfactory as that shown in Figures 6–39 and 6–40.

The best defensive alignment when two players are back to stop the opponents' fast break is the tandem formation. In this system, the front defender's responsibilities are to stop the dribbler, then drop back to cover the side opposite the ballhandler's pass. The rear defender covers whichever player receives the first pass.

The original ballhandler, 25, should avoid the temptation to continue into the lane after passing the ball. She will likely be open in the vicinity of the free-throw line, but if she ventures into the lane and complications arise, she will be called for a three-second lane violation.

Once an offensive cutter—for instance, 3 in Figures 6–39 and 6–40—receives 25's pass, she will take the shot if the rear defender fails to cover her, or pass to a teammate if the rear defender covers her as expected. The front defender cannot cover both players without the ball, so 3 will pass to whichever player is left unguarded. Such decisions are by nature necessarily split-second, and require a great deal of drill to be made successfully and with any consistency in games.

Beating the Zone Presses 205

Figures 6-39, 6-40 Basic Three-on-Two Fast Break with Defensive Coverage.

Figure 6-41 Three-on-Two Fast Break, Alternate Defensive Coverage.

One of the greatest problem areas in finishing the fast break arises when the wing cutters arrive at their respective edges of the free-throw lane far ahead of the ballhandler.

This situation, usually the result of the cutters' having moved downcourt near the center of the court rather than following the sideline lanes until they reach the free-throw line extended, will often result in a deflected pass or turnover as the pass receiver tries vainly to shoot or relay the ball to her teammate on the other side of the basket. Since the inside defender is directly between 3 (or the other wing) and the basket when the ballhandler passes, she will also be between the pass receiver and her supposedly open teammate on the other side of the lane—and the front defender will probably be dropping back to steal the attempted lob pass. (If it's a bounce pass, the rear defender will likely block or deflect it.)

Proper laning for finishing the three-on-two fast break is as follows: the players assuming the wing positions on either side of the court should stay wide along the sidelines until they reach the area of their free-throw line extended. (The more highly skilled the players, the farther they may be from the sidelines, although they still should resist the temptation to move downcourt at full speed, regardless of the dribbler's location on the court.)

When the ballhandler's dribble is finally challenged, she picks up the ball immediately and passes to one of the cutters. We try to teach our players to *slide* toward the front defender in their last two or three dribbles, in order to be able to catch and pass the ball quickly as the defensive point guard steps toward them and to stop quickly once they have passed the ball.

It is important for the cutter who receives 1's pass to be in position to relay the ball cross-court to her teammate cutting to the basket; and in order to achieve such a situation, the pass receiver should be in the act of cutting toward the basket, and not already stationed near the basket. Both passes may be either chest- or bounce-passes, depending upon the type of pass necessary in a given situation, but lob passes should not be thrown by any of the players involved in finishing the fast break. Participants should be drilled extensively in the use of both chest-passes and bounce-passes as they are likely to be used in finishing the fast break.

Young or inexperienced players should be taught that, when an outside defender pressures their passes, the pass to their right will be easier for them to make than the pass to their left. Why? Because right-handed players won't have to bring the ball across their bodies to make the pass. On the other hand, a pass to their left will likely go behind the receiver if the defensive point guard exerts sudden, unexpected defensive pressure on an inexperienced ballhandler: she will not only have to react to the point guard's movement toward her, but she will also have to bring the ball from the right side of her body where she was dribbling to her left side to make the pass. The added time required to react to the point guard's defense, pick up her dribble on her right side, and transfer the ball to her left side before passing will increase the likelihood of the pass being intercepted. (If the ballhandler tries to pass to her left from the right side of her body without bringing the ball across to her left side, the point guard will probably deflect or steal the pass.)

A simple movement by the ballhandler can almost invariably ensure a wing cutter an open layup—if the ballhandler is capable of properly executing a fake. The dribbler brings the ball downcourt to a position close enough to deny herself passing options. Suddenly, the ballhandler stops in a balanced position, *fakes* a pass to one wing by turning her head and torso toward that player and extending the ball as if passing, then bringing the ball back to her body quickly, turning and passing to her other teammate cutting to the basket.

The point guard is frozen in position by the dribbler's penetration. If the point guard drops back to cover a cutter to the basket, the ballhandler will have the open shot inside the circle, the equivalent of a free throw. At the same time, the inside defender must react to the ballhandler's fake, since her responsibility is to cover whichever player receives the pass.

The other wing player will, therefore, be open for the uncontested layup in most cases—*if* the ballhandler's fake is convincing enough to fool the defense.

Another of the seemingly countless problems confronting coaches in establishing a fast breaking system is that of teaching players to deal with the outside defensive coverage. If, for example, the ballhandler picks up her dribble prematurely (i.e., before she is challenged by the outside defender), as shown in Figure 6-42, the front defender will drop back into side-by-side coverage of the cutters with the rear defender, leaving the ballhandler with three alternatives: (1) the unwanted outside shot beyond the top of the circle, (2) the even more dangerous passes to the cutters, (who by now are covered), and (3) waiting for her teammates to arrive.

Thus, it is imperative that the ballhandler be able to both challenge the defense and make the pass to a cutting teammate when the outside defender responds to her challenge. The dribbler leading the fast break should not automatically pick up her dribble whenever she reaches the free-throw line; in fact, it is sometimes possible to drive on the outside defender—in effect, forcing double-coverage on the two defenders. (See Figure 6-43.)

As 25 closes on the front defender, instead of picking up her dribble

Figure 6-42 Defensive Coverage When 1 Picks Up Her Dribble Too Early.

and passing to a teammate, she continues dribbling around X_5's loose defensive coverage. The inside defender moves up to stop 25's layup, leaving 3 open for a pass and uncontested layup. (Player X_5 will not drop back to guard 3, since: (1) no switch has been called, and (2) she has no way of knowing when to release from 25 to drop back to cover 3.) Player 25 may dribble either way around X_5, but the move to her left—X_5's right—will likely be more effective against opponents who tend to overguard the ballhandler toward her weaker hand.

It was explained previously that the ballhandler should not penetrate beyond the free-throw line after passing, lest she inadvertently decrease the receiver's passing angle to her teammate cutting to the basket from the other side of the court, bringing the other defender into position to interfere with the pass. An exception to this rule exists, however, in the form of a rarely used special pattern shown in Figures 6-44 and 6-45.

In this pattern, the wings follow their passing lanes to the baseline rather than to the basket. Instead of stopping at the free-throw line after passing, 25 cuts to the basket in front of X_5 for a return pass and layup. Player 25's movement takes advantage of the tandem defensive alignment and strategy. (Player X_5 is supposed to stop the dribbler, then drop back to

Figure 6-43 Forcing Double-Coverage, Three-on-Two Fast Break.

Figures 6-44, 6-45 Baseline Cutter Pattern, Three-on-Two Fast Break.

cover the weak side cutter, with the inside defender covering the pass receiver.) Thus, when the rear defender covers the wing pass and X_5 drops back to cover the opposite wing, 25's cut to the basket will be left momentarily unguarded.

Three-on-One Fast Break. In three-on-one fast breaking situations, the ballhandler will not face defensive coverage outside, so she will probably take the ball inside the free-throw lane before passing in order to give herself a shot close to the basket in the event that she elects to shoot rather than pass. If she elects to pass, her pass will be delayed and angled closer to the basket than in three-on-two coverage, and will result in a layup rather than a second pass. (Some coaches prefer that their dribbler stay outside the lane in three-on-one as well as three-on-two fast breaks, since two-pass sequences will almost invariably result in three-second lane violations.)

The movements used to set up the layup—for example, faking a pass to one cutter and passing to the other—are identical to those used in the three-on-two sequence except that, as stated previously, they are likely to occur closer to the basket in the three-on-one fast break.

Figure 6-46 Basic Three-on-One Fast Break.

Three-on-Three Fast Break. Three-on-three fast breaks may appear to possess no special advantages for offensive teams, since numerical equality negates most of the options described previously. However, in certain situations—for example, cases in which a team's lack of height means that their fast breaks will provide much of their offensive thrust—the fast break may be vital in equalizing disadvantages, even when the defense is able to send three players back to stop the fast break.

It should be obvious that, whether the defense sets up 1–2 (Figure 6–47) or 2–1 (Figure 6–48), the defensive players will match up with the ballhandler and cutters. Of course, the matchups may favor the offensive players, but the prudent coach will plan ahead for those occasions in which the matchups favor the defense.

The simplest pattern to confuse the matchups is the pass-and-cut with weak side screen shown in Figure 6–49. In other circumstances the pattern might be easily defended, but one must remember that the pattern is run at high speed and the defenders have been rushing back to their positions rather than resting comfortably and anticipating such moves.

Figure 6-47 Matching Up Defensively from 1–2 Formation.

Beating the Zone Presses 213

Figure 6-48 Matching Up Defensively from 2–1 Formation.

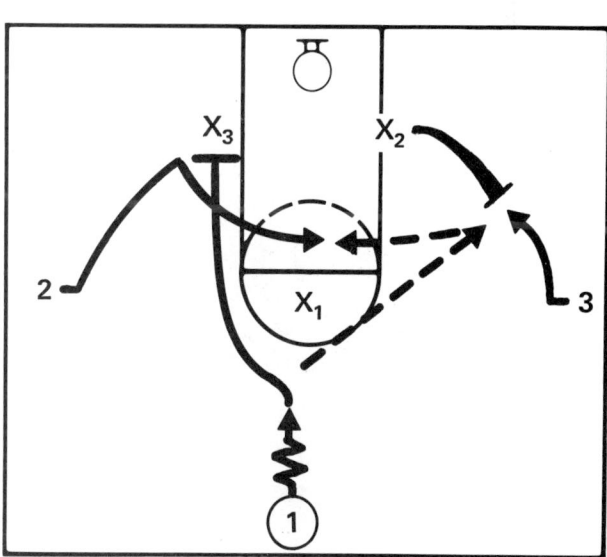

Figure 6-49 Pass-and-Cut with Weak Side Screen.

Ballhandler 1 passes to 3 and cuts to the weak side to screen for 2. Player 2 cuts behind the screen to receive 3's pass. (Note: the ballhandler's dribble is to the corner of the free-throw line in order to allow a fourth offensive player to enter into the fast break, as shown in Figure 6–50.)

Four-on-Three Fast Break. The three-player fast break is not necessarily stymied when the opponents can muster three players back on defense, not even when the defenders are capable of stopping such basic maneuvers as the pass-and-cut with weak side screen. When six players—three from each team—are downcourt, the seventh player, if a member of the offensive team, will afford an advantage for the offensive team.

Generally, the fourth offensive player downcourt will be either the sixth or seventh player in the fast break, depending upon whether two or three defensive players are back on defense. The first two offensive players, the outside (wing) cutters, will cut to the basket. The ballhandler, instead of dribbling to the center of the free-throw lane, will veer to the corner of the lane in order to provide an outside opening for the fourth offensive player—Player 3 in Figure 6–50.

In Figure 6–51, Player 2 screens for 3 cutting behind X_3 along the baseline. Player 4's cut ensures that X_2 will not move across the lane to help cover 2 and 3. Figure 6–52 shows the movement to the other side of the court, with 4 screening X_1 away from 1, and 2 cutting behind 3's

Figure 6-50 Basic Four-on-Three Fast Break Pattern.

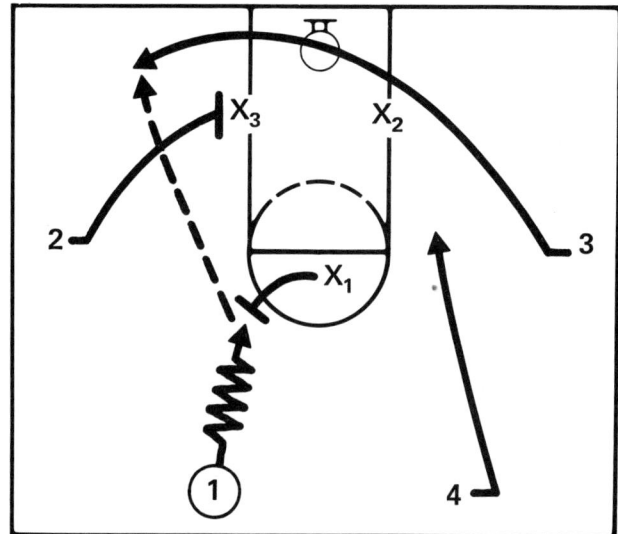

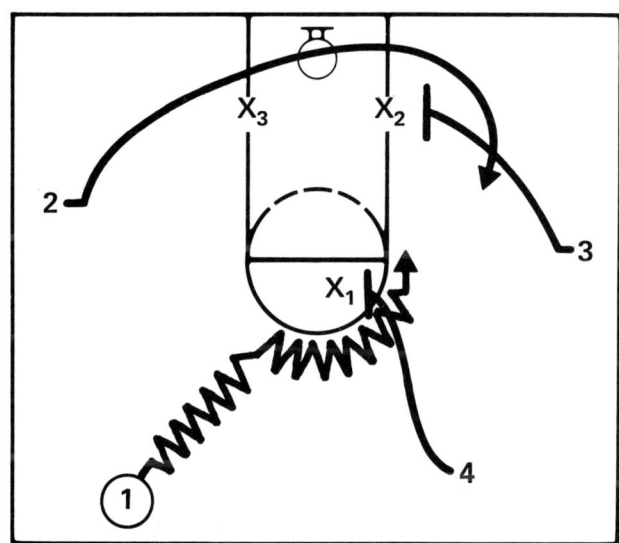

Figures 6-51, 6-52 Variations of Basic Four-on-Three Fast Break Pattern.

screen. These moves, while slightly more time consuming than regular fast breaking patterns, are certainly within acceptable time limitations for most teams. Of course, any number of other patterns could be devised to take advantage of the four-on-three situation, as long as the time factor is taken into consideration. After all, the four-on-three advantage will not last indefinitely.

COMBATTING THE HALF-COURT ZONE PRESSES

As most coaches will readily testify, the half-court zone pressing defenses can present formidable obstacles to teams attempting to bring the ball downcourt. That this is so is due at least in part to the confusion surrounding the half-court zone presses and their usage. Why, for example, does a team select a half-court zone press rather than a full-court pressing defense? Do the half-court presses possess advantages unknown to the full-court presses? Are there common elements among the half-court zone presses that can lead to better understanding of all half-court zone pressing defenses? Answers to these and other questions are vital to a team's chances of attacking, or merely surviving against, the half-court zone presses.

Teams often resort to half-court presses when their opponents are capable of consistently spreading their full-court defensive coverage beyond the limits of its effective coverage. Dropping back into half-court coverage thus serves to give the defensive team more time to set up its coverage, and to confine both the ball and the defensive players to a smaller area of the court. Half-court zone pressing defenses generally are more effective on small or narrow courts, where confinement of the ballhandler is underscored by the limitations of the court itself.

On the other hand, the act of dropping back into half-court defensive coverage allows the offensive team to prepare to beat the press, too, and although the ball is confined to a certain extent, passing beyond the first line of defensive coverage will practically guarantee high-percentage shots or scoring opportunities off the resulting fast break.

Success in using half-court pressing defenses depends on three factors: (1) controlling the dribbler, first by close single-coverage and later by double-teaming; (2) cutting off the passing lanes; and (3) denying the long passes that lead to easy baskets. Conversely, beating the half-court zone presses requires confident ballhandling that can attack the double-team before it is sprung, spreading the defense and sending cutters into the passing lanes and making the long passes to the corners or along the sidelines when defensive coverage so dictates.

Even-Front Half-Court Zone Pressing Defenses. Even-front half-court zone presses are used less frequently than odd-front alignments, and when they are used, they usually rotate into an odd-front alignment in a manner similar to that shown in Figure 6–53.

The object of rotation is, of course, to provide individual coverage of the dribbler prior to trapping, since premature trapping in the half-court area increases the likelihood of fast breaking by the offensive team.

The most likely even-front alignments seen in half-court pressing defenses are: 2-2-1, 2-1-2, and 2-3. As mentioned previously, these alignments rotate into odd-front alignments, and they will also provide

Beating the Zone Presses 217

Figure 6-53 Defensive Rotation from Even-Front Half-Court Zone Pressing Defense.

coverage of the passing lanes as described in the section of this book dealing with odd-front half-court zone pressing defenses. Thus, methods of attacking such defensive coverage will be found in the next section of this chapter.

It is possible to trap the dribbler from an even-front half-court alignment, but such techniques are seldom effective because the dribbler is not controlled, or turned toward either sideline, prior to the trapping movement.

The weaknesses of such a trapping system are illustrated in Figures 6–54, 6–55, and 6–56. The three non-trapping defenders must cover the two half-court corners, the baseline corners, and the large area around the top of the circle—a difficult task for only three defenders. Such coverage simply leaves too many open areas in the offensive half-court capable of being exploited by the remaining four offensive players.

In Figures 6–54 and 6–55, as the outside defenders trap 25 at the middle of the court, she passes to a wing, who is quickly covered by X_{23}.

218 Zone Offenses for Women's Basketball

Figure 6-54.

Figures 6-54, 6-55, 6-56 Beating the Half-Court Trap at the Middle of the Court.

Figure 6-56.

Player 25 cuts between the trapping defenders for a return pass. Figure 6–56 depicts a variation in which 32 rather than 25 cuts to the opening for 2's pass.

Odd-Front Half-Court Zone Pressing Defenses. The odd-front half-court zone pressing alignments—1–3–1, 3–2, 3–1–1, and 1–2–2—are superior to the even-front alignments in at least one respect, that they do not require defensive rotation prior to the trapping movement.

Of the four alignments listed, the 1–3–1 and 3–2 are perhaps the most frequently encountered. (The 3–1–1 and 1–2–2 alignments are variations of the 3–2.) Half-court zone coverage from these basic alignments may differ markedly, depending to a great extent upon the point (defensive) guard's ability to control the dribbler and prevent the long pass and subsequent layup.

The first point to consider in combatting the odd-front half-court zone presses is whether the trapping movement will occur in the backcourt or after the dribbler crosses the half-court line.

The advantages for the defensive team of backcourt trapping are twofold: first, not having crossed the half-court line, the ballhandler is likely to commit a ten-second backcourt violation when the trap is sprung; and second, the long pass downcourt will necessarily be longer, and thus entail greater risk for the offensive team than when the ballhandler is allowed to dribble across the half-court line.

The major disadvantage of backcourt trapping to the defensive team is that the area for effectively spreading the defense is slightly larger than in front-court trapping. Thus, it is important for the offensive team to anticipate the trap, spread the offensive players, force the double-team, and attempt to fast break when trapping fails to contain the ball or force a turnover.

The element of surprise is the chief ingredient in effective front-court half-court trapping. Once the ballhandlers dribble past half-court, they tend to relax slightly, expecting the defenders to drop back into normal zone defensive coverage when they fail to force the ten-second backcourt violation.

Regardless of on which side of the half-court line the trap is sprung, however, the defenders will follow a predictable course of events in setting and springing their traps.

Controlling the Ballhandler. The superiority of odd-front to even-front half-court zone pressing alignments is due to the facility involved in aligning the defensive personnel to match up or achieve one-on-one control of the ballhandler. (The term *controlling the ballhandler* refers to a defensive player's assuming one-on-one coverage of the dribbler and turning her toward one sideline or the other.)

The point at which defensive coverage of the ballhandler begins varies with defensive intentions. If the offensive team is capable of completing the long pass regardless of the defensive coverage, one or more defenders may "cheat" downcourt to begin their coverage in their offensive midcourt area. If the defensive team intends merely to trap in the backcourt, the point defensive guard's position will be in the vicinity of the half-court line. And if the trap is to be sprung in the front-court, she will set up in the vicinity of the opponents' midcourt area.

Trapping the Dribbler. After moving into, or assuming, one-on-one coverage without forcing the ballhandler to pick up her dribble, the point guard will turn her toward a sideline, where a teammate will move up to trap her. This teammate—X_2 in Figure 6–57—will apply strong defensive pressure to the dribbler in order to force her to reverse pivot toward point guard X_1 (and probably pick up her dribble as well).

Cutting Off the Passing Lanes. As the trapping movement is being set up, the other defenders will move into position to steal the ballhandler's most likely passes. If the ballhandler does not pick up her dribble, she likely will have the ball stolen, batted away from her, or tied up by one of the trapping guards. And if she picks up her dribble, she still

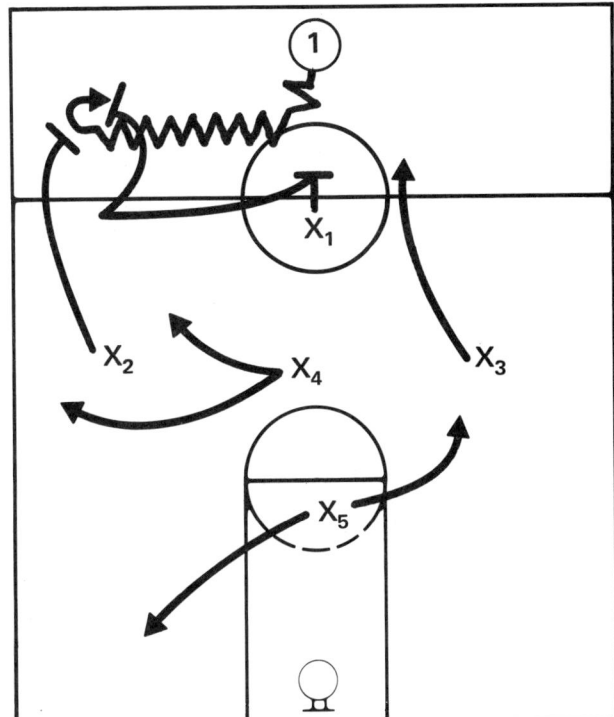

Figure 6-57 Setting Up the Defensive Trap.

must pass to a teammate beyond the reaching hands of the trapping players and defenders playing the passing lanes.

Although alignments and specific areas for trapping, cutting off the passing lanes, etc., may differ from team to team, the general features are the same for all half-court zone presses: controlling the ballhandler, trapping, cutting off the passing lanes—these steps will always be found, and in that particular order. Thus, the first step in preparing to combat the half-court presses lies in knowing where the opponents like to assume control of the dribbler, and where they intend to spring the trap.

As mentioned previously, half-court traps almost always occur along the sidelines because the ballhandler's dribbling and passing options and routes are reduced from those areas. It is possible to trap in the middle of the court, of course, but the passing lanes are broader in that configuration, and the defensive coverage spread to a far greater extent than is possible in sideline trapping.

In sideline trapping, the opponents will send one player to cover the cross-court primary passing lane, one player to cover the ball-side primary passing lane, two players to trap the dribbler, and one player to cover the possible long passes, particularly on the side of the court the dribbler is facing. (See Figure 6–58.)

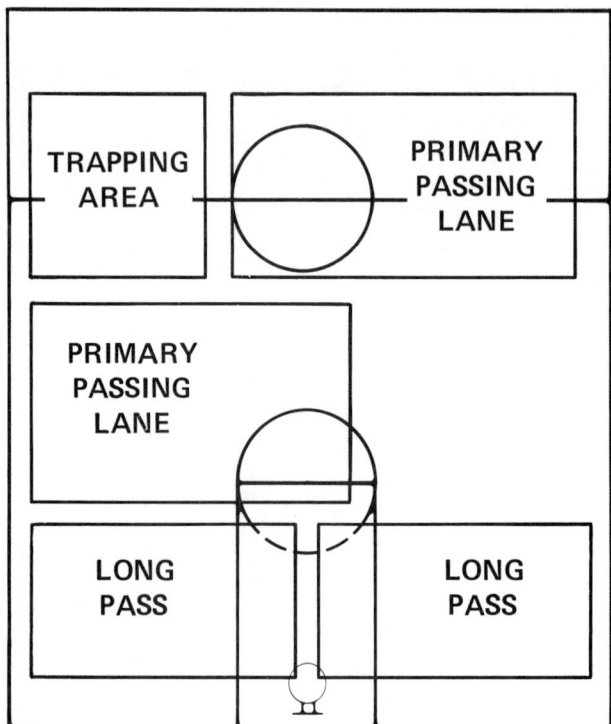

Figure 6-58 Corner Trapping Defensive Coverage, Half-Court Zone Press.

Two methods exist for combatting the half-court zone presses: forcing the double-team and spreading the defense into single-coverage.

In the first method, forcing the double-team, the ballhandler brings the ball down the center of the court and, upon receiving defensive pressure, veers quickly toward the nearest defensive player along the sideline. (See Figure 6–59.) This attacking movement forces the defenders to double-team the dribbler, but instead of being led into it as before, she is now prepared to deal with the double coverage on her own terms, since it is *she* who instigated the action rather than the defense.

At the same time ballhandler 25 is forcing the defense into premature double coverage, her teammates are moving into the open areas of the court away from the ball in order to spread the defense to the limits of its coverage. (Note: young or inexperienced ballhandlers should, in forcing the double-teaming, go to their right if they're right-handed, since they will likely be unable to make the passes necessary to beat the press while dribbling left-handed. Too, if they have to maintain a closed stance while dribbling in order to protect the ball, they may not be able to see open teammates.) When the defense dictates offensive movements by virtue of effective coverage, the primary passing lanes will likely be closed to all but the most highly skilled passers. However, when the

Figure 6-59 Forcing the Double-Team Against Half-Court Zone Pressing Defense.

ballhandler dictates the speed and direction of her movement, it will be virtually impossible to stop her from passing to an open teammate.

In Figure 6–59, X_5 is initially responsible for both deep offensive players, since 25 may not be able to throw the ball that far. As 25 reaches the point where she might be able to make the pass, a defender will cover her and begin influencing her one way or the other. If the defender controls 25's dribble, the deep defender will slide toward the deep ball side player. The player in the baseline weak side corner will be open to a greater extent than the other deep corner, but the dribbler facing unexpected double-teaming will likely be unable to see her. Similarly, if the defense turns 25 back to her left, the deep defender will move toward the other corner to cut off *that* passing lane. Openings may be found in the defensive coverage at this point, but not without a great deal of searching by the harried ballhandler.

On the other hand, when 25 forces two defenders to guard her, the inside and middle defenders will be unable to react quickly enough to stop 25's passes. Until absolutely sure what the ballhandler is doing and how the outside defenders are going to stop it, the inside defenders dare not commit themselves to specific coverage lest they inadvertently guess wrong and surrender the easy layup. (See Figure 6–60.)

Figure 6-60 The Consequences of Guessing Wrong Defensively.

Beating the Zone Presses   225

If a wing defender is forced to cover the ballhandler prematurely, the middle defender will have to cover the ball side wing. And if the deep defender moves toward the ball side corner, the weak side baseline corner will be open. (If the weak side wing drops back, the pass to 30 will lead to a three-on-two fast break, or at least will get the ball into the offensive court without difficulty.)

An even better pattern exists to attack the defense when the middle defender covers the sideline passing lane: the player in the weak side baseline corner cuts to the top of the circle for 25's pass, and the weak side wing cuts to the basket for a pass from high post. (See Figure 6-61.)

Generally, the defense will not overcommit itself against forced double-teaming—it's simply too risky. Zone pressing and trapping defenses are aggressive by nature and always involve considerable risk; however, the risks are minimized when the defenders control the flow of the ball and the offensive players. On those occasions when the defenders cannot control the movement of the ball or the ballhandler(s), they will

Figure 6-61 Fast Breaking from Forced Double-Team.

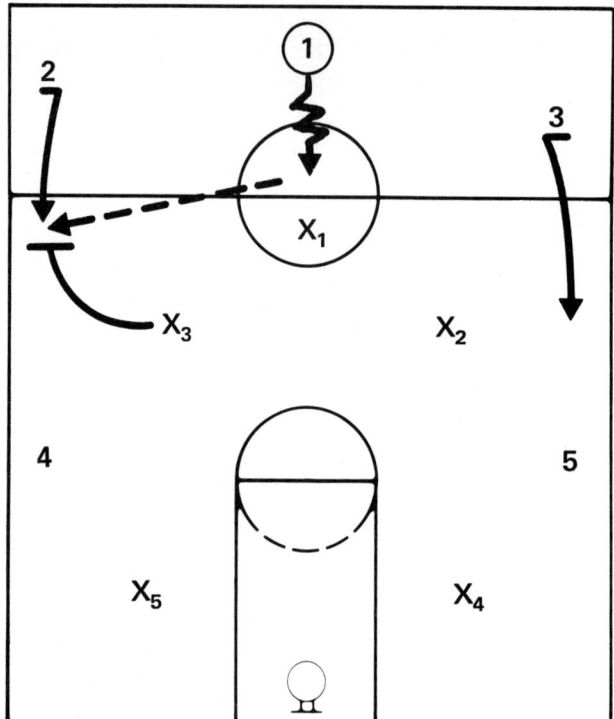

Figure 6-62 Spreading the Defense for One-on-One Coverage.

likely drop back into more conservative coverage until they decide how to re-establish defensive control. Teams will use attacking defense only when it is to their advantage to do so. When they cannot limit the number or extent of passing lanes available to the ballhandler, they are seldom willing to gamble on the outcome. The stakes are too high.

The second method of combatting the half-court zone presses involves spreading the defense for one-on-one coverage. This strategy is most easily effected by matching up with the defense and passing to a wing. (See Figure 6–62.)

Of course, the basic movement by itself will not always avoid double-teaming, but the sideline pass accomplishes two things unknown to basic attacking movements: first, the pass receiver along the sideline still has her dribble if and when she needs it; and second, she cannot be turned by the defenders.

The importance of these points cannot be stressed too strongly, since they go directly to the heart of what the defensive team hopes to accomplish: to control the dribbler, then suddenly turn her by trapping so that she will have to pick up her dribble while some of her teammates are out of her line of sight. When the ball is *passed* to the half-court corner rather than dribbled, however, the new ballhandler has no need to

Figure 6-63 Splitting and Spreading the Defense, Ball in the Half-Court Corner.

reverse pivot; she will merely dribble to her right or her left, as indicated by the defensive coverage—if, indeed, she decides to dribble at all! It is difficult to control or turn a dribbler who hasn't begun dribbling.

In Figure 6–63, Player 25 has already passed to 3 in the half-court corner. Player 25 cuts through the middle, and, if open, receives 3's pass; if not, she continues to the sideline. Player 30 moves closer to 3 in order to avoid long cross-court passes if 3 is double-teamed.

Notice that the defensive coverage is still largely uncommitted, with the exception of the defender covering 3. Who will cover 25's cut through the middle and to the sideline? The point guard might cover 25 the first time, but she cannot cover 25 all the way to the sideline and remain in zone coverage. Say the middle defender covers 25 at the sideline. Who then covers 30? Probably the point guard, except when she tries to trap 3. The weak side wing will then drop back to cover the weak side baseline, and the deep defender will slide across to cover the pass to the ball side baseline. After such defensive coverage has been established, 3 will simply dribble across the half-court line against one-on-one coverage.

Despite the lengthy description and analysis, the entire maneuver will take only three or four seconds. Player 25 will cut as shown immediately after passing the ball. If 25 isn't open for a return pass, 3 will consider the long pass if open, then dribble across the half-court line against her defender. And if the point guard drops off 30 to double-team 3, she will merely pass to 30, who will dribble into the front-court. (The weak side wing dropped back to cover the weak side baseline pass.)

Incidentally, it is probably better to have the deep offensive players set up at the ten-second mark along the sidelines and break to the baseline corners rather than setting up in the corners. Their downcourt movement will tend to keep the deep defender(s) thinking deep rather than coming up to steal passes in the primary passing lanes. Even when players can't make the long passes, you want the opponents to think you're interested in them.

The defensive team's alternative in covering the pass to the wing at half-court is to double-team her. Such a situation is ideal for fast breaking, since the advantage shifts strongly to the offensive team when the ballhandler who is being trapped still has her dribble. Yet so many teams

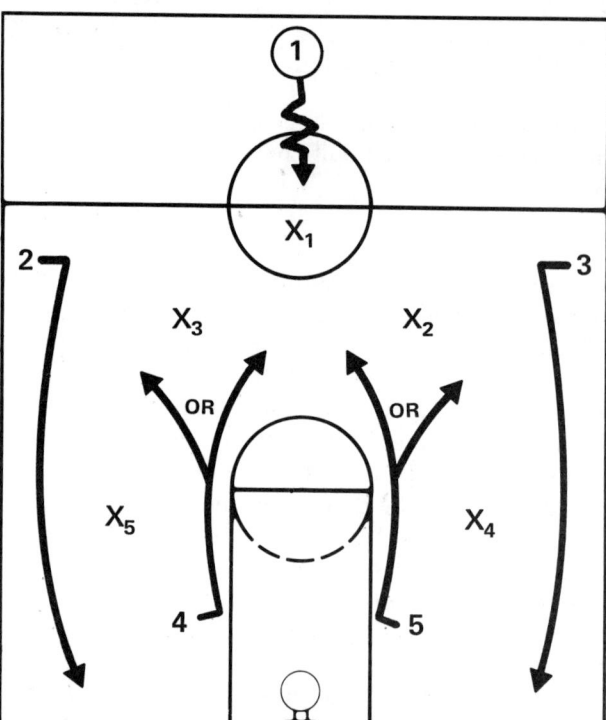

Figure 6-64 Tandem Cutting Pattern, Basic Movements.

try this useless show of aggression that it warrants closer inspection.

All kinds of fast breaking possibilities arise when 3 in the corner passes cross-court: the direct pass to the ball side baseline cutter for a layup, for example, if the deep defender moves back to cover weak side; or 30 passing to the baseline corner and cutting to the basket in a three-on-two or three-on-one fast break; or 30 advancing downcourt with the ball until challenged, then passing inside for a two-on-one fast break. Whatever the case, it is almost a certainty that double-teaming after the pass to the wing at half-court ranks among the poorest decisions a defensive team can make in half-court pressing, and the offensive team should be alert for opportunities to fast break off such coverage whenever it arises.

Tandem Cutting Pattern. An alternate method for combatting the various half-court zone pressing defenses is shown in Figure 6-64.

From a 1–2–2 alignment, the post players cut high as the wings cut to the baseline corners. This movement is almost certain to ensure an open pass, either to the corners if the deep defenders move up to cover the shorter passes, or to the cutters toward the ball if the defenders stay back.

As 1 dribbles toward the half-court line, 4 and 5 cut toward the ball,

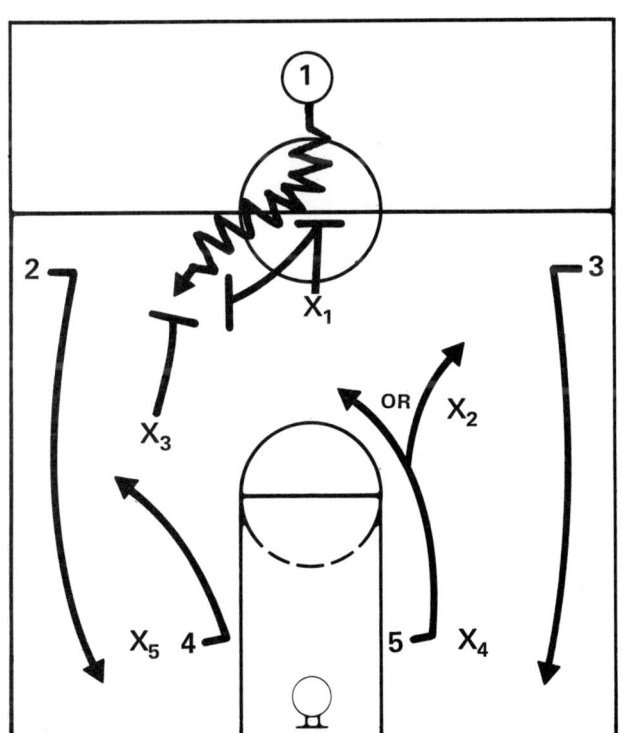

Figure 6-65 Combatting the Half-Court Trap, Tandem Cutting Pattern.

and 2 and 3 cut toward the corners. If X_4 and X_5 move up to cover 4 and 5, 2 and 3 will be open along the baseline, probably for a layup as well. On the other hand, the deep defenders may stay back to cover 2 and 3, in which case 4 or 5 will be open if X_2 or X_3 trap the dribbler with X_1. (See Figure 6–65.)

The defenders' third alternative in covering the tandem cutting movements is to match up with the cutters, with X_5 taking 2, X_4 covering 3, X_2 picking up 5, and X_3 guarding 4. (X_1 is, of course, on 1.) While such coverage will undoubtedly hinder 1's passing alternatives, it will lessen the defenders' chances of trapping the dribbler.

An important point that should not be overlooked is that, when the press is beaten, the offensive team should take the ball to the basket whenever possible. Four-on-three offensive advantages are common when the trap fails to contain the ball, and teams should take advantage of their numerical superiority at every opportunity.

7 Zone Offensive Drills

Practice is the best of all instructors.
Publilus Syrus
Maxim 439

Zone defenses are designed for two general purposes, namely: either to hide a team's defensive shortcomings of some kind or another, or to deny the offensive team certain advantages that it otherwise might have. For whichever reason, however, we can safely assume that the following will be true:

1. Openings in the zone coverage will be found (and reached) less frequently when they occur inside than outside.

2. The seams, or overlapping areas of responsibility within the zone coverage, will shift with movement of the ball and, to a lesser extent, with movement of the offensive players. Attacking these openings will be determined to a large extent by the players' ability to identify and move the ball to such areas promptly.

3. Every zone defense (except matchup) will leave at least one area of the court open to exploitation, although good zone defensive coverage will tend to dictate which areas the offense may attack.

4. No zone offense is likely to succeed against good zone defense unless a team possesses at least one good ballhandler, an outside shooter capable of at least occasionally tossing one in from 15–18 feet out, and the threat of inside penetration.

The primary role of drills within this framework is to familiarize players with the process of finding, cutting, and passing into or around the zone as the defensive players and openings shift with the movement of the ball.

1. The Penetrating Dribble. As has been mentioned elsewhere, the term *penetrating dribble* refers to a series of dribbles directed toward the basket, a defensive player, or between two defensive players. Such movement on the part of the ballhandler tends to freeze the defensive player(s) in position, and thus broaden perimeter passing lanes.

Figure 7-1 depicts the effect of a typical freezing movement directed against a single defender.[1]

If 25 fails to penetrate from the 1–2–2 alignment shown in Figure 7-1, the outside defenders will be able to cover the passes to the wings. Of course, the offensive team may not care whether or not the outside defenders cover the wings, but the point is that such coverage will eliminate the outside shot from the wing positions, or at least alter the length or location of such shots—as well as keeping the taller players inside on defense.

[1] The penetrating dribble generally tends to freeze *all* defensive coverage along the perimeters of the zone, regardless of whether the movement is directed toward one, or between two, opponents.

Figure 7-1 Freezing a Single Defender, Penetrating Dribble.

Zone Offensive Drills

In drilling players in using the penetration dribble against one player as shown in Figure 7-2, the coach should stress that: (1) the ballhandler should not penetrate to within an arm's length of the defender, and (2) the ballhandler should throw a chest pass or bounce pass (not a lob pass) in order to give the wing shooter time to get set.

Of course, the angle of the penetrating dribble may be altered to suit the desired pattern or defensive alignment. Examples of various angles of dribble penetration for purposes of freezing the defense are shown in Figures 7-3 and 7-4.

It is advisable in all three cases to have the receivers moving into position rather than standing still, to receive the pass, and thus simulate game conditions as nearly as possible.

Dribbling into two defenders is more difficult than dribbling toward a single defensive player. First, the passing angle, although broader, is more difficult, since the defenders are wider apart; and second, the passer is open to double-teaming when she changes her mind and decides not to make the pass. Finally, a lob or bounce pass may be the only way to get the ball to a teammate along the perimeter of the defensive coverage, and such passes are always risky against zone defense.

The two most common areas of penetration by dribbling between two defenders are shown in Figures 7-5 and 7-6.

In Figure 7-5, the dribbler's penetration effectively forces the inside defenders to cover the passes to the wings, since the guards will not have time to stop the dribbler and still drop back to cover the wings and the high post will have no way of knowing which side to cover until the ball is actually passed. Similarly, the dribbler's penetration between the wing

Figure 7-2 Penetrating Dribble, Directed Toward a Single Defender.

Figures 7-3, 7-4 Alternate Methods of Drilling Penetrating Dribble Against a Single Defender.

Zone Offensive Drills 235

Figures 7-5, 7-6 Freezing Two Outside Defenders, Penetrating Dribble.

and point guard in Figure 7–6 will force X_{55} to cover initially both the ball side corner and low post position. (If the weak side inside defender moves across to cover ball side low post, X_{23} will have to drop back to cover weak side low post, leaving the weak side high post unguarded. However, the ballhandler's penetrating movement will likely eliminate those two movements by the defenders.)

The best rule of thumb for advising players how far to dribble into the two defenders is, *continue until at least one defender commits herself to guarding you rather than dropping back to cover a wing*. When one or both defenders can no longer cover a wing, the ballhandler should pick up her dribble and pass quickly to the wing. Even a single step forward by either of the defenders will suffice to give the wing time to set herself, catch the pass, and shoot, if the ballhandler is capable of making quick, accurate passes to the wings sliding into position.

One individual drill deserving special mention at this time is a passing drill pertaining specifically to the pass off the penetrating dribble. For want of a better name, we'll call it:

2. The Fake-and-Pass Drill. Two players stand facing each other across the free-throw lane. A third (defensive) player stands between them, guarding the player with the ball. The object of the drill is for the ballhandler to use a fake-high, pass-low (i.e., throw a bounce pass), or fake-low and throw-high technique to pass the ball to her teammate across the lane. Lob passes are not permitted, nor are quick passes made before the defensive player is ready.

Any pass in which the offensive player does not fake at least once before passing is banned, since the purpose of the drill is not merely to play keep-away, but also to provide practice in the faking movements sometimes necessary in passing the ball after penetrating between two defenders.

3. Pass-and-Cut Drills. One of the most effective maneuvers in zone offense is the pass-and-cut. A single pass-and-cut pattern is shown in Figure 7–7, with a slightly more involved double pass-and-cut sequence with partial outside rotation shown in Figure 7–8.

Among the advantages of pass-and-cut patterns are: (1) They provide offensive continuity when accompanied by outside rotation toward the ball, (2) they provide at least the appearance of inside penetration while enhancing outside shooting possibilities, and (3) they are easily learned even by young or inexperienced players. Regardless of whether a team uses pass-and-cut sequences in its zone offensive patterns—it is difficult to avoid using them in action-oriented patterns—players should become familiar with pass-and-cut sequences.

The patterns shown in Figures 7–7 and 7–8 may be used to practice passing and cutting, with defenders added in any zone defensive align-

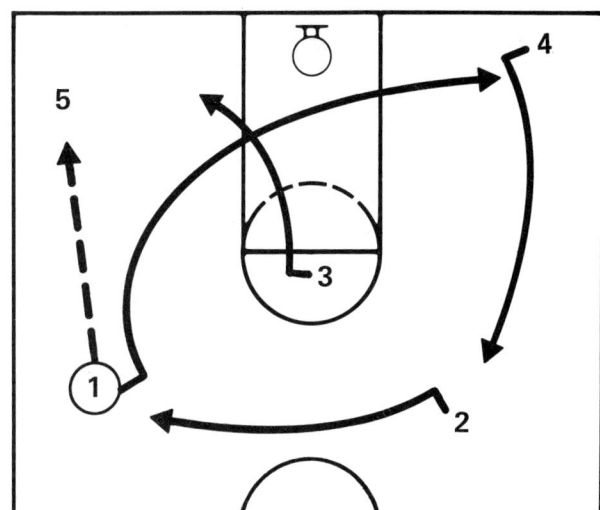

Figure 7-7 Single Pass-and-Cut Pattern with Outside Rotation.

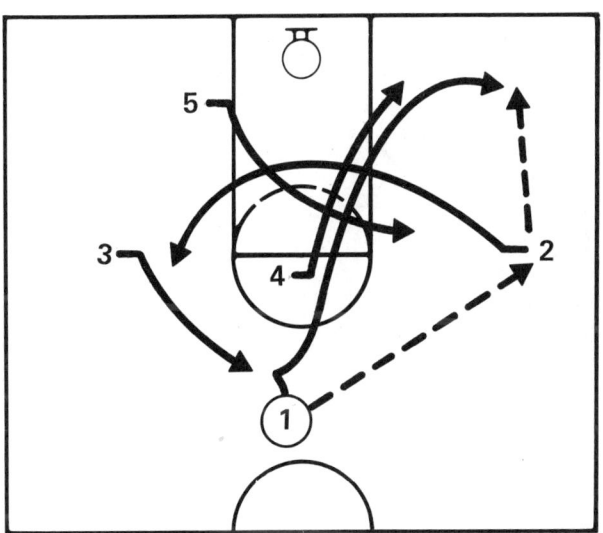

Figure 7-8 Double Pass-and-Cut Pattern with Partial Outside Rotation.

ment desired. Once players begin to comprehend the pass-and-cut sequences in drill, with or without defensive coverage, they may practice freelance movements based on recognition of open court positions. For instance, in using a freelance technique from the 2–1–2 offensive alignment shown in Figure 7–9, 1 may cut to either the ball side corner or weak side low post after passing to 5. (In either case, 2 will fill 1's vacated position, and 4 will fill 2's position.)

If 1 cuts to the corner (Figure 7–9), player 5 will pass to either 1 or 2 and cut through the lane to weak side low post. However, if 1 cuts to weak

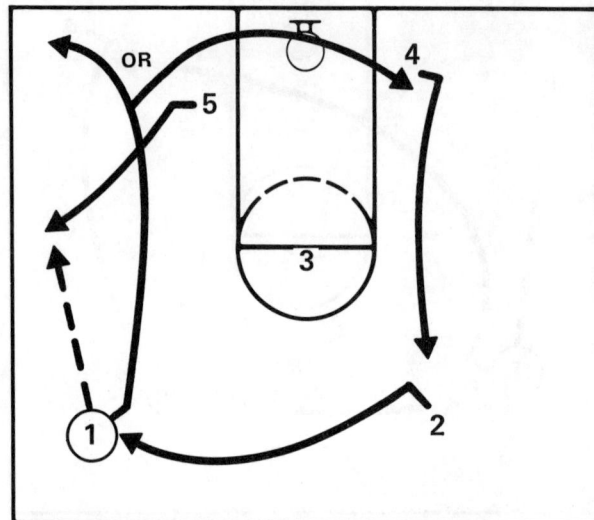

Figure 7-9 Beginning a 2-1-2 Freelance Pass-and-Cut Pattern.

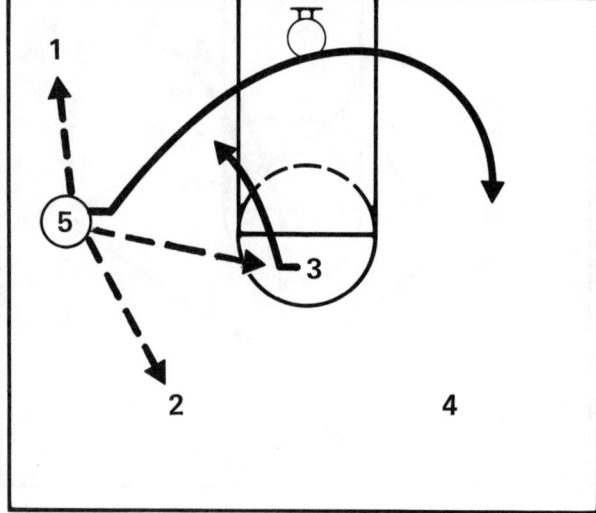

Figure 7-10 Player 5's Options After 1's Cut to the Corner, Freelance Pass-and-Cut Pattern.

side low post, 3 may cut to the ball side corner to provide 5 with the same passing options. (See Figure 7-11.)

If 5 passes to 2, the ball side corner player will fill 5's position. When 5 passes to the corner and cuts, however, the player in the corner will have to either stay in the corner until the next player filling the wing position passes and cuts, or dribble out of the corner herself. (Cutting from the corner is nonproductive in almost every instance.)

Thus, the freelance pattern continues, with players passing to either

Zone Offensive Drills 239

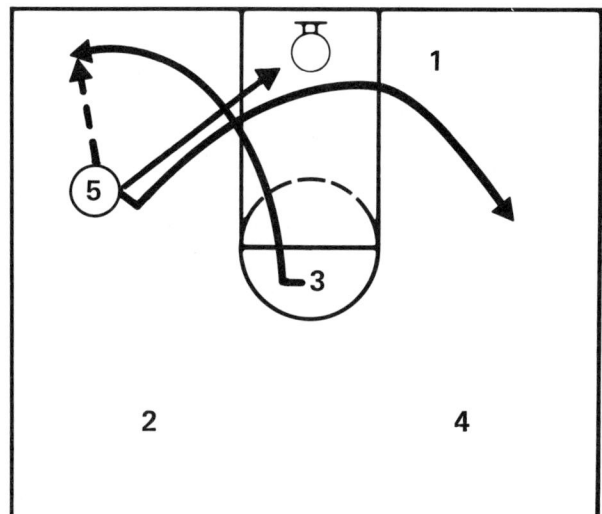

Figure 7-11 Player 5's Options After 1's Cut to Weak Side Low Post, Freelance Pass-and-Cut Pattern.

side, rotating outside toward the ball, cutting either away from the ball or to the ball side corner, and filling positions not quite randomly, but as court balance and offensive continuity dictate.

4. Sliding (Perimeter) Dribble and Inside Cuts. Sometimes a coach may want her ballhandler to dribble around the outside of the zone coverage, perhaps to watch the defenders adjust to ball position or look for openings in the coverage. Or, a player with the ball in the corner may want to watch the defense as she dribbles out to the wing position in order to pass inside quickly if the occasion arises. In both cases, the dribbler may use a sliding movement for better vision and ball control.

The offense may also be geared to a cross-court weak side pass from an overload position, as our inexperienced 17–6 squad used in 1976–77. (See Figures 7–12 and 7–13.)

Our weak side wing was the only decent outside shooter and one-on-one player on our team. Since opponents tended to gear their zone coverage toward her, we had trouble finding room for her to operate in until we came up with the pattern shown in Figures 7–12 and 7–13. If a wing defender stayed back to cover her, she cut toward the weak side corner, and if an inside defender stayed back, she moved toward the weak side high post. Admittedly, the cross-court passes were dangerous, but at least they denied the opponents the double coverage they would otherwise have been able to use in guarding her. (Incidentally, we ran the same pattern to her side of the court, too, not so much in hopes of making the same pass to 3 as to try to pick apart the defensive coverage and allow the wing to take the open outside shot or drive the baseline.)

Figures 7-12, 7-13 Sliding Dribble and Cross-court (Weak Side) Pass.

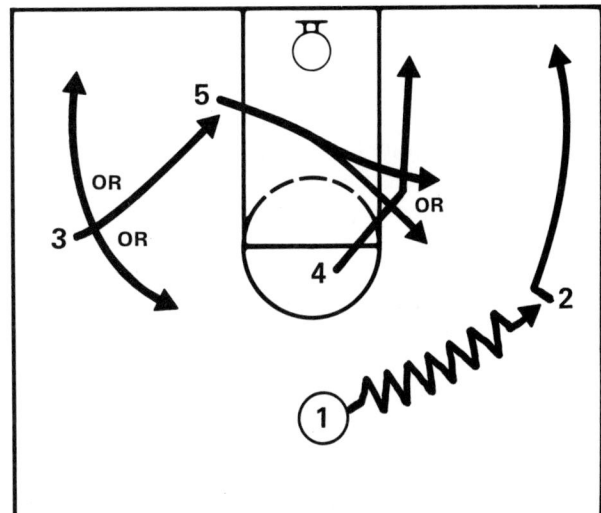

Figure 7-14 Inside Cuts with Sliding Dribble.

Openings arising out of sliding along the perimeter are likely to be of fleeting duration, since they do not occur as a result of blind side cuts or quick movements into open areas. Thus, passes must be made quickly, although the inside cuts may be relatively slow.

Sliding movements are ideal for practicing inside cuts, especially when a team uses a high-low post interchange or other tandem post movement pattern. The sliding movement allows the cutters inside to watch the defenders' movements as they shift their coverage.

As 1 slides to her right, 4 slides to the high post position and continues down to low post (or the corner if 2 clears), facing the ball all the way. Player 5 then: (1) cuts into the lane and, failing to get the ball, (2) continues to the vicinity of high post. (Player 4's cut must precede 5's cut in order to draw the inside defenders toward the baseline.)

The direction of both the dribble and the inside cuts may be varied, of course. Numerous cutting patterns have been shown in this book, any of which may be adapted to this drill.

5. Screening Drills. Although the point is debatable, many coaches feel that screening is less effective against zone defenses than it is in player-to-player coverage, since screening requires at least two offensive players in the same general area of the court. This in turn increases the likelihood of two defensive players moving into that same area, which detractors say reduces both offensive players' maneuvering room. Regardless, it is imperative that players learn to set screens properly, whether for zone or player-to-player usage.

Post Screens. The same screening drill may be used in five-player form, with inside passes occurring as the players work themselves open.

Ball-and-player rotation for the drill is shown in Figure 7–18.

In Figure 7–15, high post 3 reverse pivots or steps out to screen the defensive point guard, allowing 25 to dribble past her. Figures 7–16 and 7–17 depict a high-low post interchange with screen. It has been mentioned elsewhere that the screen isn't really necessary against zone defense, but the drill itself provides good practice in inside screening techniques. (Player 32 must be careful to leave the lane after screening, or else she will be called for a three-second lane violation. Thus, she obviously must exit from the lane on weak side, since there isn't sufficient time for her to move into the lane, set her screen, and move back across the lane to the ball side of the court.)

In Figure 7–19, low post 5 screens for 4 cutting across the lane along the baseline. The "2–3 baseline screening offense" uses just such screens to free players for 10–12 foot baseline shots.

Perimeter Screens. Since post screens are those set by players occupying high or low post positions, perimeter screens include screens set by players other than post players, although post players may be involved in screening as well. Since these screens occur most frequently along the perimeter, the term *perimeter screen* has been chosen to designate these screening movements.

Screens are possibly most effective against matchup zone defense, since the purpose of the matchups is to achieve player-to-player defensive

Figure 7-15 High Post "Step Out" Screen.

Zone Offensive Drills 243

Figures 7-16, 7-17 High-Low Post Interchange with Screen.

244   Zone Offenses for Women's Basketball

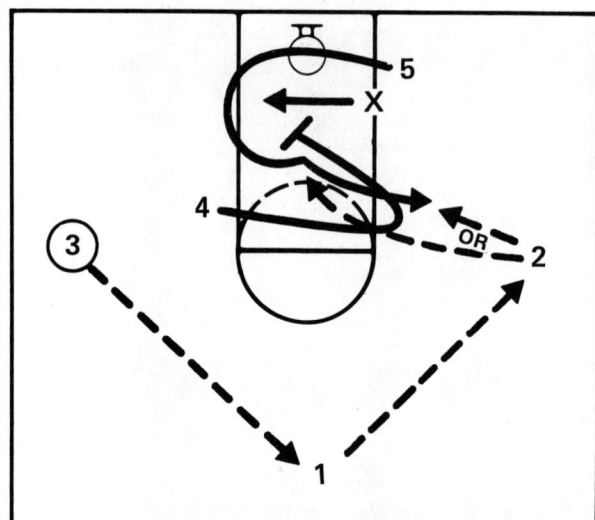

Figure 7-18 High-Low Post Interchange, Continuing with Ball and Player Rotation.

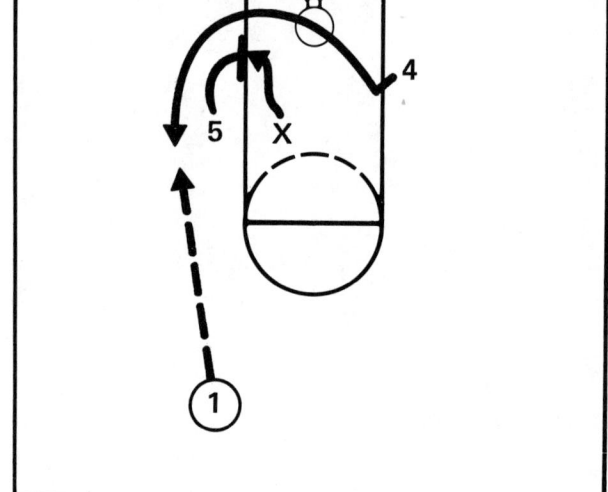

Figure 7-19 Low Post Baseline (Pivot) Screen.

coverage from a zone alignment. Thus, it is possible to use player-to-player set plays or continuity patterns to practice perimeter screening.

The possibilities for perimeter screening are endless. The ones shown may be considered representative not only in terms of execution, but also in their location on the court. For example, the single- and double-screens shown in Figures 7–20, 7–22, 7–23, and 7–24 are designed to free a cutter for a shot along, or near, the baseline, while the screens by 3 in Figures 7–21 and 7–24 permit the ballhandler to penetrate into outside shooting positions or set the overload herself.

Zone Offensive Drills 245

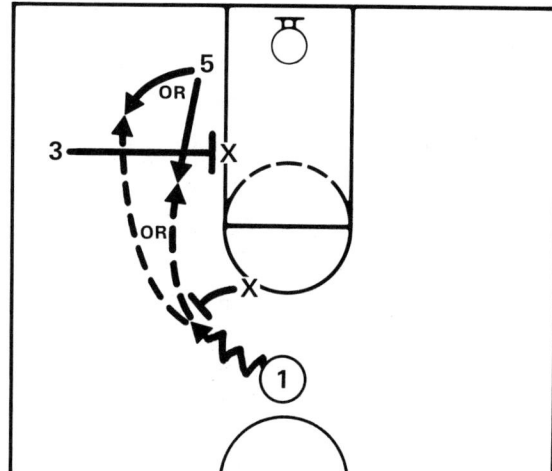

Figure 7-20 Inside Screen, Outside Cut.

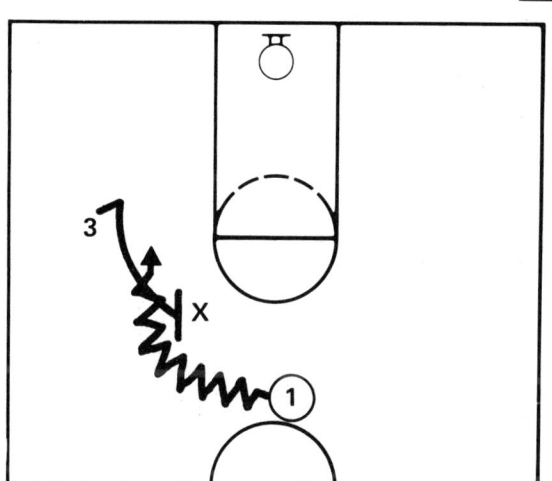

Figure 7-21 Outside Screen.

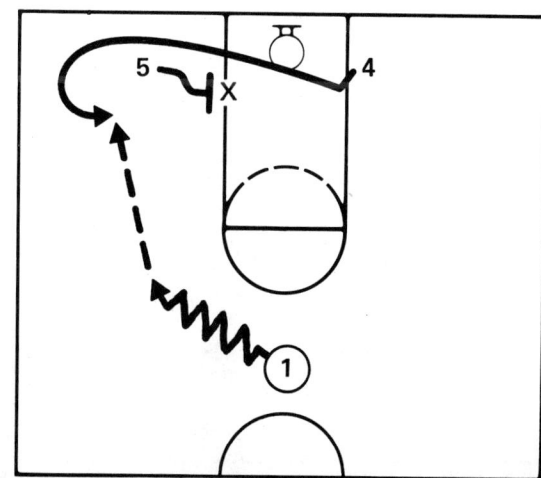

Figure 7-22 Baseline Screen.

246 Zone Offenses for Women's Basketball

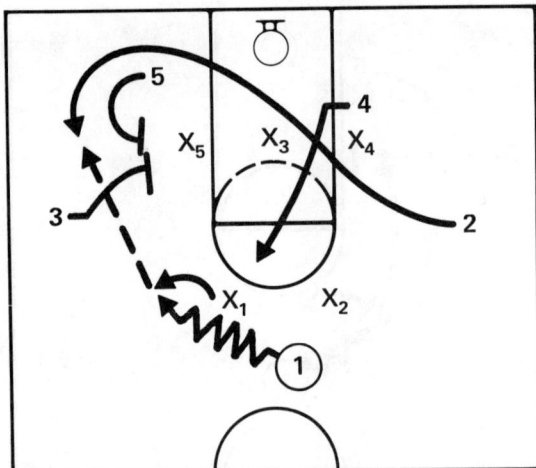

Figure 7-23 Baseline Double Screen.

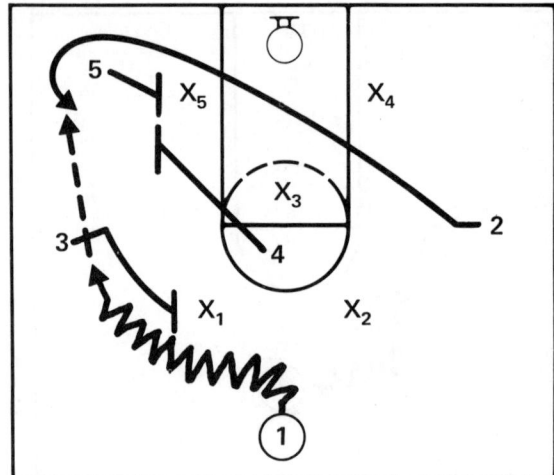

Figure 7-24 Baseline Double Screen, Outside Screen Combination.

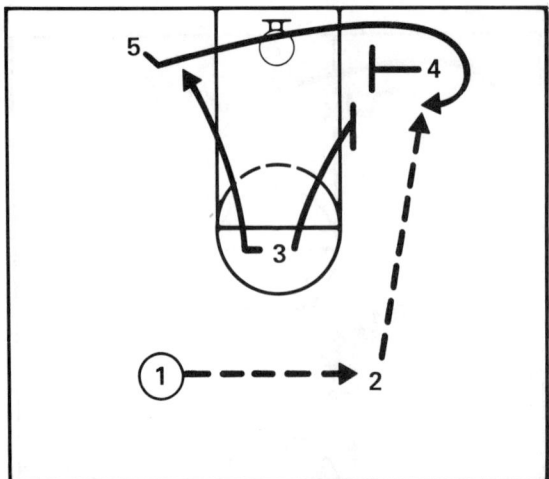

Figure 7-25 Screen (or Double-Screen) Away From the Ball.

Two or three points concerning zone screening deserve further consideration at this point.

1. Concerning outside screens for the dribbler, such screens are not as likely to work against odd-front zone defenses as they are against even-front zone coverage, since the defenders will merely switch when the screens are set, as shown in Figure 7-26. (The defenders may switch against the screens set in Figure 7-24 too, but the high post defender will have to come outside beyond the limits of her coverage to guard the ballhandler. Also, two or more screens are required to force such a defensive change against odd-front coverage, whereas a single screen will suffice against even-front coverage.) The difference lies in the court position of the outside defensive players—X_1 and X_2 in Figure 7-24, X_1 and X_3 in

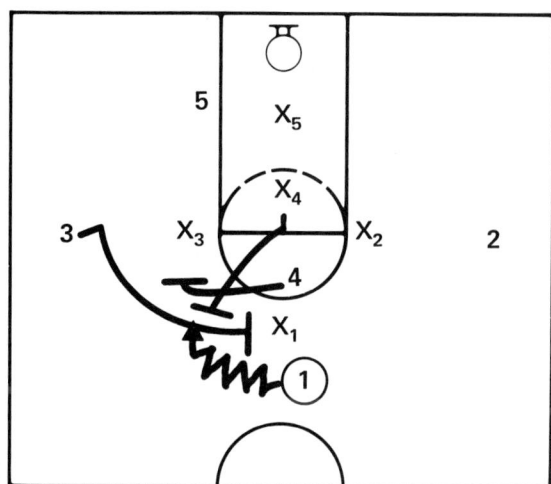

Figure 7-26 Defensive Switching Against Outside Screen.

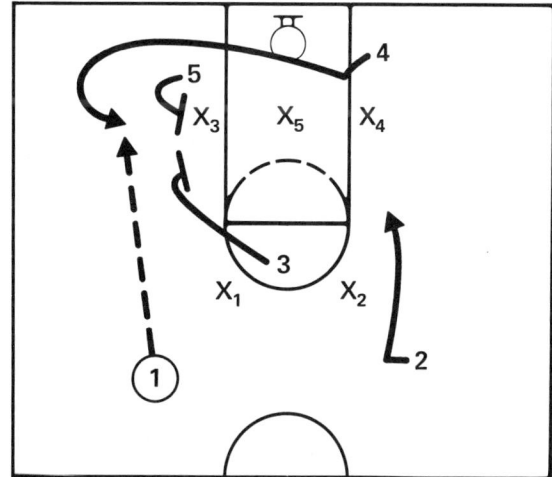

Figure 7-27 Setting Up the Baseline Double Screen.

248 Zone Offenses for Women's Basketball

Figure 7-28 Attempting to Cover the Double Screen from 2–3 Zone Defense.

Figure 7–26. Player X_3 can and will support X_1 in 1–2–2 zone defense, but X_2 cannot support X_1 in 2–1–2 zone defense.

2. A second consideration concerning screens is that—in my own experience, at least—double screens such as those shown in Figures 7–23, 7–24, and 7–25 are more effective against zone defenses than single screens. Since players in zone defense usually set up inside the lane, single screens must necessarily be set in the lane, too, or else risk movement and subsequent offensive fouls by the screening player as the defender cuts around the screen to cover the pass receiver.

With double screens, however, the defenders' cuts are longer, and the coverage is spread to a far greater extent than is possible in covering single screens effectively. Figures 7–27 and 7–28 illustrate the problems presented to the zone defensive coverage from two different standpoints.

Three players are in deep coverage in 2–1–2 or 2–3 zone defense. When 3 joins 5 to set the double screen for 4 as shown in Figure 7–27, player X_3 will have to cover 4 in the corner, and only X_5 will be in position to cover 5 and 3 if 4 decides to pass inside. At that, X_5 will be hard pressed to stop the inside pass, and X_4 will in most cases be unable to assist X_5 to any great extent.

In drilling the double screen pattern, 4 should be taught to look first to 5, then 3, since X_5 will probably cover 3 initially rather than 5. Once the inside pass to 5 has been established, however, X_5 will likely cover 5, which will mean that 4 will have to look to 3. The pass to 3 may also be made from the intermediate wing position when 4 passes back to 1.

Glossary

Aggressive Defense Style of defensive play in which the defenders attempt to force offensive players into perilous situations or ballhandling errors rather than staying back and waiting for them to make mistakes.

Automatics Spontaneous offensive movements designed to counteract defensive coverage of a set play or continuity pattern.

Back Court The half-court away from the offensive team's basket.

Backdoor, Going Backdoor Cut, or cutting, behind a defensive player, especially toward the basket, to receive a pass from a teammate.

Balanced Alignment Any offensive alignment with an equal number of players on both sides of the court.

Ballhandler The player in possession of the ball, especially the dribbler.

Ball Side (of the court) The side of the court the ball is in.

Baseball Pass One-handed pass thrown baseball-style, usually covering the length of the court.

Baseline The boundary line at either end of the court.

Basic (Zone) **Defense** Zone defense in which emphasis is placed upon coverage of the low post position and the ballhandler, with lesser emphasis upon the other ball side and weak side positions. Basic defense is generally passive in nature, denying the ball inside and giving up certain shots in order to prevent giving up higher percentage shots elsewhere. Also known as *containing* defense.

Blind Without looking, as a blind pass; or, that which cannot be seen by a player, as a blind screen.

Blocking Out The act of moving between an opposing player and the basket, especially for rebounding purposes.

Boards The backboards.

Bounce Pass Any pass that bounces before it reaches the receiver.

Box-and-One (Combination) **Defense** Defense in which four players set up in a 2–2 zone defense, and the fifth player assumes player-to-player coverage of a given offensive player.

Break Sudden, rapid offensive movement from one area of the court to another.

Center Colloquially, a team's tallest player; or, one who plays the high and/or low post positions offensively and defensively.

Chest Pass The basic pass in basketball, thrown with two hands from chest level.

Clear, Clearout The act of one or more offensive players' leaving an area in order to allow a teammate to operate freely in a one-on-one confrontation.

Collapse To drop back inside.

Combination Press/Pressing Defense Any pressing defense combining properties of both zone and player-to-player defense.

Combination (Zone) **Defense** Defense in which part of the team is in zone coverage, and the rest of the players are using player-to-player coverage. The three principal types of combination defense are the diamond-and-one, the box-and-one, and the triangle-and-two.

"Containing" Zone Defense See Basic (Zone) Defense.

Continuity Offense Any offensive pattern in which the basic movements may be repeated any number of times without the necessity of realigning the offensive players in their original positions.

Control Offense Any offensive pattern used for the purpose of holding or controlling the ball.

Corner Any of the four corners of the half-court; also, the offensive positions located 15–18 feet from the basket and 3–4 feet from the baseline on either side of the court.

Cover To guard or defend an offensive player or area of the court.

Criss-Cross Scissoring movement by two offensive players.

Cross-Court Across the court.

Cut, Cutter Any offensive player moving, or any movement, from one area of the court to another. Distinguishable from **Sliding** by the increased speed of the movement.

Cutting Off Passing Lanes Defensive technique of playing in the passing lane between the ball handler and her intended receiver.

Deep Near the basket.

Defense That phase of the game in which a team is not in possession of the ball.

Defensive Balance The practice of keeping an offensive player outside to protect against the opponents' fast break.

Defensive Rotation Shifting defensive alignments and assignments in an orderly manner within a zone defense to meet a specific need, as in matching up.

Delay Offensive strategy in which a team considers scoring secondary to maintaining possession of the ball.

Delay Trapping Pressing defensive technique in which trapping is delayed until the defenders match up with the offensive players.

Diamond-and-One (Combination) **Defense** Defense in which four players set up in a 1–2–1 zone defense, and the fifth player assumes player-to-player coverage of a given offensive player.

Disguising an Offense The act of deliberately aligning an offense incorrectly, or in such a manner as to conceal the basic positions from which the movements will come.

Double-Teaming Two defensive players' guarding a single offensive player. Distinguishable from **Trapping** in intent: double-teaming is generally used to keep the ball away from a specific player, not to steal it from her or force a turnover.

Downcourt Toward a team's offensive basket.

Drive Rapid dribbling movement toward the basket, especially for a layup.

Even-Front (Zone) **Defense** Zone defensive coverage featuring two players setting up outside.

Facing the Basket Standing in such a position that not only one's head, but feet as well, are pointing toward the basket.

Fake Feinting movement in one direction to permit a genuine movement in another direction.

False Splitting Pattern Alignment in which the offensive team appears to be splitting the defense, but actually permits the opponents to match up defensively.

Fast Break Offensive technique of sending players downcourt faster than the defense can get its players back to stop them.

Filling the Passing Lanes In fast breaking, cutting into or along the preferred passing lanes and routes downcourt.

First Line of Defense In pressing defenses, that part of the defensive alignment nearest the ball or the defensive team's offensive basket.

Five-on-Four Offensive advantage featuring five offensive players and only four defensive players, usually occurring at the end of a fast break.

Following the Ball Moving toward the side of the court the ball is on, especially inside.

Forcing a Double Team Offensive technique of purposely dribbling into a double-team before the defense is prepared to trap the ballhandler.

Forwards Colloquially, a team's inside players other than the tallest player.

Four-on-Three Offensive advantage featuring four offensive players and only three defensive players, usually at the end of a fast break.

Four-Player Fast Break Fast break involving four offensive players.

Four-Player Overload Offensive alignment with four players on one side of the court.

Freelancing Using one-on-one movements or random cutting sequences, as opposed to running a pattern offense or set play.

Freezing (a defensive player) Any offensive movement that keeps a defensive player from moving or altering her coverage.

Freezing the Ball Offensive strategy of holding the ball rather than working for shots, generally from a spread formation.

Front Court, Forecourt That half of the court in which the offensive team attempts to score.

Fronting Defensive technique of standing between an offensive player and the ball, especially inside.

Full-Court Press Defensive pressure applied throughout the full length of the court as the offensive team attempts to bring the ball downcourt.

Guard To defense; colloquially, the team's smallest players, or those who play outside offensively and defensively and assume the team's ballhandling responsibilities.

Half-Court Press Defensive pressure applied throughout the defensive half-court as the offensive team brings the ball downcourt.

High Near the free-throw line or top of the circle.

High-Percentage Shot Any shot likely to be made, or any shot preferred by the offensive team.

High Post Offensive position at the center, or along the edges, of the free-throw line.

Inbounds Pass Any pass made from out of bounds following a dead ball situation.

Influencing (a Pass or Dribble) Defensive technique of maneuvering an offensive player or the ball toward or away from a given area of the court.

Inside Near or toward the basket.

Interchanging The act of two offensive players' exchanging positions.

Intermediate Wing Positions Offensive positions on either side of the court located midway between the wings and the point.

Jogging Running at a leisurely pace, especially without high knee- or heel-lift.

Key Movement or signal that directs movements of other players; also, colloquially, the area of the free-throw circles.

Lane The free-throw lane.

"Laning" In fast breaking, the practice of assigning specific lanes to offensive players.

Layup Shot taken at the end of a drive to the basket.

Lob Pass Pass with a high, arcing trajectory, usually over one or more defensive players.

Low Near the basket, as in low post.

Low-Percentage Shot Any shot unlikely to be made more often than occasionally, or any shot not desired by the offensive team.

Low Post A court position on either side of the basket, located just outside the free-throw lane and near the baseline.

Matchup, Matching Up Defensive technique in which each defensive player shifts into player-to-player coverage within a zone defense.

Midcourt That area of the court immediately adjacent to, and on either side of, the half-court line.

Middle Generally, the area in and around the free-throw lane.

Odd-Front (Zone) Defense Zone defensive coverage featuring one or three players setting up outside.

Offense That phase of the game in which a team possesses the ball.

One-on-One Confrontation or matchup involving one offensive player and one defensive player, especially in potential scoring situations.

One Pass Away from the Ball See Primary Receiver.

One-Up, One-Back (Alignment) Two players setting up one in front of the other. Also called **Tandem** alignment.

Opening Space between two defensive players.

Outlet Pass After transition from defense to offense, the pass that begins a fast break; also, a pass outside that allows the offensive team to reset its alignment or continue its pattern when the defense has stopped its basic thrust.

Outside Away from the basket.

Overguarding Defensive maneuver in which a defensive player stands or plays diagonally between, or in front of, an offensive player in relation to the ball.

Overload An offensive technique involving setting or cutting three or more players to one side of the court; or, setting or cutting more than one player into the same area of a zone.

Overplaying See Overguarding.

Overshooting Shooting the ball too hard, a trait shared by most poor shooters.

Pass-and-Cut Offensive technique in which the ballhandler passes to a teammate and cuts to any of several areas of the court (e.g., toward the basket, the weak side, or behind the pass receiver).

Passing Across a Zone Passing the ball cross-court from wing to wing, or diagonally from wing to corner or corner to wing.

Passing Lane The space between the player passing the ball and the intended receiver.

Passive Defense See Basic (Zone) Defense.

Pattern Offense See Set Play and Continuity Offense.

Penetrate To dribble into or between two defensive players for the purpose of either driving or freezing one or more defensive players.

Perimeter The area along the outer edges of zone defensive coverage.

Picking Up the Dribble Catching the ball with both hands at the end of a dribble.

Pivot Turning movement with one foot firmly planted on the floor; also, colloquially, any offensive player occupying the high- or low-post position.

Player-to-Player Defense Style of defense characterized by each player's guarding, or being responsible for, specific offensive players, as contrasted with defending an area, or zone, of the court.

Playing the Passing Lanes See Cutting Off the Passing Lanes.

Point The area around the top of the circle.

Posting Setting a player at, or cutting her to, a high- or low-post position.

Press, Pressing Defense Style of play characterized by defensive pressure applied over the full length of the court, three-fourths of the court, or half of the court.

Pressure Defense Applying close, aggressive defensive coverage to one or more offensive players.

Primary Receiver Any player in position to receive a pass directly from the ballhandler, especially a preferred pass receiver in a given situation.

Primary Shooter A team's preferred shooter in a given situation.

Reverse Pivot Pivoting movement backward and away from one's original direction, as in dribbling to the baseline and reverse pivoting toward the middle of the court.

Revolving An offensive technique of moving players from position to position in an overload offense without rotating the ball to the other side of the court.

Roll Sliding or pivoting movement away from a teammate (and usually toward the basket) following a screen.

Rotation (of the ball and/or an offensive player) Going from one side of the court to the other within an offensive pattern.

Run-and-Jump Defense Defensive maneuver similar to trapping, except that the defenders switch defensive responsibilities instead of trapping.

Running the Clock Playing offensively without attempting to score.

Safety Valve An offensive player who remains outside as a secondary pass receiver for an outlet pass in case an offensive pattern or movement fails to produce the desired results.

Sagging Dropping off, or moving away from, an offensive player, usually to provide additional defensive coverage elsewhere.

Scissoring Criss-crossing movement by two offensive players, often around a high post player.

Screen Offensive technique of blocking the path of a defensive player to free a teammate.

Seam The areas between defensive players' zones of responsibility in a zone defense.

Segment Drill Any drill emphasizing a single aspect of a larger pattern.

Set Play A series of offensive cuts, screens, or other movements designed to yield an open shot or scoring opportunity.

Set Up To assume basic or original positions.

Shuffle Offense A type of continuity offense featuring multiple cuts and screens toward and away from the ball.

Side-by-Side (Alignment) Any two teammates, especially offensive players, setting up side by side.

Single-Coverage One-on-one defensive coverage.

Sinking *See* Sagging.

Slide, Sliding Movement by an offensive player from one area of the court to another, usually at a leisurely or measured pace.

Slowdown Offensive strategy stressing patient shot selection.

Splitting Setting offensive players along the outside and/or inside seams of a zone defense.

Splitting the Post Scissoring movement by two outside offensive players around a third player, usually at a high post position.

Spread Formation, Spreading an Offense Aligning offensive players wider than normal, either at the wing, intermediate wing, or corner positions, and usually with the intent of widening the defenders' zones of responsibility. Delaying tactics usually feature spread alignments.

Stack An offensive alignment with two players setting up low on one or both sides of the court.

Stall, Stalling Effort by the offensive team to run the clock by maintaining ball possession without trying to score.

"Streaker" The first offensive player downcourt in fast breaking, usually sent downcourt as soon as her team gains possession of the ball.

Switch, Switching Defensive maneuver in which two or more defensive players swap defensive assignments. In zone defense, switching is usually automatic.

Tandem (alignment) Any high-low offensive alignment; or, any one-up, one-back defensive alignment, as in defending a three-on-two fast break.

Ten-Second Backcourt Violation Violation due to the offensive team's inability to move the ball beyond the half-court line into its front court in the prescribed ten seconds.

Three-on-Two Offensive advantage featuring three offensive players and only two defensive players, usually at the end of a fast break.

Three-Player Fast Break Fast break involving three offensive players.

Three-Player Overload/Delay Offensive alignment or tactic involving three players primarily, with other players filling less demanding or active roles.

Throw-in The inbounds pass.

Top of the Circle Those areas of the free-throw circles nearest to the half-court line.

Trailer In fast breaking, a player who does not enter into the fast break initially, although she may become involved if she is the fourth offensive player downcourt when three defenders are back to stop the fast break.

Transition Changing from defense to offense (or vice versa), especially the critical three or four seconds in fast breaking immediately after regaining possession of the ball.

Trapping An aggressive defensive maneuver in which two or more players harass the ballhandler simultaneously, attempting to steal the ball or force a turnover.

Triangle-and-Two (Combination) **Defense** Defense in which three players set up in a 2–1 or 1–2 zone defense, and the other two defenders assume player-to-player coverage of two offensive players.

Turning the Dribbler Overguarding the dribbler in such a manner as to make her reverse pivot away from her originally intended direction.

Turnover Any offensive mistake that results in the defensive team's acquiring possession of the ball without the offensive team having taken a shot.

Two-on-One Offensive advantage featuring two offensive players and only one defensive player, usually occurring at the end of a fast break.

Two Passes Away from the Ball Any court position that normally requires two passes to rotate the ball from one position to another (e.g., passing from corner to wing to point, or from wing to point to the other wing).

Two-Player Fast Break Fast break involving two offensive players.

Unbalanced Having more players on one side of the court than the other.

Weak Side The side of the court away from the ball.

Weave An outside pattern featuring player and ball rotation from one side of the court to the other; often used as a slowdown or delay offense.

Wheel A type of continuity offense featuring player rotation, cuts, and screens toward and away from the ball.

Wing Offensive position, or player occupying that position, located near the sideline along the free-throw line extended.

Zone Defense Style of defensive play characterized by players' defending areas of the court, or zones, rather than specific players.

Zone Press Pressing defense from a zone alignment, and with players assuming zone defensive responsibilities.

Zones of Responsibility Areas within a zone defense for which individual defensive players are responsible.

Bibliography

Barnes, Mildred J. *Women's Basketball*. Boston: Allyn and Bacon, 1972.

Bell, Mary M. *Women's Basketball*. Dubuque, Iowa: William C. Brown Co., 1964.

Cousy, Bob and Frank Power, Jr. *Basketball: Concepts and Techniques*. Boston: Allyn and Bacon, 1970.

Eaves, Joel. *Basketball's Shuffle Offense*. Englewood Cliffs, N. J.: Prentice-Hall, 1960.

Gardner, Jack. *Championship Basketball with Jack Gardner*. Englewood Cliffs, N. J.: Prentice-Hall, 1961.

Harris, Delmer W. *Coaching Basketball's Zone Offenses*. West Nyack, N. Y.: Parker Publishing Co., 1976.

Jucker, Ed. *Cincinnati Power Basketball*. Englewood Cliffs, N. J.: Prentice-Hall, 1962.

McGuire, Frank. *Offensive Basketball*. Englewood Cliffs, N. J.: Prentice-Hall, 1959.

Meyer, Margaret and Marguerite Schwartz. *Team Sports for Girls and Women*. Philadelphia: W. B. Saunders Co., 1957.

Miller, Donna Mae and Katherine L. Ley. *Individual and Team Sports for Women*. Englewood Cliffs, N. J.: Prentice-Hall, 1955.

Neal, Patsy. *Basketball Techniques for Women*. New York: Ronald Press, 1966.

Pinholster, Garland F. *Pinholster's Wheel Offense for Basketball*. Englewood Cliffs, N. J.: Prentice-Hall, 1966.

Ridl, Charles. *How to Develop a Deliberate Basketball Offense*. Englewood Cliffs, N. J.: Prentice-Hall, 1966.

Rupp, Adolph F. *Rupp's Championship Basketball*, 2nd ed. Englewood Cliffs, N. J.: Prentice-Hall, 1957.

Santos, Harry G. *How to Attack and Defeat Zone Defenses in Basketball.* West Nyack, N. Y.: Parker Publishing Co., 1966.

Schaafsma, Frances. *Women's Basketball.* Dubuque, Iowa: William C. Brown Co., 1966.

Sports Illustrated, ed. *Sports Illustrated Book of Basketball.* Philadelphia and New York: J. B. Lippincott Co., 1962.

Stutts, Ann. *Women's Basketball.* Pacific Palisades, Calif.: Goodyear Publishing Co., 1969.

Sweet, Virgil. *Specifics of V Offense.* Valparaiso, Indiana, 1966.

Teague, Bertha F. *Basketball for Girls.* New York: Ronald Press, 1962.

Vannier, Maryhelen and Hally Beth Poindexter. *Individual and Team Sports for Girls and Women.* Philadelphia: W. B. Saunders Co., 1960.

Warren, William E. *Team Patterns in Girls and Women's Basketball.* Cranbury, N. J.: A. S. Barnes & Co., 1976.

Wooden, John. *Practical Modern Basketball.* New York: Ronald Press, 1966.

———. *1976–77 Basketball Rule Book.* Elgin, Illinois: National Federation of State High School Athletic Associations, 1976.

Index

Automatics, 46

Balance, defensive, 9, 48
Box-and-one defense, 36–37

Combination defense: 35, 38
  offenses against, 142–143
"Containing" zone defense, 41
Control offenses: 143–155
  defined, 143–144
  five-player weave, 148–150
  four-player delay patterns, 150–155
  three-player patterns, 146–147, 151–155
  when a team is ahead, 147–148
  when behind in a game, 144–145
  zone patterns as, 146

Delay offenses: see *Control offenses*
Delay trapping, 172–174
Diamond-and-one defense, 36–37
Drills, zone offensive, 231–250

Even-front zone defenses, 13–17

False splitting patterns, 89, 92–94
Fast breaking: 184–216
  establishing lanes in, 199–201
  faking in, 204
  finishing the fast break, 201–216
  four-on-three, 214
  laning in, 190–194
  philosophy, 159–160
  principles of, 189–190
  three-on-one, 211
  three-on-three, 212–214
  three-on-two, 204–211
  two-on-one, 199–205
"Follow the leader" overload rotation, 80–82
Freelance offense, 46
Freezing one or more defenders, 94–96
Freezing the ball: see *Control offenses*

Half-court zone presses: 216–221
  even front, 216–219

Half-court zone presses (cont.)
  fast breaking against, 225
  odd-front, 219–220
  offenses against, 222–230

Inbounding against presses: 163–169
  contested throwins, 163–169
  uncontested throwins, 163

"Keying" zone offenses: 127–134
  low post keys, 131–134
  point guard keys, 129–131

"Laning" zone defense, 22–24

Matchup zone defense: 24–27, 134–137
  considerations in attacking, 135–137
  from 1–2–2 alignment, 110–111
  zone offenses against, 137–138

Odd-front zone defenses, 13–14, 17–21
"One-up, one-back" bring-in alignment, 164
Overloading: 51–87
  against matchup zone defense, 137–138
  as a strategy, 45
  basic movements, 62–64
  defined, 3, 51
  four-player patterns and alignments, 4–5, 73–79
  maintaining an overload, 66–67
  multiple rotation system, 79–82
  positions and strategy, 53–62
  rotation patterns (ball and player), 67–70
  strengths, 53
  three-player patterns and alignments, 4–5, 62–73
  weaknesses, 51–53

Pass-and-cut (against presses): 181–184
  drills, 236–239
Penetrating against zone defense: 46–47, 94–115
  drills, 232–236
Player rotation, 44

Revolving rotation overload pattern, 70–73
Rotation in cutter pattern, 101
Run-and-jump defense (full-court), 174–177

Safety valve, 162–163
Screening: 45, 46
  double screen, 112–113
  drills, 241–249
  from splitting alignment, 96–99
  high-low screening offense, 123–125
  on weak side, 86–88, 125–127
  2–3 baseline screening offense, 117–120
"Side-by-side" bring-in alignment, 163
Splitting patterns: 89–115
  against even-front zones, 96–99
  against odd-front zones, 99–114
  defined, 5–6, 44
Spreading:
  against half-court zone press, 226–229
  against zone press, 160–161
Stalling: see Control offenses

Trapping zone defense: 27–35
  full-court, 158, 170–171
  zone offense against, 139–141

"V" offense, 120–123

Weak side cutter pattern: 83–88
  full-court, 181

Zone defenses:
   attacking weaknesses of, 3–6, 8–9, 42–44
   basic coverage, 11–21
   principles of, 231
   reasons for using, 2–3
   versatility of, 9–11

Zone offenses:
   principles of, 42–49
Zone pressing defense:
   offensive considerations, 158–162
   philosophy, 157–158